Raw Spirit

Raw Spirit

*In Search of the
Perfect Dram*

Iain Banks

LARGE PRINT

Oxford

First published in Great Britain 2003
by
Century, one of the publishers in
The Random House Group Ltd

Published in Large Print 2004 by ISIS Publishing Ltd,
7 Centremead, Osney Mead, Oxford OX2 0ES
by arrangement with
Century, one of the publishers in
The Random House Group Ltd

British Library Cataloguing in Publication Data
Banks, Iain, 1954–
    Raw spirit: in search of the perfect dram.
    – Large print ed.
    1. Banks, Iain, 1954– Travel – Scotland
    2. Distilleries – Scotland
    3. Whisky industry – Scotland – History
    4. Whisky – Scotland – History
    5. Large type books
    6. Highlands (Scotland) – Description and travel
    I. Title
    914.1'15'0486

ISBN 0–7531–5305–X (hb)
ISBN 0–7531–5306–8 (pb)

Printed and bound by Antony Rowe, Chippenham

For Gary and Christiane

And to the memory of James Hale

This book really couldn't have been written without the help of a lot of other people. I would like to thank my wife Ann, Oliver Johnson, John Jarrold, Toby and Harriet Roxburgh and everybody else at Ballivicar, Martin Gray, Les, Aileen and Eilidh McFarlane, Jim Brown, Dave McCartney, Ken MacLeod, Tom and Michelle Obasi, Roger Gray and Izabella, Mic Cheetham, Gary and Christiane Lloyd, Ray, Carole and Andrew Redman, Bruce, Yvonne, Ross and Amy Frater, Jenny and James Dewar, Andrew Greig and Lesley Glaister, my uncle Bob, everybody I met and talked to in the distilleries I visited — with particular appreciation going to all the managers and the long-suffering though invariably helpful tour guides who were prepared to answer my idiot questions — all at the Scotch Malt Whisky Society and, lastly and firstly, my parents.

Contents

Introduction — Out of our Heads 1

1. These Drugs of Subtle Virtue 6
   The Land Rover: a paean....................11
   Great Wee Roads: a digression................21

2. Does not Rhyme with "Outlay" 28
   Pronunciation: a word.......................30
   Once upon a time: distilling as cottage
   industry 35
   Distillery aesthetics: a highly partial
   overview....................................37
   Childhood: a sentimental detour 48

3. Exploding Custard Factories....................53
   Whisky: the how-to bit.......................55
   Notes: a note 71

4. To Jura 80
   Willy's Definitive Dram Definition.............82
   The Toby's Party/The Balcony Scene story.....87

5. The Heart of the Water....................103
   The midge: microscopic megascourge 107
   Les and Iain's Guide to Sensible Sailing 115
   Loch Shiel: an appreciation, with
   reservations.................................116
   The SMWS: home from home 121

Drinking: you'd think it would be obvious 126
And that's one of the good ones 129

6. WhiskyLandWorldVille! 134
   Altitude problem 146

7. Break for Curry 165
   Scotland: land of contrasts (not).............170
   The Highlands: their identification and use ..172
   Highway the hard way: a road bore writes ...184

8. Fear and Loathing in Glenlivet.................192
   The Jag: all the fruity flavour of yesteryear...192
   Substances: the usual disclaimer 200

9. The Awemsys of Azshashoshz 225
   Azshashoshz: that etymology in full..........227
   Head crash: talking on empty 240
   McCartney: the case for madness.............243
   Ditto Brown: telling who your real friends
   are 247

10. Welcome to the Land of Heederum-
    Hawderum...................................255
    Happy cars: in defence of anthropo-
    morphism...................................256
    What Happened to My Car 280

11. The Smell of a Full Scottish Breakfast in the
    Morning 287
    How much? Nested digressions around
    Aussie wine.................................289
    Writers: What Not to Say 310
    Stop Press Handy Anti-Midge Tip...........322

12. Porridge and Scottishness, Football
     and Fireworks 323
     Fitba and the Greater Morality 338

13. Just the Whole Gantry, Then 351
     Why Roger and I have mixed feelings about
     Brad..371

14. The Ends of the Country......................384
     Welcome to the Free World 384
     Illegality: a thought experiment 404
     Orkney: a Handy Hint on blending in.......408

15. Tunnel Biking 415
     Last rant before the end......................428
     Redman's Blues 434

16. A Secret Still 436

     Pronunciation Guide..........................445

Everything in here is true.
Especially the bits I made up.

Introduction

Out of our Heads

"Banksie, hi. What you up to?"

"Well, I'm going to be writing a book about whisky."

"You're what?"

"I'm going to be writing a book about whisky. I've been, umm, you know, commissioned. To write a book about it. About whisky. Malt whisky, actually."

"You're writing a book about *whisky*?"

"Yeah. It means I have to go all over Scotland, driving mostly, but taking other types of transport — ferries, planes, trains, that sort of thing — visiting distilleries and tasting malt whisky. With expenses, obviously."

"You serious?"

"Course I'm serious!"

"Really?"

"Oh yeah."

". . . Do you need any help with this?"

★　★　★

Beginning with something ending; in these perverse times this seems somehow appropriate. But first, a sort of mission statement:

This is a book more than nominally about single-malt whisky, about the art of making it and the pleasure to be had in consuming it. It is also, partly, about the business of selling and promoting the stuff, about the whisky industry in general, about drink in general, even about mood- or perception-altering substances in general. It's not *just* about whisky, because drinking whisky is never about just drinking whisky; we're social creatures and we tend to drink in a social context, with family, friends or just accomplices. Even if we resort to drinking alone, we drink with memories and ghosts.

It's a book about the land and country I love, about Scotland and its people, its cities, towns and villages and the landscape around them. It isn't going to be a book of detailed tasting notes — frankly I don't have the nose, appearances being deceptive — though there will usually be a brief description of a whisky's generally accepted character, and occasional attempts to describe a particularly favoured dram in a more personal manner where I think I can get away with it. It's not a guide book to Scotland, either, though a few restaurants, hotels, cultural sites, scenic areas and tourist traps are bound to be mentioned.

I'm going to travel to the far north, to Caithness and Orkney; to Dumfries and Galloway, to Skye and Mull and Islay, to Speyside, Moray, Aberdeenshire, Perthshire, Argyll, Clydeside, Lothian and wherever else I can find distilleries. I'm not going to every single one (though I do intend to sample the wares of each, including some that are closed or no longer exist) because frankly they're not all worth seeing once you've a general idea how distilleries work, and also because they're not all set up to receive visitors and — after a few feet-finding, hand-holding pro-style tours at the start — I'm not looking for any special favours just because I'm writing a book.

It will — appropriately, given the subject matter — be a staggered tour; I'll be taking in distilleries in clusters and individually over single weeks and day trips, returning to my home in North Queensferry in between (at least partly because I'm intending to buy a full bottle of as many single malts as I can, and, with about a hundred distilleries in Scotland, plus the closed ones, I'll need to get back fairly frequently to off-load and free up some boot-space). North Queensferry — The Ferry, as we locals tend to call it — is where I lived until I was nine, and it's been my home for the last thirteen or so years. I have family here, and it's home, too, to a lot of memories. It's my hub, my docking station, and I make no excuses for returning here to recharge.

Roads, cars (quite a lot of roads, and quite a lot of cars, come to think of it . . . and one motorbike) are going to feature heavily in the book, as well as ferries, trains and aircraft and any other forms of transport I can find which can be shackled into the narrative if there's the even the least semblance of an excuse for it.

This is a search for the perfect dram, undertaken in the full knowledge that such a thing probably doesn't

3

exist. That doesn't matter; it's a quest, and any quest is at least partly its own point. And besides, you never know.

This book will, inevitably, be about me, my family and my friends too, especially those friends who have been persuaded — with, you may not be surprised to learn, no great deal of body-part manipulation involved — to take part in this project. As a natural result, old adventures — several of them involving no illegal activity whatsoever — and ancient anecdotes of dubious and disputed authenticity will be ruthlessly exhumed, exposed, exaggerated and exploited. This, let's face it, is a book about one of the hardest of hard liquors and for all this Let's be mature, I just drink it for the taste not the effect, honest, Two units a day only stuff . . . it is, basically, a legal, exclusive, relatively expensive but very pleasant way of getting out of your head.

And, talking about being out of our heads, this book can't help being about the war. You know the one; the Iraq war, Gulf War II, This Time It's Personal. My travels are starting just as the war begins, which makes it kind of hard to ignore, and, anyway, what's happening around me as I make my way across Scotland, visiting distilleries, has to have some bearing on matters; I don't intend to ignore the people or the places or the scenery or the weather around me as I make these journeys and I can't ignore the political environment either, both at home and abroad. This is not as peripheral as it might sound in a book about whisky; the stuff, certainly as we know it, has always been up to its pretty little bottle-neck in politics.

So. That ending at the beginning. Yesterday morning, on what was officially the first day of spring, my wife and I cut our passports in half and sent the remains to Mr Blair's office in Downing Street.

CHAPTER
ONE

These Drugs of Subtle Virtue

"Hiya, Banksie! Written any good books lately?"

"Not if you believe certain critics, but I'm going to be writing one about whisky."

"A book about whisky?"

"Yeah. Malt whisky."

"You're kiddin!"

"Not as such."

"This mean you're going to have to do the 'R' word?"

"The 'R' word? Oh! Research? Yeah, basically. Goin to have to drive round Scotland, or, well, be driven round Scotland, take trains, ferries, planes and such, go to distilleries, taste whiskies, that sort of —"

"And they're going to pay you for this?"

"They've already started."

"Right. I see. D'you need a hand?"

Friday the 21st of March 2003 is a good three-ferry day. It starts kind of weirdly; I get up very early and print up a load of A4 posters with your standard anti-war slogans: NO BLOOD FOR OIL, NOT IN MY NAME, and TONY BLIAR (my personal favourite, though probably not really all that effective). While those are printing I watch the breakfast news coverage of our bouncing, day-old war. I plaster the posters across the Land Rover: one in a transparent sleeve taped across the spare wheel on the rear door, six on the side windows. There's even one on the sunroof, though I think I must have been getting a bit carried away by this stage; the only people ever likely to see that one are passing helicopter pilots and people who happen to be walking over motorway bridges as I drive below.

After I've taken the scissors to our passports, I compose a brief covering letter, send an email explaining why we're doing what we're doing to the *Guardian*'s letters page and head into Inverkeithing to send the passports' remains via registered mail to 10 Downing Street.

I come home and say goodbye to Ann; I'll be away almost a week on Islay. After that, though I'm supposed to be making for the west coast, I head into central Edinburgh and drive around for a bit, trying to show off my posters along Queensferry Road, Charlotte Square and George Street before crossing Princes Street and going up the Mound past the temporary Scottish Parliament building to the castle and down the Royal Mile, then back to Princes Street.

In the city centre, on this bright, fresh, sunny day — singularly inappropriate for my mood, but there you go, that's the pathetic fallacy for you — a few people notice the posters and some of them nod or give a thumbs up; the people who disapprove just tend to look away. But most people don't look in the first place. Maybe I should have used coloured sheets of A4, or even just printed the words in something other than black, however big the font and however starkly pointed the gesture seemed at the time. Maybe I should have honked my damn horn.

I head west, out past the airport for the M8 through Glasgow, to cross the Clyde from Gourock to Dunoon.

Looking down at the trucks and cars sitting on the open vehicle deck on the ferry, I can't even see the poster on the Land Rover's sunroof; it's one of those stippled black glass sunroofs that just hinges up a little rather than slides right back, and because of the fine black mesh effect on the glass the writing on the poster is only visible from directly above.

I stand in the sunlight, listening to the cries of the wheeling gulls as I drink a Styrofoam cup of tea and munch on a soggy, microwaved shell pie. I watch the depressingly decrepit remains of what used to be the modestly majestic Gourock Pier fall astern to be replaced by the arse-out aspect of the old tenements whose more respectable fronts face out into the main street on the far side. A glitter of windscreens in the seafront car park where a few guys stand with fishing rods, then the outdoor swimming pool and the rising slope of pleasant Victorian sandstone villas and early and late twentieth-century bungalows. I look around, at the canted streets, budding trees and whin-covered slopes, crowned by the folly on top of Tower Hill to the

8

east, at the hills and mountains to the north and west, at the broad river, disappearing to a bright horizon in the south.

I used to live here, in Gourock. I used to work there, on the pier.

When I was young, from the age of about ten into my mid-teens, I'd lie awake at night in the summer in my bedroom high above the bay and the great curve of Gourock pier. Each fair night, in those warm months, I'd hear, through a cracked open window, the sound of a distant engine, puttering quietly away from the quayside a half-mile or so away. It came from one of the dozen or so ferries and steamers which always tied up there during the summer season.

It was the end of the Clyde's golden age, when not that many people had cars and a lot of Glaswegians still took day trips and whole two-week holidays doon the watter, to resorts like Largs, Dunoon and Rothesay. I worked on the pier — catching mooring ropes and hoisting gangways, mostly — for a couple of summers while I was at University in the early seventies, along with a couple of full-time pier porters and one or two old school pals from Gourock High. In retrospect, I feel privileged to have been there, witnessing the end of an era. We caught the ropes off the *Waverley* — the world's last sea-going paddle steamer, and still to be found thudding and splashing its way round the seaside resorts of Britain during the summer — and we watched the newfangled hovercraft come roaring up the beach near the Pilots' Station at the downstream end of the pier, spitting stones from under its skirts like bullets and generally making a nuisance of itself. As I say, the *Waverley*'s still hanging on in there, but the hovercraft never really caught on; some eras come and go almost before you realise they've started.

Now all the great steamers are gone and just the car ferries survive; there are a few small boats running across the Clyde to Helensburgh and Kilcreggan, and the odd booze cruise — sometimes on the *Waverley* if it's on the Clyde — to somewhere further afield, but that's your lot, and many of the old piers are crumbling away. Even Gourock pier, home to the Dunoon ferries, is mostly a ruin. The trains stop outside, further down the platforms instead of running on into the long galleried curve of the serried glass roof, most of which has been demolished, and even the pier's surface has disappeared once you go beyond the car ferry's ro-ro ramp; all that's left are the concrete foundations which used to support the wood and tarmac above.

It all looks a bit like somebody's mouth just after they've had most of their teeth removed. I think if you'd never seen the place before you'd find it ugly just on first principles, but for somebody like me, remembering how handsome it used to look, it's saddening too.

I hear there are plans to redevelop the whole seafront in Gourock and — always providing it's not just the usual excuse for developers to cram the maximum number of tiny flats into the one space with minimal facilities — it can't happen soon enough.

Public space/private space. I cheer myself up, partially, by gazing at the Defender.

10

The Land Rover: a paean.

Ah, the Land Rover. It is, to give its full title, a Land Rover Defender 110 County Station Wagon Td5. It's the particularly agricultural-looking model of the Land Rover stable, the ugly one in a family not noted for being overburdened with outrageously good looks in the first place. It has straight up-and-down sides and flat-plane glass all round (except for the wee curved windows set into the edge of the roof which are for looking up at mountains, allegedly). Engine sounds like a bucket of bolts in a tumble drier.

And, for some strange reason, I love this vehicle.

I never thought this would happen. I am a petrol-head, I confess. I like cars, I like motorbikes, I'm pretty fond of most modes of transport but I especially love stuff I can drive myself, because I just plain enjoy driving. My favourite fairground ride was always, and is still, the dodgems, for that very reason; you are — at least marginally — in control. Once I accepted that going the wrong way round and trying to hit as many people as possible — while exciting — was against the rules and promptly got you thrown out, I played it the other way round, trying to have as *few* collisions as possible; this was slightly less exciting, but much more satisfying. (The attraction of the modern extreme theme-park ride, where the competition amongst the designers seems to be to discover who can terrify the captive customer the most in the shortest time, almost entirely escapes me).

I strongly suspect that if I still lived in the south-east of England I wouldn't enjoy driving so much — or I'd do a lot of track-day stuff — but because I'm lucky enough to live where I want, in Scotland, and Scotland, away from the central belt (indeed still in places within it) is full of great driving roads, I have a deeply full and fulfilled driving life and a rather splendid ongoing relationship with my vehicles of choice and the roads I use them on.

So what am I doing driving a three-tonne diesel device with the aerodynamics of a scaled-up half-brick and apparently officially classed as a bus? And not just driving it, but really getting a kick out of driving it? I mean, this thing is trapped in the sixties: no air conditioning, no central locking, not even electric windows, and as for *air bags*: Ha! Air bags? *Air* bags? Defenders aren't especially soothing and pleasant places to be when they're the right way up and the road ahead is smooth and straight; you weren't seriously expecting to have a *crash* in comfort, were you?

What on earth do I see in this motorised Portakabin, this crude, noisy, rattly, stilt-tyred throwback with a comedy heating system that takes twenty minutes from cold to produce the first slight, damp hint of just-about-above-ambient-temperature air from its wheezing vents, whose turning circle is rivalled for tightness by your average canal narrow boat, whose front seat belts are cunningly sited so that they naturally fall into a position where they jam the door when you close it and whose aerodynamics are bettered by most motor homes and several bungalows? What can be the attraction?

Well, for one thing, the Land Rover has been chipped; something called a Stage Two Conversion has upped its horse power by 50 per cent, replacing — or at least reprogramming — the original engine management chip and fitting a beefier turbo (the "T" in Td5 stands for "Turbo", and it's a five-cylinder diesel engine).

This does not exactly transform the Land Rover into a Ferrari, but it does mean you can keep up with normal traffic and can tackle long motorway inclines without the ignominy of having to slow and change down from top gear (it has five forward gears, but could use a sixth). Keeping the original gears means that you do tend to have to whisk through them pretty quickly on the way up — there aren't many cars where you can comfortably change up to top gear at 40, even while going uphill — and the thing does feel a bit overrevved at motorway speeds. Still, there are useful peaks of acceleration to be found. You can sweep past startled slower drivers and caravans in the Land Rover, too, in other words; you just have to remember to slow down for the bends.

And you can *do* things to them; customise them, fit what is, in effect, chunky Landy jewellery to them, like ladders up the back, wading snorkels up the front, vehicle-long roof-racks, foot-plates on the wings so you can stand on them without scratching them, dinner-plate-sized driving lights, rear spot-lights, front towing hitches (they pretty much all have rear towing hitches).

13

There's even stuff you can do yourself if you're not utterly mechanically incompetent; I took off its four wee spring-loaded side-steps all by myself and replaced them with beefy-looking running boards over a year ago and they *still* haven't fallen off yet. On the inside, the long-wheelbase ones in particular let you stow vast quantities of junk in them. This is a vehicle with almost no conventional cubby holes or storage bins to speak of; what it has instead is a ludicrous number of nooks and crannies, once you start looking for them, mostly behind and under its many, many seats.

And you can fit a winch, the better to extricate yourself from awkward ditch-involving situations where even your low-ratio, differential-locked four-wheel drive and mud-plugging tyres won't get you out of your sticky predicament. Or so I'm told. Personally, I've never used the winch for that, but it has come in handy for boat-pulling-out duties and once got our old Drascombe Lugger (that's a boat, honest, not rhyming slang) onto the trailer and then the trailer out of the sea in circumstances probably no other vehicle but a tractor would have prevailed in.

The only trouble with all the ironmongery up front is that you're making an already deeply pedestrian-unfriendly vehicle even more lethal. Of all the things on the road you don't want to walk out in front of, a tooled-up Defender must figure pretty near the top of the list. The first thing you'll hit — no, let me correct that; the first thing that will hit *you* — is an industrial-looking winch capable of hauling five tonnes or so attached with extreme rigidity to a beefed-up

14

bumper you could hang a lifeboat off which is in turn bolted to an exceptionally sturdy steel ladder chassis which is attached to everything else. There is no give there, anywhere.

("Does this thing have crumple zones?"

"Yes. They're called other cars.")

In the Defender's defence, all I can say is that, realising all this, you do tend to drive even more carefully, especially in towns, given the sort of mess you could make of other people or lesser vehicles if you hit one.

The impressive view is useful here. Being so high up gives you a much better idea of what's going on between and beyond parked cars and, on the open road, helps with planning overtaking manoeuvres. The Defender's windscreen starts about where most cars' roofs top out and from a Defender — especially one like ours, fitted with tall 750 series tyres which would hardly look out of place on a tractor — you even get to look down on Range Rover drivers. And walls. You and your passengers get to look over walls and hedges and fences; even a totally familiar route opens up the first time you drive it in one of these beasts.

Other Defender advantages: they're hard to lose. Take your average car into a crowded supermarket car park, forget exactly where you left it and you can spend ages searching for the thing. A Defender is different; as you push your trolley out of the supermarket's front doors you can easily spot a Defender because it's the object blocking out the sun in the near, middle or far distance, depending. And, talking about supermarket trolleys, Defenders laugh in the face of those savage despoilers of metallic-finish car bodywork. Honestly; you can still feel deeply proud of and even attached to the thing, but you just stop caring about dings, dents and scratches.

In fact, a Defender doesn't really look quite right until it's got a few dents in its aluminium panels (Defenders look somehow distinctly embarrassed when they're all clean and gleaming, too, and as for the alloy wheels you sometimes see them fitted with . . . dearie me). Plus the high floor — at hip-height on me, and I'm just over six feet — is perfect for loading heavy stuff, much more spine- and disc-friendly than a low car boot, however commodious.

And, with a little experience, you can throw Defenders about to a surprising degree; they lean a lot and you're kept very aware indeed that you're driving something over two metres tall and only five feet wide, but, to some degree, they can be hustled. You can even get the tyres to squeal, though such larks do tend to alarm one's passengers and as a result are very much not recommended. They are also very much not recommended because that squealing noise from the rubber bits generally means you are a frighteningly small speed increment away from executing a series of spectator-spectacular but incumbent-injurious rolls-cum-somersaults immediately prior to becoming an embedded part, or parts, of the nearby scenery.

Last advantage. This really only affects people in London for now, but if I read the rules correctly, you can drive a Land Rover like mine into the central charging zone of London without having to pay the congestion charge. I'm not saying you *should*, of course, but I think in theory you could.

This is because a 110 County Station Wagon of this vintage has at least ten passenger seats. In theory it has eleven, believe it or not, but that includes the central seat in the front right beside the driver, where your passenger basically gets sexually assaulted every time an even-numbered gear is selected. Most people replace this effectively useless so-called seat with a cubby box for storing handy Landy stuff. As a result of this bizarre proliferation of seats and seat belts, the vehicle is effectively classed as a bus, and while it does mean that you face the added expense of an MOT from year one of ownership, not year three, this would easily be outweighed for Londoners by the benefits of even just a couple of weeks' free driving into the city centre.

Still a fine, bright, sunny day. Not warm, but mild, even on the water. The ferry shoulders its way through the knee-high waves; Gourock's drawn-out southern limits draw away and I walk to the other side of the boat to watch Dunoon and Argyll come closer.

What the hell am I doing here?

It all started a few months ago, with my agent. The way things are supposed to when you're a professional, after all. I was sitting at home in North Queensferry reading the paper and minding my own business on a cool October day when the phone rang.

"Hello?"

"Banksie. It's Mic. I may have something for you."

My agent is called Mic Cheetham; she's one of the best, kindest, nicest people I've ever met, but that's in civilian mode; as an agent she has the great and invaluable merit of treating the authors she represents like her cubs. She's the tigress, and you don't get between her and them, or even think about doing anything unpleasant to them, unless you want to be professionally mauled. Mic is a very good friend but when she's in full-on agent mode I'm just mainly glad that she's on my side. What was Wellington's remark about his troops? "I don't know what effect they'll have upon the enemy, but, by God, they frighten me." Something like that.

Anyway, Mic knows through years of experience and a deep tolerance of my congenital laziness that at least 95 per cent of the proposals that people contact her with concerning spiffing projects they want me to be part of she can either say No to without even asking me — though she'll always mention it later — or promise to pass on but with the warning that there's relatively little hope that I'm actually going to say Yes.

And if Mic says she might have something for me, it must be a proposal worth thinking about. The last time she sounded like this I ended up driving a Formula One car round the Magny-Cours circuit in deepest France for *Car* magazine and having a great time (with reservations; I discovered I'm really a pretty rubbish track driver).

"Uh-huh?" I said, successfully containing my excitement.

"How do you fancy being driven round every distillery in Scotland in a taxi and drinking lots of whisky? And then writing a book about it? For a not insubstantial sum. What d'you think? Eh? Hmm? Interested?"

I was so excited I think I took my feet off the desk.

I thought quickly (no, really). "Can I drive the taxi?"

"Then you can't drink."

"I'll do the drinking later."

"Then I don't see why not."

"Why a taxi anyway?"

"I think they're going for the incongruity factor; a black cab round the Highlands, puttering through the misty glens beneath the fearsome peaks, that sort of thing."

"These people are from London, aren't they?"

"Where else? Plus they thought you might share some witty repartee with a garrulous Glasgow cabbie."

"So they don't know me; good, good . . ."

"Anyway, Banksie, what do you think?"

"Can we ditch the taxi? I mean, they're fine in cities, but some of these distilleries are hundreds of miles away in the middle of nowhere."

"What do you propose to do? Walk?"

"No, I'll just use my own wheels. I'll drive myself. To drink. Ha!"

"So you'd be alone?"

"Yes."

"Then where's the witty repartee?"

"Maybe I can get some of my pals to come along and help with the driving and the tasting and the repartee

19

side of things. Some of my friends are quite witty. Well, they're always insulting me. That's the same thing, isn't it?"

"Of course it is, my dear."

". . . Hmm. And we are talking expenses included here, right? Petrol, hotels? Umm . . . More petrol?"

"Of course."

"And you really think they'll fall — they'll agree to this?"

You can hear somebody smile over the phone sometimes, just by the quality of their voice. "Leave it with me."

"Brilliant! I'll do it!"

Which is why I find myself standing on the deck of this ferry, heading for sunny Dunoon, about to start the research phase of — gee! — my first non-fiction book. This next week on Islay should be fun if I don't let the war get me down. And then there's Jura, of course; I want to get across to Jura this time, to visit the distillery there and maybe get to see Orwell's old house near the northern tip, and even — just possibly — finally see the Corryvrecken, the great tidal whirlpool between the north of Jura and the south of Scarba which I've heard about and seen some footage of (and mentioned in an earlier book or two) but always wanted to experience for myself. I mean; a whirlpool! One so ferocious you can hear it from miles away! How cool is that?

From Dunoon along the coast road — past the peaceful-again Holy Loch where the old US Polaris subs had their floating dock and support ships — to the first of the Great Wee Roads we're going to encounter in this book. Officially it's called the B836 but I'm really bad at recalling road numbers so to me it's filed in my head as the Great Wee Road To The Left Just Outside Dunoon Before You Get To The Younger's Botanical Gardens That Takes You Towards The Kyles Of Bute, The Colintraive Ferry For Bute, Tighnabruich And The Ferry For Tarbert. Or something like that.

At the head of Loch Striven I pass a field filled with huge dark brown wooden poles lying on the grass in the hazy sunlight. They look like oversize telephone poles, but must be due to carry power lines. The smell of creosote fills the Land Rover's cabin. Sometime round about here I realise I'm going to miss the next ferry to Tarbert, where I've been hoping to drop in on some old friends — and thus complete a clean sweep of ex-editors this weekend — so I take a detour to Otter Ferry via a precipitous wee road curling over the hills towards Loch Fyne.

Great Wee Roads: a digression.

A Great Wee Road in my terminology just means a small road that isn't a main route and which is fun to drive. Often it will be a short cut or at least an alternative route to the main road. It will virtually never be quicker than the main-road route but it will be a pleasure to drive, perhaps partly because it has less traffic, partly because it goes through lots of beautiful scenery and perhaps because it has lots of flowing curves, sudden dips, challenging hills and/or fast straights (though GWRs rarely have many of those). A GWR can be extremely slow — often *way* below the legal limit — and still be enormous fun, it can even be a single-track road, quite busy with traffic and so somewhat frustrating, and yet still be a hoot, and some roads only really become GWRs when it's raining and you have to slow down.

Anyway, that single-lane-with-passing-places route over to Otter Ferry — snaking up some deciduously wooded slopes towards the broad flat tops of the low hills and their close-ranked bristles of pines — is definitely a GWR.

By the side of Loch Fyne I head north again and back down Glendaurel, finally having to press on once more as I've ever so slightly underestimated the time required — again — and so end up gunning the Defender up the long curving slopes towards the viewpoint looking out over the Kyles of Bute (this is one of the best views in Argyll, maybe one of the great views of Scotland; a vast, opening delta of ragged, joining lochs, flung arcs of islets and low-hilled island disappearing into the distance).

This must be the first time — certainly the first time in decent weather — I haven't stopped to take in that great sweep of view. The Land Rover tackles the hill fast in top gear, leaning mightily on the bends but still seat-of-the-pants secure; it feels good, but I'm annoyed at myself for not being able to spare the view more than a glance as I whiz by the car park at the summit.

★ ★ ★

Getting on to the ferry from Portavadie to Tarbert is a bit easier than it used to be; last time I was here you had to reverse onto the boat, which must have been fun if you were towing a caravan. Back then, a few years ago now, my car was the only vehicle on the ferry, which felt kind of romantic somehow. I was on the way to meet an ex-girlfriend for lunch; a strictly platonic visit, but, still, there was a certain poignancy there.

A year or so later the same ferry figured at the start of the first episode of the TV adaptation of *The Crow Road*, with young Joe McFadden playing the central character, Prentice McHoan, standing all alone on the deck, coming back to his family home for a funeral. I remember watching that first episode on a pre-transmission video and being very nervous — *The Crow Road* was the first book I'd ever had successfully adapted for the screen — and when I saw that first image, and made the connection with the ferry journey I'd taken a year or so earlier, I had one of those It's-going-to-be-all-right Good Omen feelings that I'm not sure atheists like me are really allowed to have (but appreciate now and again all the same), and relaxed, deciding that probably this was going to be a good adaptation. Which, I'm happy to report, it was.

For the whole journey I've been listening to a mixture of the radio and some ancient select tapes; the radio for the latest news on the war and the old compilation tapes because I'm still feeling a bit emotional about the war, I suppose, and want something nostalgic and comforting to listen to. I've brought my Apple iPod too, along with the adaptor that lets it communicate with the Land Rover's tape player (CDs are *far* too hi-tech for Defenders of this vintage; I counted myself lucky it hadn't arrived with a seventies-stylee eight-track) but I haven't bothered connecting it.

So my listening consists of a mixture of breathless embedded journalists telling me how much progress the US and British troops are making, dashing across the sands towards Baghdad and Basra, and old songs from the decade before the first Gulf War.

Tarbert to Kennacraig, where the ferry for Islay leaves, takes ten minutes. The voyage to Port Ellen lasts a couple of hours, the late afternoon becoming night. On the boat I sit in the bar reading the paper, soaking up the war, then read some of the whisky books I've brought along as research. I drink a couple of pints. Usually if I'm going to be driving later I don't drink alcohol but if I'm on a long ferry journey with a very short drive at the far end I'll allow myself up to the legal limit. Two pints of Export is safe enough, though it's also heading up towards my other limit, when I start thinking, Hmm, quite fancy a fag.

Blame the dope. When I first started smoking the occasional joint it was always resin crumbled into tobacco — I don't think I *saw* grass for about ten years after my first J — and later, especially during what you might call binge smoking sessions, when my pals and I were arguably too wrecked to roll another number or load just one more bong, it was just sociable as well as a hell of a lot easier to have a straight, smoke an ordinary cigarette. So as a result I have a sort of sporadic, part-time addiction, and have decided that yes, that old piece of poisonous propaganda my generation were peddled is actually true, cannabis does lead you on to stronger and much, much more lethal drugs. Well, one, anyway; specifically, to tobacco, if that's what you mix it with. Ah, the joys of cretinous prohibition (. . . we'll be returning to this theme later. Just in case you're under any illusions).

But it's odd; when I'm sober I hate the smell of cigarette smoke. I'm the kind of person who tells people smoking on non-smoking trains to put their fag out. (Thinks: Hmm, I believe the technical term for this is "hypocrite"? No?) I even do this on the last train, when people are often drunk and seem to think that makes it okay to smoke, and I've been known to do this even when they're bigger than I am or there's more of them.

However. Just let me sink a few pints or a few whiskies or a few whatever and — especially if I'm with people who smoke — I start thinking that a cigarette would just round the buzz off nicely. Usually I manage to resist. Sometimes, very drunk, feeling extremely socially relaxed, I succumb, and start cadging fags off my pals.

And, while I may not pay for my habit in financial terms — apart from the occasions when I feel I've smoked too many of somebody else's fags, when I'll go and buy them a packet . . . though they're never my fags, you understand; they're my friends', because I

25

don't really smoke, see? — I do pay. Extensive research has revealed that my hangovers are consistently between 50 and 100 per cent worse the next morning if I've been smoking, compared to the control group of Standard Bad Hangovers And Their Usual Indicators (number and type of painkillers required, extent of sighing and quiet moaning, ability to string more than three words together, depth of desire to consume large greasy breakfasts, etc.).

On the ferry I also have a Cal Mac chicken curry and chips with lots of tomato sauce. This is, I realise, your basic poor/horribilist cuisine, and almost as awful a confession as owning up to smoking, but it's become something of a tradition for me on Caledonian MacBrayne ships, especially on the five-hour journey from Oban to Barra, where Ann and I spend a week or so most years.

We're talking the sort of curry you used to get in school, like chip shop curry or a Chinese restaurant curry; curry like they almost don't do it anywhere else any more (and for good reasons); frequently all glutinous with too much cornflour and with the chicken meat often boiled and simmered down to fibres, the whole thing coloured a suspicious-looking dark, mustardy yellow, doubtless loaded with sodium and E-numbers. Plus the chips are rarely better than okay. However, as a strange sort of slumming-it treat, it works for me. I actually look forward to one of these when we're planning trips to Barra, and I was genuinely pleased to find that they had the same dish on the Islay service.

On the Barra trip I always know to take a dumpy little bottle of tomato sauce with me so I have a decent helping with which to slather the chips, but even without that and being forced to use a handful of those annoying little sachets instead, it is a joy. Albeit a guilty one.

Of course, when I get to where I'm going I find that my hosts have cooked some fresh-off-the-farm's-own-fields lamb with gleaming new potatoes and a selection of succulent vegetables, and I feel really guilty about the mass-production time warp pseudo curry I've just eaten on the boat, but that's just the way it goes. Anyway, I have a couple of glasses of wine, and then another couple of glasses of wine . . . and then a second dinner partly out of politeness but partly also because it all just looks and smells so good.

And that, I strongly suspect, is the start of a process which sees me put on nearly a stone in weight during the laughingly entitled "research" phase of this book.

CHAPTER
TWO

Does not Rhyme with "Outlay"

"Banksie, what's this about you writing a book about whisky?"

"It's true. They're going to pay me to drive round Scotland, or be driven round Scotland . . . whatever, visiting distilleries and drinking whisky."

"So it wasn't a joke?"

"No, not a joke."

"And you're sure it's not a dream you've, like, mistaken for reality?"

"Definitely. I have a signed contract. Want to hear it rustle?"

"Just wanted to be sure. So, you'll be wanting help with this . . ."

The first signpost you see coming off the ferry at Port Ellen on Islay has only two words on it; it points right to ARDBEG and left to BOWMORE. Brilliant, I thought; a road sign that is made up 100 per cent of distillery names; a proclamation that you are on an island where the making of whisky is absolutely integral to the place itself, where directions are defined by drink!

This was, patently, a great place to start the distillery tour. I love Islay whiskies. There are seven working distilleries on the island — pretty good given that there are less than three thousand people on the place — each producing their own distinctive whiskies, and I have a deep affection for all of them. I have favourites amongst those seven basic malts, but they're basically all in my top twenty Scotches. This may, I suppose, change over the course of the next two or three months as I visit distilleries throughout Scotland and taste whiskies I've only ever heard of before (and in a few cases, never heard of before), but I doubt it'll make that much difference; it's hard to believe there are tastes as dramatic as the Islay malts that have somehow escaped the attention of me and my pals.

The reason I've taken to them so much is, I suppose, that Islay whiskies are just generally bursting with flavour. Actually, make that bursting with flavours, plural. I came to the realisation many years ago that I like big, strong, even aggressive tastes: cheddars so sharp they make your eyes water, curries in general, though preferably fairly hot, Thai meals, garlic-heavy Middle-Eastern mezes, chilli-saturated Mexican dishes, hugely fruity Ozzie wines, and thumpingly, almost aggressively flavoured whiskies (for the record the things I don't like are: Brussels sprouts, marzipan, cherries and Amaretto. Plus one other category of foodstuff that we'll come to later ... it's a bit embarrassing).

Distinguishing between the different styles of Islays, the most obvious micro-area lies in the south, on the short stretch of coast — extravagantly frayed, wildly indented, profusely hummocked and multifariously cragged — facing south-east towards the Mull of Kintyre.

The three southern coastal whiskies of Islay — with Laphroaig in particular providing the most radical example — constitute what is almost a different drink from whisky. The distinction is that sharp; I know several people who like their drink, love their whisky — be it the stuff you'd serve to somebody who's severely overstayed their welcome or the special reserve you'd only bring out for the most special of special occasions — who hate Ardbeg, Lagavulin and Laphroaig with a vengeance. Of the three, they usually especially hate Lagavulin and Laphroaig, and, out of that pair, reserve their most intense aversion for Laphroaig.

Pronunciation: a word.

In the paragraph above there are, in order of appearance — and coincidentally alphabetical order — one that's fairly self-evident (Ardbeg), one that's not as tricky as it might look to the untutored eye at first sight (Lagavulin), and one definitely iffy example (Laphroaig). Here's the trick: there's a pronunciation guide at the back of this book, [not included].

I've even underlined the relevant bit to emphasise in each name because that might just make all the difference between success and failure when you're trying to order a specific dram from a hard-of-hearing or just plain awkward bar person, especially late on when you might be drunk and slurring your words. Don't say I'm not good to you.

And can we please deal with the difference between "lock" — which is either a thing found on a door or a way of raising or lowering a boat on a canal — and "loch", which is generally the name given to a body of water in Scotland which in England would be termed a lake? The "ch" sound (as in loch, broch, and indeed och) is a soft, sibilant noise made at the back of the mouth with the tongue drawn back and upwards. It sounds a bit like distant surf, if you want to get romantic about it. What it does not sound like is "ck".

Well, unless we're talking about either of the occurrences in Bruichladdich. Or Glen Garioch in Aberdeenshire.

And let's not even mention the Lake of Menteith.

One last thing; back when I lived in London, in the early eighties, an ad agency was running a campaign for the Duty-Free shops at Heathrow and one of the posters I'd see in the tube stations showed a bottle of (if I recall correctly) Laphroaig, with the byline "Islay for less outlay". This implies the two relevant words rhyme, and is wrong. The first bit of the island's name sounds like "Isle" and the end is just "la". That simple. So let's not have any more of these gratuitous cross-border mispronunciations.

Now, those southern Islays. Some people can't stand the taste of the three but keep trying every now and again, wishing that they could appreciate these strange, fierce, acerbic whiskies the way other people obviously do, others are just perplexed that anybody would want to drink such bizarre-tasting stuff but leave it at that, while others seem to hate them the way you'd despise an especially loathsome politician. Their most intense regret, bewilderment or venom, respectively, is generally reserved for Laphroaig, as the most intensely different — even wilfully incongruous — example of Extreme Whisky.

The comparison I think is most apt in the wider field of drink is probably Chateau Musar. This is one of my favourite red wines in the world, but it is profoundly different from other reds, especially other reds generally considered to be worth a place on a decent wine list. It is spicy. In fact, it's spicy in a way that is utterly different from what a wine taster will normally mean when they apply the word "spicy" to any other fine wine. It's a bit like the difference between somebody having red hair and somebody wearing a red wig the colour of a British postbox; the word "red" is the same, but once you know the context, once you know what sort of red is being talked about, the image you have of the person being described alters drastically.

So with Chateau Musar; it's so different from any other fine red wine it practically needs a separate category of drink to define it (in *Michael Broadbent's Vintage Wine*, an authoritative and astoundingly comprehensive overview of 50 years of wine-tasting, it merits a categorisation all of its own).

Chateau Musar is made by a man called Serge Hochar — son of Gaston, who started the enterprise — in circumstances which have, over the years, certainly — and frequently — merited the description "difficult". When other wine makers talk about a difficult year they mean there was a late frost or a too-damp September; when Mr Hochar says it was a difficult year you suspect he means that there were landmines to remove from between the vines or that there was an unexpectedly high number of extremely brief, sudden and entirely unannounced visits from the Israeli Air Force. Chateau Musar is from Lebanon. Specifically, it is from the Bekaa valley, notorious over the decades as the location of training camps for terrorists/freedom fighters (the reader is invited to choose as appropriate to their dogma). Wags have been known to shake bottles of the stuff by their ear, claiming to be listening for the tell-tale chinking sound of shrapnel.

Despite all this, Mr Hochar has succeeded in producing a vintage every year apart from one, and not just producing any old harshly ropy but high-novelty-value gut-rot, either; Musar is in every sense a fine wine.

But very different; again, some people, solely through taste rather than prejudice, can't stand the stuff. Just like Laphroaig it is sometimes referred to as an acquired taste, though I'm not sure about this. I suspect more people stick with their original reaction to both drinks rather than start out hating only to end up loving.

Whatever; Laphroaig in particular is a hell of drink, especially if you don't like it. It's oddly peaty (oddly because there's much less peat involved in the making of it than in most whiskies we think of as peaty) and positively bursting with smells straight out of the medicine cabinet, the quayside, a road repair depot and even an industrial plant (mouthwash, disinfectant, iodine, cough sweets . . . actually make that cough sours . . . seaweed, tar, diesel, oil . . .). Pungent, no-holds-barred stuff, though arguably not quite as remorselessly astringent as it used to be.

I think the truth is that, as well as having changed somewhat over the years to a *slightly* mellower formulation, Laphroaig is just a very slow-maturing whisky; it still has enormous, restless, raw energy and character at an age when most other whiskies would be starting to take on too much of the character of the barrel they've been matured within, turning woody. Not this stuff. At ten years it's ferocious, full of antagonistic flavours, sweet and sour and tarry, redolent of peat, pepper and burnt toffee. It shouldn't all work together — and as I say, for some people, it never will — and yet it does, magnificently. Five years later it's still powerful, though more balanced, slightly sweeter, less demanding, and deeper, while at 30 years it's finally getting to the Hmm, just about perfect stage (apparently — I've never tasted Laphroaig this old; I'm relying on usually reliable sources here).

Lagavulin, barely a whisky-barrel's throw away along the coast, is a close second on the in-your-faceness stakes, which was kind of the idea, as the guy who had the place built, Sir Peter Mackie, was trying to make a whisky like Laphroaig. What's there on the site now is the result of a combination of three separate distilleries, themselves the distillation of about ten distinct bothies-with-stills which used to make spirit back in the pre-excise days when it was all just a cosy wee cottage industry and everybody was basically semi-pro.

Once upon a time: distilling as a cottage industry.

In the old days people made whisky because it was just part of the life of being a crofter (a croft being the Scottish term for a small farm). You grew barley, you harvested it, and what you couldn't feed your family or your animals with, you could either sell, or make into whisky, which you could also use yourself, or sell. Turning barley into whisky was a good way of storing your surplus; barley goes mouldy in a damp climate. Whisky doesn't.

To people like this, making beer or whisky from their crops was as much part of their lives as sowing the seeds at the start of the season or bringing in the harvest at the end. To them the government was a distant entity with little day-to-day relevance to their lives; when, during the gradual commodification and commercial exploitation of whisky, the politicians decided that people would no longer be allowed to make their own whisky unless they did so on an industrial scale, and paid the government for the privilege, it must have seemed as outrageous to the crofters as if they were to be taxed for heating a kettle of water, or making soup. Little wonder the excise men, charged with policing these new and generally hated laws and bringing in the loot they would produce, were so despised, obstructed and vilified.

Lagavulin — made in pear-shaped stills which are so pear-shaped they look like they were deliberately modelled on pears — has a dry, salty taste, and is usually more sherry-influenced than a similarly aged Laphroaig, though still reeking of smoke and peat. For a long time this was my second favourite Islay, a short nose ahead of the wonderful Ardbeg.

My tastes do seem to have changed over the years, and these days I'd put Bowmore near the top of the list just under Laphroaig. Bowmore is north and west of the south coast's Big Three, on the — relatively — balmy coast of Loch Indaal. As a producer, Bowmore has a richness throughout its range of whiskies that makes it one of the handful of very best distilleries in Scotland; as well as the 12, 17 and 21-year-olds they have others with names like Legend (eight to ten years old), Mariner (fifteen) and Darkest (probably about the same age as Mariner, though there's no age stated). There are lots of other expressions available given sufficient time and money, but that's enough to be going on with for now.

Put it this way; those mentioned above range from merely very good indeed to utterly stunning, with a power and opulence of taste bursting through the older whiskies that beggars belief. There's intense smoke — though like summer bonfires, not just peat fires — whin scent on a sea breeze, plus the entire contents of a well-stocked florist. Just the most glorious, life-affirming stuff. I can accept that people might not like Laphroaig and maybe the other south coasters, but if you can't find a Bowmore to fall in love with, you may have to consider very seriously the possibility that you're wasting your money drinking whisky at all.

Distillery aesthetics: a highly partial overview.

Many distilleries are quite beautiful. A lot, probably the majority, are set in scenery which is somewhere between rather lovely and utterly magnificent. There is, obviously, no real link between the nobility of the distillery's environs or its architectural attractiveness and the worth of the whisky made there. There are a few quite gorgeous distilleries, jewels in fabulous settings or just extremely interesting architecturally, which produce whisky of no great singular merit (though they often contribute significantly to fine blends). On the other hand there is, for example, Glenlivet, which — while it rests within some perfectly pretty Speyside hill-and-glen scenery — from any direction I've ever come at it from, looks like a bit of a mess, sprawling across its hillside in a bedraggled mixture of building styles, proportions and textures which end up being anything but easy on the eye.

And it doesn't matter, because Glenlivet is rightly regarded as one of the great Speysides, indeed one of the great single malt whiskies. It would be nice if it was produced in something obviously befitting its intrinsic stature, something of either perfectly natural, almost organic vernacular elegance, or of painstakingly careful design by Lutyens or Sir Richard Rogers, but that would just be a bonus, and it's better that the attention of all concerned is on the whisky itself, not the buildings, rather than the other way round.

The Islay distilleries are all pretty spoiled when it comes to setting. The two least favoured are Bruichladdich and Bowmore, the former because it's just a pleasant assemblage of buildings by a nice wee village on a stretch of shore which is by turns sandy and rocky, with a broad, shallow sea loch in front and low, tree-lined hills behind (see, it's actually in a pretty damn spiffing situation, but we're talking relative values here); the latter because it's in a roughly similar context on the opposite side of Loch Indaal and is part of the town of Bowmore. In fact, the distillery's so integrated into the rest of the town that, when its stills are producing, the excess hot water helps to heat the municipal swimming pool next door. Again, Bowmore, Islay's effective capital, is a fine, attractive little town and no disgrace at all to the smart, tidy distillery on its southern perimeter, it's just that the other Islay distilleries are so much more dramatic in their surroundings.

The three south coasters look out to the long arm of sea that is the . . . well, to be honest I'm not sure. Even after scrutinising my dad's old Admiralty charts I can't decide whether it's a sort of out-pouching of the Irish Sea, part of the Atlantic or the start of the Sound of

Jura. Anyway, it's deepish water, and can be wild in a winter storm. Small islands — more like jagged scatters of rock — pierce the waters offshore and the distilleries look sort of nestled into the broken folds of the sea-facing land, as if they've squatted there amongst the boulders, lochans and trees and then sort of wriggled about to get themselves hunkered down and comfortable.

They look elegant. They have whitewashed walls, black roofs and black detailing, pagodas standing proud, clipped lawns and a general air of discreet pride. Handily, all of them have their names in VERY LARGE LETTERS painted in black on their tallest seaward walls, so if you take a photo from the right angle you never need to scratch your head and mutter, Well, I *think* it looks like Laphroaig, but maybe it's Ardbeg . . .

Caol Ila and Bunnahabhain sit in even more dramatic scenery, wedged at the bottom of steep hillsides as though teetering on the brink of falling into the sea, looking respectively across and up the Sound of Jura, with the Paps of Jura rising in an appropriately, if colossally, mammiform manner across the water. There used to be a quite spectacularly complete but rusty wreck lying at a steep angle up on the rocks just along the coast from Bunnahabhain — I remember seeing it from the ferry as we approached from Colonsay, a dozen years or so ago — but the same stormy seas that drove the ship there in the first place have pounded it to pieces since and there's little left to see now.

Given its remote and wild situation it seems almost odd that Bunnahabhain produces what is in some ways

39

the lightest, least dramatic Islay whisky; it's still quite oily and salty while being moderately sherry-sweet and has a hint of peat, but it's a mellow drink compared to the others, and also compared to its dramatic, thrown-down setting. I feel I'm kind of damning it with faint praise here, but it's actually a very fine malt, and if all the Islays were as ferociously heavy hitting as Laphroaig, brandishing their peat, smoke and iodine in your face, the island would lose a great deal; Bunnahabhain is more the strong, silent type, and none the worse for that. Quite a lot of it goes into Black Bottle, making it perhaps the best reasonably-priced blend on the market, certainly for Islay lovers.

On Islay I'm staying at Ballivicar farm, near Port Ellen, with Toby and Harriet Roxburgh. Toby is a rotund, ruddy figure, avowedly Scottish yet with an accent he himself describes as "cut-glass". Toby has the best basilisk stare I've ever encountered (though never, happily, in anger) and once told the late Robert Maxwell to "Fuck off!", and lived — and remained employed — to tell the tale. I think hopper loads of respect are due on that count alone.

Educated and erudite, witty and well read, Toby is a man I first got to know as the person who bought *The Wasp Factory* for paperback, when he was editor of Futura. Later he took on *Consider Phlebas*, my first science fiction novel, and we really got to know each other at the first SF convention I ever attended, in 1986. I say got to know; what I mean is I lay on the floor in the bar under a table with a pint of beer balanced on my chest, wondering vaguely why the ceiling seemed so close, while Toby generously plied my wife with champagne.

It was at the same convention, Mexicon II, that I first encountered John Jarrold. A famous fan — I have no intention of attempting to explain the intricacies or even the basics of British SF Fandom In The Late Twentieth Century, Its Customs And Mores; you'll just have to accept concepts like that of a famous fan — John later became a respected editor, and not just of science fiction.

John and I haven't met up for some time and neither of us has seen Toby and Harriet for years, so a rendezvous on Islay has been arranged, John flying in earlier on the Friday afternoon from Hastings via Heathrow and Glasgow. We'll meet up with photographer Martin Gray tomorrow. Martin has taken on the unenviable job of trying to take a decent photograph of me for the book's cover. My editor for this book, Oliver Johnson, will appear on Monday, arriving on the plane that will take John back down south.

John sits in the Roxburghs' kitchen, having just finished some of the lamb I at first refuse and will later tuck into. He is resplendent in an impressively thick white cable-knit jumper and what certainly appears to be an equally impressively thick white cable-knit beard and moustache. John has a seemingly photographic memory for Shakespeare, the words of every musical ever committed to celluloid and the dialogue from most films of the past 50 years. This, coupled with a profoundly ingrained desire to share this knowledge

41

with you, does, of course, make him a *deeply* annoying person to watch a film with if you haven't already seen it and he has, but it's a small price to pay.

Well, that and the fact that when he starts quoting Shakespeare and you think, Ha, I know this bit! and join in, you inevitably find that the segment you know only extends to cover the next couple of lines, whereas the verses John's regaling you with seemingly stretch on, through and indeed occasionally beyond the next Act. Never mind, the guy's a joy to be with and he did arguably save my life once, on a hotel balcony in Brighton very early one morning back in the late eighties, so I shouldn't criticise just because he knows stuff I don't (we'll come to the dangerous details of the balcony scene and Toby's "Just a Few Drinks for Friends" Party later).

Harriet, Toby's wife, is equally wonderful and even more ruddy-cheeked than her husband, with a great, pealingly infectious laugh and a neat ability to control a fully loaded quad bike while remaining undistracted by a small platoon of accompanying dogs and children. She drives a mean chariot too (they have a chariot made from plywood, an old car axle and what looks like bent scaffolding poles which gets lashed onto the Clydesdale and pulled round the fields with Harriet and a bunch of bouncing, whooping, yelling children aboard. No idea why). Harriet is usually to be found tramping across the farmyard with a bucket of something noisome or just plain smelly swinging from each arm.

The Roxburghs and their farm present an image which, for all its eccentricities, encapsulates fairly representatively what British farming at a certain scale — i.e. not gigantic — has become. Heads are kept above water by extreme, almost tortuous diversification, so that as well as the animal husbandry side (involving both sheep and cattle, and both enterprises perpetually and grotesquely complicated by a brain-boggling array of EU and DEFRA rules and regulations for which the adjective "Byzantine" seems woefully inadequate, hinting as it does, relatively speaking, at a regulatory scheme of sweet reason and minimalist elegance compared to the carbuncular reality), money is made from the holiday flats converted from stables attached to the main farm building, from a pony-trekking business and livery sideline, from a waste-paper-shredding scheme and from Toby's one-week-a-month job as editor of the *Ileach*, Islay's very own newspaper. NB: regardless of how Islay itself is pronounced, Ileach, which means somebody from Islay, is pronounced "Eelich". Sorry about this continual pronuncial complexity, but as my computer occasionally informs me in its Stephen Hawking voice, It's not my fault.

When we arrive at the farm, Belinda, Toby and Harriet's daughter, has not long returned from maternity hospital in Glasgow. Living on an island like Islay for any substantial amount of time will, unless you keep in very rude health indeed, eventually convince you that helicopter air ambulances are very noisy and not that glamorous after all. Belinda has returned with

43

her tiny, beautiful brand new baby daughter called Beth, sister to Rachael. Rachael is four and very strong willed. She is an uninhibited singer at bath time and hums when she draws. A lovely, single-minded, head-down-determined, even grumpy child, it's too early to tell whether she's inherited the female Roxburgh laugh from her mother and grandmother. I like her a lot. Belinda is married to Robert, who is chef at the nearby Machrie Hotel and does wonderful things with local scallops, venison and beef.

We're driving out to the Machrie for lunch when we see a buzzard. "Oh wow," I say. "A buzzard! Look." Ann and I are big fans of buzzards; we're members of the RSPB but not very dedicated ornithologists, and a buzzard is one of the few large birds we're able to identify confidently. They're becoming much more common than they once were but it's still literally remarkable for us to see one near where we live. The specimen we spot on the way to the Machrie is a big, slow-flapping adult, making its way empty-taloned across the fields to a nearby telephone pole, to perch and scan.

"Ha!" Toby says bitterly, glaring at the thing. "Buzzards. They're the reason we don't have any songbirds at Ballivicar."

"Oh," I say, crest rapidly falling. What a townie you're showing yourself to be, Banks, I think.

"And as for the otters —"

"You have otters?" I say, delighted again. "I *love* —"

Toby growls. "Damn things keep eating the ducks."

"Ah."

Islay is a fertile, fecund place which is surrounded by — almost infested with — wildlife. There are orcas, dolphins and seals off the coasts, feeding on unseen numbers of fish and crustacea. There are three species of deer scattered through the forests and hills, each of them apparently pursuing lives largely dedicated to jumping out in front of cars at night with the absolute minimum of warning, in — one has to assume — some misplaced spirit of sportingness. There are multitudinous birds of prey, including those songbird-snaffling buzzards, clouds and carpets of wintering geese — just passing through to refuel from and leave fertiliser on the fields (again, at least three different species) — pheasants (plump, brightly coloured birds prone to wandering around fields, hedgerows, verges and any intriguingly tarmacked surface with a distracted air, looking vaguely lost, as though they have the sneaking suspicion they should be somewhere else . . . basically road kill waiting to happen), otters (boo! hiss! *Bad* otters!), hares — *lots* of hares, usually seen bounding away on back legs that somehow look too long for them, as though they've borrowed them from a young gazelle — rabbits, plus a whole slew of smaller creatures that are generally only seen in squashed form, decorating the lumpy, undulating, peat-floated road surfaces of Islay with brown-red splodges of fur, meat and bone. These are, especially when fresh — and indeed preferably twitching — of enormous and consuming interest to the noisy flocks of crows which would otherwise be happily employed looking for sheep recently fallen on their backs so they can peck out their

45

eyes or get stuck into their juicily vulnerable nether regions.

There's so much wildlife on Islay it even interferes with the whisky-making. Worst culprits are the geese, who've been known to devour entire fields of barley destined for the honour of becoming whisky, but this hasn't stopped fish and mammals from trying to get in on the act as well; the day we went to Bunnahabhain they were taking apart one of the cooling columns in the still room because a trout had got into the system from the sea, wedged in the heat exchanger and stopped the whole operation in its tracks. It was even — and evenly — cooked, due to the proximity of the place it got stuck to the hot bits of the pipe work, though whether anybody actually ate it afterwards is not recorded. They were discussing putting a better baffle plate or something on the inlet pipe when we left and talking about how that otter managed to get itself wedged in the same place last year.

It may not exactly be the Serengeti, but living on any farm, especially one in a place with as many wild animals around as Islay, seems to constitute a rapid lesson in the brusque realities of animal life and death; if you didn't accept the red-in-tooth-and-claw stuff before you get involved with country life, you very soon will. I suppose it's one reason why farming seems to be a largely hereditary occupation, and why many people who think it'll be nice to work with animals on a more permanent basis end up having a very short career in the business.

I've never met a farmer yet who didn't have a whole herd of grisly animal horror stories (often as not involving choice phrases like "prolapsed uterus" or "maggot-infested wounds"). They are only too willing to share these tales with you in gaspingly forensic detail, presumably to remind you of the non-monetary cost of the food in your belly (food which, given the sheer gawd-awfulness of some of the stories, they are often in considerable danger of shortly being able to inspect for themselves). Even the purely arable farmers without a true beast to their name seem to have a stock of tales fit to turn the stomach of a starving vulture.

Life at Ballivicar strikes me as a complicated, often physically and emotionally strenuous but ever-involving and frequently rewarding existence of sustained bucolic chaos, surrounded by chemicals and feed stuffs, hay and manure, machinery, vehicles and tack, by chickens, cats, dogs, sheep, cows, ponies, horses, that ever-present cornucopia of local wildlife and a glorious, bewildering squall of absurdly apple-cheeked children running roaring around in dusty paddocks; barefoot, yelling, caked in muck and generally having what certainly looks like a totally brilliant time. You find yourself having an engrossing conversation with a bright, happily snot-nosed four-year-old who's come up to ask your name and show you a length of plastic pipe they've decided is a trumpet; you look around in the sunlight at the primary surroundings; bright green grass, rich red earth and pure blue sky and you think, Grief, who'd raise a child in a city?

Then you think, Well, billions do, because they have to, because that's the way the modern world's been moving for centuries and there doesn't look like much around to reverse that course. And suddenly you worry about the child you're talking to, imagining this sunny openness, this cheery, inquisitive innocence being transplanted to the big bad city where instead of being one of the most happily beautiful things you've seen, it becomes a liability, a point of weakness, to be exploited by those unscrupulous enough to treat trust as gullibility and people as collateral, to be damaged.

Finally, though, with a little more thought, you accept that what you see before you still represents such a great start in life, that just as a childhood spent in the muck and glaur, eating dirt and falling into the nettles turns out to be a much more effective way of inoculating a child against infections and allergies to come than keeping them antiseptically spotless and clean, so this farmyard, outdoorsy life of crowded rough and tumble must have its own full suite of lessons about trust and betrayal, allegiances and self-reliance that will translate to any future situation; children are more resilient than we fear and wiser than we think, and we probably worry more than we need.

Childhood: a sentimental detour.

It seems to me that almost nothing in life is so important as being loved and cared for as a child. Maybe only an early death ever means more, has more bearing on the ultimate shape of an existence. Even a

48

vast lottery win or some other great stroke of fortune means little in comparison, because the legacy of one is liable to affect so profoundly the reaction to the other.

Somebody who's been loved, who has been brought up to feel respect for themselves and to feel and show respect for others, who has felt cherished and cared for and has been sheltered from harm as much as possible while never being deceived into thinking that life will essentially always be painless, has something more valuable than inherited fortune or title, and stands a far better chance of coping with whatever challenges life subsequently throws at them than somebody with only material advantages. Nothing guarantees success or even survival, and any auspicious start can be overwhelmed by future calamity, but the chances of avoiding tragedy are better — and even the journey to any eventual bitterness all the easier — with a childhood informed by love.

I have to confess an interest here; I had the great good fortune to be born to parents who loved me and did all they could do to give me the best possible start in life. I was an only child and so I suppose I had all the love they had to spare, and perhaps I was even more cherished than I might have been otherwise because my parents had had a child a couple of years before me, Martha Ann, who was born with spina bifida and died after only six weeks.

For whatever reason, I started life with all the taken-for-granted advantages of the only child, plus a few more, maybe, because my father — faced, say, with the best cut of meat from a joint — would smile and

49

wave it aside and say, "Oh, let the boy have it. He's growing."

And that was always the way it was, and so I grew up kind of assuming that matters should be arranged largely for my convenience and I should have the pick of things. In fact, this assumption of superiority was so ingrained that I usually wouldn't even mind if somebody else was occasionally given precedence. I'd just smile tolerantly and think that was nice for them; really whatever they'd just got should be mine, obviously, but it was good that other people got a share of the spoils now and again, even if they didn't really merit it, and I could even take pleasure in my own — albeit imposed — magnanimity.

The only area where I conceded rank on a continuing basis was in general smartness; there was a pretty blonde girl in my class in North Queensferry Primary School called Mary Henderson. Mary always came top in tests and I was always a worshipful second (there was one time after she'd been off school ill for several weeks when the positions were reversed, but even in Primary Two I knew that didn't count). Brains and beauty. Naturally I fell as completely in love with her as it's possible to fall at such an undeveloped age, and Mary became my first girlfriend, from the age of five to when we were both nine, and I left the village. It didn't entirely end there — not that she ever knew — because I kind of fell hopelessly in love with her when I was fourteen, but that's another story. We kept in sporadic touch and, years later, when she was working

50

for a firm of lawyers in Edinburgh, she sold me my first flat in the city.

In any event, I had a happy childhood.

A lot of people who've read *The Wasp Factory* and have fallen for those old nonsenses about people only writing about what they know and first novels always being autobiographical seem to think I must have had a really awful, disturbed and even abused childhood, but it just ain't true.

Years ago the launch party for *Canal Dreams* was held in Edinburgh. This was a first for me; all my book launches until then had been in London, however my publishers had finally given in to years of me whining that we always had these shindigs in London where they were frankly a bit lost in amongst all the other launches and general media clutter; wasn't it time to have one in Scotland where it might be a bit more of an event? So they'd relented. Desperate, after my years of wheedling, to make sure that the evening wasn't some awful one-man-and-his-dog affair where almost nobody turned up, I'd invited as many of my family as possible along, including my parents. The book shop was full, I'd done the usual reading and answered various questions, everybody seemed happy and I was sitting signing copies at a table when a young male exchange student from the States said, as I scribbled over his book, "Gee, I just read *The Wasp Factory*; you must have had a really disturbed childhood."

Ha-ha! I thought. For once I can deny this with *witnesses*! "Nope," I said. "And I can prove it." I

51

pointed. "See that little old grey-haired lady there? That's my mum; ask her about my childhood."

The guy wandered off and, a few signed books later, I heard my mother's voice floating over the assembled heads; "Och, no, Iain was always a very happy wee boy."

Consider my case well and truly rested.

CHAPTER
THREE

Exploding Custard Factories

"Banksie, this true you're writing a book about whisky?"

"Yeah, they're going to get me to drive —"

"You'll be needing a hand. Count me in."

Mr Jarrold and I, slightly hungover, spend a quiet, pleasant, sunny Saturday going round lots of closed distilleries so I can take photographs of the distillery names in VERY BIG LETTERS painted on their whitewashed walls. At first I'm a bit mystified that the distilleries are closed on a Saturday — I'd kind of been hoping to get off to a flier here and be able to tell Oliver the Editor how determined I've been to start doing my research — but then these are basically light industrial units with a five-day week which happen to have guided tours and Visitor Centres as well; they're not — certainly before Easter and the start of the season — full-time tourist haunts, and that is part of their charm.

We have lunch with a view of Loch Indaal and the harbour in the Harbour Inn. This was only supposed to be a snack, but somehow it turned into a full three-courser when we started reading the menu. I stare at my pudding and consider the merits of not bothering to eat it but just strapping it directly to my waist, for which it is surely destined, but then eat it anyway. Then we wander/waddle round to the Bowmore whisky shop and stock up on a case full of whisky; basically one each from all seven of the working distilleries on the island, plus an old Port Ellen. Port Ellen distillery, forming the western limit of Port Ellen the town, no longer produces its own whisky but instead provides the malted barley for five of the other distilleries on Islay, and so still plays a significant part in the island's economy and the overall quality of the Islay whiskies.

The Bowmore whisky shop is very well stocked indeed and I get a bit carried away, spending an eye-wateringly large amount of money effectively buying the oldest version of each of the whiskies on offer (actually, distillers don't call them versions, they call them expressions, which I suppose does sound slightly classier. Also, buying the oldest was a bit stupid without doing more research; age isn't everything).

All I can say is it seemed like a good idea at the time.

We drive around a bit afterwards, taking more photos and getting very good at spotting the distinctive pagoda-shaped ventilators — relics of the old drying floors where each distillery used to malt its own barley — that tend to denote the presence of a distillery.

"That'll be another of those distinctive pagodas there, then."

"It will indeed . . . Hey, look! There, outside that house; a life-size plastic goose! Hey, there's loads of them! And they're only 35 of your Earth pounds! I'm going to buy one! Maybe two!"

"You really have lost all sense of value, haven't you, Iain?"

". . . wonder if they light up. Hmm? Sorry, what?"

Whisky: the how-to bit.

(If you already know how whisky's made, you may want to skip this section. Well, unless you're one of these know-all types who wants to look for mistakes or something.)

Whisky is made from barley, which is a type of grain that grows well in Scotland's relatively cool, damp climate. You harvest the barley, soak the stuff in water to start it germinating, then dry it off again to stop it actually sprouting too far. The idea is to turn the starch in the barley into sugar. (Barley's not much use as it is; I mean all you can do with it is let it turn into another barley plant or eat it, basically. Sugar you can do something useful with, i.e. start the process of turning it into drink.)

It's during the drying process that you can add the peaty flavour. In the old days peat fuelled the fires that dried the germinating barley, and naturally some of the smell of the smoke got into the barley. Back then every distillery would do its own malting. Malting is what the whole process so far is called, and it produces malted barley, or just plain malt, hence the name malt whisky.

Once steeped (nothing especially technical in the word — just Scots for "soaked") the germinating barley would be laid out on enormous malting floors inside the distillery and guys would walk up and down, dragging boards behind them to turn the barley over now and again, basically ploughing it to let the air get at every grain. The whole malting process can take from one week to nearly two. Only a few distilleries still do this themselves: Balvenie on Speyside, Bowmore and Laphroaig on Islay, Springbank in Campbeltown on the Mull of Kintyre and Highland Park just outside Kirkwall, on Orkney. The rest source their grain from specialist malt mills, specifying the level of peatiness they want.

Then you mill the malted barley — stopping before it's milled too finely, when it would just be flour — until you have stuff called grist.

At this point distilleries have been known to explode.

No, seriously. Any fine organic dust mixed with air in the right proportions will explode if there's a source of ignition like a spark (a bad explosion in a custard factory must sound perfectly hilarious unless you're actually present at the time), and because barley's grown in the soil it usually arrives with a few tiny stones in it. The stones can get caught in the metal rollers in the milling machine, produce a spark, ignite the malt-dust and Bang! So distillers take some care to make sure all the stones are removed from the barley before it goes into the milling machine.

After this you make beer in a teapot, transfer it to a bucket and then boil it in a kettle. Thereafter: barrel, bottle and serve.

Okay, this simplifies the process a little and glosses over vast amounts of skill and potentially decades of time, but them's the basics.

The grist goes into a large cylindrical metal vessel called a mash tun; these usually hold many thousands of litres. Hot water is added, the resulting mixture is stirred to keep things going, the water is allowed to drain through the sieve-like floor of the mash tun and the process is repeated twice and some water's recycled. Finally drained, the mash tun contains draff, which, converted into pellets or cake, makes a really good cattle feed (sadly for the cattle, there's no alcohol left in this stuff, so if a distillery tour guide tells you they have "happy cattle" nearby, just smile tolerantly).

The stuff that's drained away is a sweet brown liquid called worts — hmm — and goes into one of the unsung containers in the whole distilling process: the underback (the mash tuns and washbacks get all the attention — it's not fair).

Then it's those washbacks. These are impressive big things which are usually made of Oregon pine and look like giant upside-down wooden buckets. Yeast is added to the worts and this is where fermentation happens. Looking into a washback once the fermentation process has gotten under way is very impressive; it's a little Corryvrecken going on in there. You'd swear it's all being kept swirling and thrashing around with a big propeller stuck in the base, but it's all just the energy unleashed from the sugars by the yeasts. In fact the only motor in a washback is usually set into the lid to power a thin bar that revolves to knock the bubbles down, otherwise the foam threatens to overflow and escape like a cheap special effect from a bad fifties science fiction movie. Handy hint: don't stick your head into a washback at this point and take a deep breath; the carbon dioxide has been known to knock people out.

Once all this excitement's died down, what's left smells like home-brewed beer and has an alcohol content of about eight per cent, so it's pretty strong by beer standards (it also tastes like shit by any standards, frankly, though it apparently acts as a highly effective laxative in doses above, say, about half a teacup).

This fairly horrible liquid is then transferred to a still, the copper-constructed, deeply glamorous, photogenic part of the whole business (photogenic, that is, if they'll actually let you take a photo; most of the Islay distilleries are pretty relaxed places and don't mind cameras, but a lot of the more corporatised mainland ones won't let you use cameras inside, citing the danger of a flash setting off the spirit fumes. I find this dubious; do they think people are still using nineteenth-century technology? You know; the little sticks like miniature builders' hods loaded with flash powder which those photographer johnnies once utilised to take daguerreotypes of hackney carriages and passing Zeppelins with. I mean, honestly).

There are two still types, usually, and they are used in succession. They are both just big kettles, heated by peat or anthracite direct flame in very traditional distilleries, or by gas- or oil-fuelled jets, or steam pipes, elsewhere. The first is the wash still; the alcohol in the mixture boiling away inside the still turns to a vapour before the water in the mixture does and rises to the top of the still to depart through a pipe called the Lyne arm. The vapour is cooled, becomes liquid and then goes to the second still, the spirit still, where the same process happens all over again.

The liquid that's sent from the wash still to the spirit still is called low wines; what's left in the wash still after it's finished its distillation — not a pretty sight or smell, as a rule — is called pot ale. Sometimes that gets added to the cattle cake too. Still no happy heifers though.

After both stills have done their bit comes a sort of testing cabinet called a spirit safe (also quite glamorous, in a brassy, glassy sort of way) where the distillers do some fairly basic chemistry experiments to decide which part of the resulting stream of clear liquid they're going to use. You can't use everything that comes out of a still; the first stuff to come out is overly strong and contains too many chemicals you wouldn't want to swallow, while the last bit is sort of all weak and pathetic and gets sent back into the wash still to try again.

That first part is called the foreshots, the good bit is the middle cut and the last bit is the feints, though sometimes you'll hear them referred to as the head, heart and tail.

There's a big rectangular tank involved at this point which receives the spirit and is imaginatively called the spirit receiving tank (another unsung container — still unfair), then it's off to the cask-filling bit.

Now, you *could* keep the spirit in bottles, ceramic jugs or even well-cleaned oil drums, but at best it would stay just as it was when it was first poured into the container (at worst it would eventually go off). The wood makes the difference. This may have been a class thing; in the old days poor people kept their whisky in bottles or flagons or a pail or something; the better off would have had empty casks in their cellars because they could afford to buy stuff like wine and sherry in that sort of bulk, and using the emptied barrels to store whisky in must have seemed a prudent and canny idea.

These days the casks used for malt whisky are usually ex-bourbon barrels brought in from the States, often broken down into their individual staves (the curved side bits, shaped a bit like these parentheses) and circular ends, to save transport costs. The barrels are reassembled in Scotland and the flavour of the bourbon adds an extra depth to the developing spirit/whisky. Sherry casks provide an even more salubrious environment for young and impressionable whisky as it matures, but they cost more — about £250 a throw compared to £50 for a bourbon cask. Some of the more adventurous distilleries have used barrels which have contained other drinks, like rum or red wine, and produced some very interesting whiskies indeed (more of this later). Whatever; after the filling, it's off to the warehouse.

The pace slackens off here.

A lot.

Three years minimum by law before you can even call what's in the barrels whisky — it's still "spirit" until those 36 months are up.

Most whisky spends at least twice that amount of time in the warehouse (wonderful, cool, beautiful, *fabulously*-fragranced places) and most single malts will age for a minimum of ten or twelve years before being allowed anywhere near a bottle. The reason these dark, quiet, usually earth-floored warehouses smell so damn wonderful (it is hard even for a heathen like me not to think of them as hallowed) is that, not to oversharpen the point, even the best-made wooden barrels leak. The fumes find their way out of the casks and into the atmosphere; they even penetrate the usually very thick walls of the average bonded warehouse, turning those walls black because there's a particular airborne fungus which thrives on just those vapours (and which, umm, is black). This happens at a rate of about two per cent per year, so a cask that's been sitting for ten years will have lost about a fifth of its contents.

This sounds wasteful but it isn't; it's a bit like the infant human brain losing synaptic connections as it grows and matures; what's left — the network of strengthened pathways in the brain or the concentrated flavours remaining in the barrel — is all the better for what's been given up. This two per cent per year loss is usually called the Angel's Share. Presumably because the Fungus's Share doesn't sound quite so romantic.

Once bottled, whisky doesn't mature or deteriorate as long as the seal remains tight, though if it is

61

uncorked and then — for some unfathomable reason — not finished, it will eventually go off in a year or two. (I am mildly horrified that this has been discovered.)

Oh; and store it upright, not flat.

That's it.

"Hello, ma darlin. How are you —?

"The phone won't stop!"

"Won't stop what?"

"Ringing! I've had all these newspapers calling the house wanting to talk to you about us burning our passports! I'm going crazy!"

"But we didn't burn —"

"Why are you always away when these things happen?"

"Good timing? Ha, just kid —"

"It's not funny!"

"Well, no, but —"

"I'm going insane here. I had some woman from the *Scotsman* on earlier —"

"I though this was why we went ex-directory. How did those — ? Never mind."

"I don't know what to do!"

"Well, take the phone out."

"I'm worried they'll come to the house!"

"That's a point; the fucking *Daily Mail* doorstepped me that time I said, Drugs; just say Yes."

"And I'm missing you. Help!"

"Well, why not come out here? Come to Islay. Harriet and Toby were, like, dreadfully disappointed when I turned up without you. A less secure person than myself could almost have formed the impression it was you they were really looking forward to seeing, not me. Bizarre though that sounds, obviously. But yeah, come on out."

"How?"

"Drive?"

"Oh, come on, you know I hate driving."

"Well then . . . train to Edinburgh, another train to Glasgow, then . . . I think there's a bus to Kennacraig. Or something like that. Probably."

"Oh, come on!"

"Right. Well. Umm . . . Fly?"

"There are no more flights till Monday."

"You've checked?"

"I've checked."

"Ah, what the hell, just charter a plane."

"What?"

"Charter a plane. Drive over to Embra airport or get a taxi and charter a light plane from there."

"What, really?"

"Well, no, not really, I was just —"

"I could look into it, I suppose."

"Well . . ."

"Is that okay?"

"Ah, well, umm."

"You really wouldn't mind?"

"I, well, I, umm, no. No, I suppose, if you're really missing —"

"Where would I find that sort of thing? Yellow Pages, I suppose. I'll call you back. Bye."

Which is how, after a succession of false starts and on-again, off-again phone calls, John Jarrold and I find ourselves at an otherwise deserted Islay airport on a Sunday afternoon, meeting Ann off a dinky little twin-engine Cessna which left Edinburgh just 40 minutes earlier.

"What was the delay?"

"First one of the engines wouldn't start, then the door wouldn't close, then there was mist over the runway, then there was no air traffic control. The pilot was called Lorna and she was only 25. I said sorry for making her work on a Sunday but she said she'd only have been doing the decorating. It was *brilliant!*"

(Me, suspiciously:) "Have you been drinking coffee?"

The rest of Sunday — after Ann has settled in, had a welcoming dram or two with Toby and Harriet and promptly gone for a snooze — I spend with Martin the photographer, revisiting most of the distilleries John and I drove to yesterday. They're still closed, of course, but looking very picturesque in the gently hazy sunshine with the calm sea lapping quietly against the rocks. We take what feels like about eighteen rolls of film, including the one that's on the back cover of the book. Real whisky, unnatural grip. That's photography.

Martin is staying with friends near Loch Gruinart, in the north-east of the island, but later comes to stay in the other self-catering flat along with Oliver, and apparently turns out to be an extremely good guitarist, though Ann and I miss the impromptu concert. Later it turns out we know people in common; Martin's done a

lot of album covers, including one or two for
Shoogelnifty; one of my favourite bands, plus I know a
couple of the guys. Actually, the last time I saw
Malcolm the guitarist was at my birthday bash in
February; I vaguely recall getting all excited about a
plan we hatched together about doing a joint
musical/literary tour of Cuba with — hopefully —
British Council money. I have a nasty feeling I was
supposed to write the letter proposing this to the BC.
Durn; I'd better tell Malc about my gratuitous
passport-destroying antics . . .

We go mob-handed to the Machrie for dinner,
utilising the bus-like carrying capacity of the Defender
to transport everybody in one go. It's on the way back
in the darkness that I'm warned about the kamikaze
proclivities of the local deer population, especially
between the hotel and the farm, and so crawl dutifully
along at 30 miles an hour, eyes peeled for antlers
craftily disguised as branches lurking with malevolent
intent amongst the roadside trees.

Each evening, I'm watching the progress of the war. It
opens without the shock and awe we've been promised,
but on the other hand there are no sudden chemical or
biological counter attacks either. Which is good,
obviously. Yet just a micron suspicious, too. I mean, if
you've got weapons of mass destruction — as we have
been so assiduously and indeed almost desperately
assured Saddam has — isn't now, when you're being
invaded by troop concentrations heading straight for
your major cities, when you'd use them?

Anyway, it all goes very quickly and smoothly for the invading forces. The Brits sort of take Basra. The US Marines cross the Euphrates.

Then everything stalls, and it almost looks like another of the nightmare scenarios is going to kick in, with stubborn resistance in depth and behind the various fronts, irregulars attacking the supply chains. Then that all fades away too and it's on to Baghdad.

Despite one or two scares, still no chemical or biological weapons turn up. I sit in the flat above the old barn each night, nursing a whisky, unable to believe this is really happening, that we've gone to war because, well, basically because George Dubya Bush and his right-wing pals wanted to, and Tony Blair was determined to do whatever Bush asked of him, seemingly happy to risk destroying the UN and sundering the EU just so that the US could have its second pushover war in two years.

But then, hey, I couldn't believe it a couple of years ago when Bush lost the election and yet got given the presidency, and hardly anybody seemed to get upset (certainly almost nobody in America was *reported* as getting upset); not much national or worldwide outrage at the fact the most powerful nation in the history of the planet had been taken over by a cross-eyed cretin backed by gang of drooling, mean-spirited, proto-fascist shitheads.

My bedtime reading, when I'm not looking at other books about whisky, is *Stupid White Men*, by Michael Moore. It's good — a little tabloid with the italics and so on, perhaps, but very to the point given the current situation. In fact painfully so; I can only take it a few pages at a time before my blood starts to boil.

This is where a stiff whisky really does make all the difference. No matter how fucked-up the world may get, a good dram will make it at least slightly more bearable.

And A-flippin-men to that.

Our first proper distillery visit — doing the tour, talking to people, checking out the visitors' shop, me assiduously taking notes — is on the Monday.

I take John to the airport and meet Oliver the Editor off the wee plane that will take John on the first leg of his long journey back south.

Oliver the Editor — Oliver Johnson — is a big, friendly, comfortable-seeming kind of guy. As well as both being writers and having a certain interest in whisky, we've definitely bonded over two more important, character-defining interests; curry, and maps. Oliver is a fellow cartophile. We've met a couple of times before. The first time was to seal the deal on the book in The Vaults, HQ of the estimable Scottish Malt Whisky Society. That's where we started, anyway, with quite a lot of single malts. Then we took in a bar across the road where I had entirely the worst whisky I've ever tasted (it was some sort of home-made blend made specifically for a regular in the bar, allegedly), whereupon we ended up in the Omar Khayyam, my favourite Edinburgh restaurant.

The second time we met was a month or two later in the middle of February when we went with Martin the

Photographer and a video film-maker to Dalwhinnie, to make a short promotional video for the book to be shown to the Random House sales force at the next sales conference. This also let Martin take some photographs, one of which ended up on the cover of the book.

Dalwhinnie was in a sense the first distillery visit of the book. (I'd been round exactly two other distilleries in my life; Highland Park in Orkney and Ardbeg on Islay.)

As an introduction to the whole business, Dalwhinnie could hardly have been bettered. We met up with some extremely helpful people from Diageo, the company that owns the place (Diageo — formerly United Distillers and Vintners — own 30 other distilleries in Scotland, giving them nearly a third of the total and making them the biggest players in the market). We were treated to some very good and extremely welcome soup on a very cold day, and given a comprehensive tour round the distillery itself and the Visitor Centre. Plus they let us clamber all over the place, taking photos from the roof and all over the grounds.

Dalwhinnie is the highest distillery in Scotland, lying at over a thousand feet above sea level. It was originally called Speyside, which is technically not as daft as it sounds given that the Spey passes about five miles due north of the distillery. It's just that the area is so not what people mean when they talk of Speyside. I confess I hadn't realised the Spey rises so far west and south of Speyside proper. In all the years I've been swinging along the road near Catlodge it had never crossed my mind that the river briefly looping around on the plain near Laggan was the glorious Spey.

As a distillery Dalwhinnie looks very proud, distinct and smart, standing on a swell of ground beyond the village, its pagoda towers rising above the surrounding trees. The day we visited there were piles of snow in the car park higher than my head, but the staff were still doing their best to make the place look presentable. Indoors there are two big onion-shaped stills and outdoors there are a couple of condensers, making use of the cool air. They had a really neat-looking and colourful program running on their computer in the still house, displaying and controlling all the valves, pipes and containers the raw materials for the whisky have to negotiate on their way through the process, which — computer and remote control apart — is pretty standard whisky-tech. Traditional, in other words.

The whisky itself represents the Highlands in Diageo's Classic Malts range, so is pretty well known these days. The 15-year-old has a light, new-mown-grass kind of smell to it, very green and scenty. There is a hint of peat and some sweetness, but it's the dry, herby notes that hold sway, making Dalwhinnie a light, zesty kind of dram, something you could put in place of a fino sherry at the start of a meal, or take, diluted perhaps, instead of a dry white wine. Not really that similar to most Speysides, then, and practically on another planet compared to an Islay dram.

★　★　★

69

After saying goodbye to John at the airport there's a quick dash to Toby and Harriet's farm so Oliver can dump his bags then he, Ann and I zip round to Bruichladdich. We're running a little late and it's on this journey, on a cheekily tightening bend sculpted into the dunes north of Bowmore, that I discover the Land Rover's ability to set its tyres a-squealing. My passengers forbear to make similar noises, but I suspect it's a close-run thing. We proceed a little more circumspectly after this and arrive safely at Bruichladdich, which faces across Loch Indaal towards distant Bowmore.

Bruichladdich is a distillery on the way back. It was closed between 1996 and 2001 and has anyway tended to be one of the Islay also-rans. Most malt drinkers would know it's an Islay even if they might not be certain how to pronounce it (with Bruichladdich and Bunnahabhain, luck has handily put the two arguably most tongue-twisting whiskies on the one island, and even had them start with the same letter). Your average malt tippler might also have a vague recollection of a light blue bottle label and a rather un-Islay-ish lack of peat on the nose, but that would be about it for anybody who wasn't already a committed fan of the stuff.

This could all be about to change; there's a new guy in charge called Duncan McGillvray who has a reputation as an adept marketeer, there are new — and very interesting-sounding — expressions on the way, new technologies and old traditions are blending harmonically and there's a general air of optimism and energy about the place. Maybe it helped that we visited on another sparklingly sunny day, though I think the sunniness was more in people's disposition. It also matters a great deal to the people we talk to — and should probably matter a fair bit to us consumers — that the distillery is owned not by some giant impersonal multinational, but by a consortium of people who live on Islay itself, so any money made here is likely, largely, to stay.

I get out my little Black n' Red alphabetically indexed notebook and prepare to start Covering The Story.

Notes: a note.

Taking notes; this is not like me. I usually just remember stuff, or very occasionally jot briefly in my diary if I happen to have it on me, or scribble something in the margin of my telephone list or CD list. Long ago in my wallet I used to carry a tiny notebook which I'd made myself; it was smaller than some stamps I've seen — I can write very small — but that was back when I was about twenty or so and having loads of ideas all the time; now I'm officially a boring old bastard of nearly 50 I don't have the same number of ideas these days and so have no pressing need to have a notebook always to hand (mind you, quality not quantity; a lot of those so-called ideas back then were just god-awful puns).

What I should really do, of course, is use a Personal Digital Assistant; one of those tiny hand-held computerette thingies you can write onto and use as sketch pads, diaries, GPS displays and god-knows-what else.

And I do have one, I just don't use it. It's a Palm Tungsten T which I was going to use to write this book on as Rog, Brad and I trundled our way through the forest and across the taiga on our way to Vladivostok on the Trans-Siberian. I had thought of taking my laptop but I'd heard things get nicked a lot on the train so I preferred something I could carry on me at all times.

I'd coveted the full-size but collapsible keyboard that connects to these things since I'd seen fellow skiffy writer Charles Stross using one in an Edinburgh pub a couple of years ago; in fact I nearly bought one of the keyboards just on aesthetic principle, to own as an object, because they are simply so damn neat, even though I didn't particularly want one of the computers themselves at the time. The keyboards fold down to a size barely any larger than the hand-held itself, and then unfold once and then twice, with bits gliding and snicking as a little sprung-loaded cradle clips up to support the tiny computer. Beautiful. Nowadays, as well as these fold-outs, you can buy keyboards made from flexible plastics which you can roll up, but even if they're lighter and better, it's the jewellery-like intricacy of the fold-out that intrigues me.

Anyway, I have one of these things but I haven't yet started carrying it around; I have a bad habit of buying glitzy bits of new technology in a fit of retail feeding-frenzy excitement and then losing interest in it for subsequent months or even years, by which time it's usually obsolete.

Later Rog borrows the hand-held/folding keyboard set-up to write stuff while he does the Trans-Siberian all by himself (Brad, too, has had to drop out).

We're shown round Bruichladdich by David Barr, the Bottlings Operations Manager, a pleasant guy with various tattoos on his arms from his time in the merchant marine. They're proud of their bottling plant at Bruichladdich. It's the only one on the island — the other distilleries ship their malts to the mainland to be bottled — and uses local water to bring the whisky to the right strength. Before all that, of course, it's the mash-tun/washback/still house standard tour with a bit of the history of the place thrown in.

Now, obviously I'm not going to detail in this book all the different tours round all the different distilleries, because that would be boring. You probably do not really need to know, for example, that Bruichladdich currently produces 300,000 bottles per year, or that the temperature of the second of the three waters introduced into the mash tun is 79 to 80 degrees centigrade, or that the distillery dog is called Tiny, all of which — along with much, much more — I duly noted down on my tour.

I've given a rough guide to whisky-making above, and it doesn't vary much between distilleries. Where it does and I think it's worthy of note, I'll let you know; otherwise, just make the relevant assumptions. The stuff

I'm looking for as I make these journeys is the interesting bits and pieces that always crop up during every tour, especially if you ask questions and keep your eyes open and senses engaged; the grace notes in a familiar theme.

What I find intriguing is stuff like the fact that now they've got their new bottling plant, next on the list of improvements at Bruichladdich is a Whisky Academy they intend to open in the summer in an old de-bonded warehouse, to teach people about whisky in depth, or the fact that a family of seven dolphins seem to have adopted the place, showing up at the same time each year in the bay across the road from the distillery, or that it has the tallest stills on the island (taller stills give the vapours inside a harder job getting out to the bit where they'll be condensed and so tend to produce lighter spirits), or that what they call their computer in the mash room is a blackboard . . . and yet they have webcams set up at various sites throughout the distillery so you can watch what's going on, live, from anywhere in the world.

It later turns out, as I discover through a *Guardian* article in early June, that Bruichladdich only got the broadband connection that makes the webcams possible due to a mistake by British Telecom. The contract was signed and legally binding before BT realised that the distillery wasn't where they thought it was. So the outgoing signals have to be bounced from Islay to Northern Ireland — admittedly only about 20 or so miles away — then away back over to Edinburgh before disappearing into the Web.

It's this mixture of tradition and newfangled that's going to keep cropping up over the next few months and (nearly) one hundred distilleries; very old tech and very new tech existing together and helping, in the end, to make and promote a drink that has itself changed and evolved over the centuries, sometimes with the grain of change in society, sometimes not.

Evolution, in the way the stuff is made, marketed and appreciated and indeed in the taste of the finished product itself, helps keep whisky interesting. At one of the earliest stages of the process at Bruichladdich we're invited to taste some of the heavily peated malt they intend to use for a future expression. This comes as a surprise because the Laddie — as it's sometimes known — is not a very peaty whisky at all, certainly not compared to the reeking giants of the island's south coast.

The peatiness of malt is measured by the parts per million (p.p.m.) of the aromatic chemical phenol it contains, and modern maltsers are able to produce accurately and consistently pretty much any degree of peatiness a distiller requests. Of the Islay whiskies, Bunnahabhain has the least peat at 5 p.p.m., while Ardbeg has the most; 50 p.p.m. In between come Bowmore with 20, Port Ellen (as was) with 25, Caol Ila with 30, Laphroaig with between 35 to 40 and Lagavulin with 40. Bruichladdich is usually the second least peated whisky, with 8 p.p.m. of phenol in the mix, but the malt we're given a few grains of to chew on is absolutely loaded; it has ten times as much as they'd usually use here; fully 80 p.p.m. It'll be a while before this monster of a dram thumps onto a bar or counter near any of us, but — always assuming that it doesn't overwhelm the seaside freshness Bruichladdich is famous for, but works with it and adds to it instead — it should be a mighty piece of work, worth waiting for.

While we've been here, a couple of guys and a digger have been tearing up a large part of the central courtyard Bruichladdich is built around; demolishing old foundations in preparation for putting down new ones, allowing glimpses of old brick-lined drains and sections of ancient wall. They're still doing this when we leave, late, to head for the south of the island, where we're due to meet Toby for lunch and have a look round Ardbeg.

If Bruichladdich feels like a place still very much in development, Ardbeg exudes an air of having already achieved the sort of transition the Laddie is aiming for. They produce a lot more whisky here (I'm not going to mention the bottles-per-whatever much more, honest); 35,000 bottles per week, or over six times what Bruichladdich does. This is the result of a lot of rebuilding, both physically and, more to the point, promotionally. Quiet through most of the eighties, Ardbeg is now owned by Glenmorangie, who have built the Ardbeg brand into something accepted (once more) as being worth mentioning in the same breath as Laphroaig and Lagavulin. They spend 35 per cent of their budget on advertising and promotion — most companies spend about sixteen per cent — and this has to make a huge difference. This all makes it sound a bit too corporate, though; the feeling you get when you're in the place is that it's been lovingly restored to and beyond past glory.

The restaurant in the Visitor Centre is exceptional; we meet Toby, apologise for being late, and have yet more wonderful Islay food. I'm convinced I can feel my belt tightening as we eat. Toby explains that a lot of Islay produce is almost-but-not-quite-organic because the farmers have agreements with the RSPB and the Nature Conservancy people that they'll let the vast flocks of migrating geese use their fields when they come through; this means that they have no choice but to use fertilisers to bring on their crops and harvest them before the geese get here; otherwise the birds would neck the lot.

Fooded, we meet up with Stuart Thomson, the distillery manager. We'd actually said Hi the day before, when Martin and I were wandering around the place taking photos and Stuart was watching one of his children learn to ride a bike (a lot of distillery managers live on site). Stuart has been busy over lunch with a party of French food and drink writers, on Islay to sample what the island has to offer.

We end up in one of the warehouses, sampling a couple of astoundingly good whiskies. One is a 12- or 13-year-old, about 62 proof, out of a bourbon cask; very phenolic, slightly carbolic but zesty, and — once it's pointed out to me — yup, has notes of American Cream Soda, which was my favourite sugary drink when I was young. This is deeply wonderful whisky, and tasting it in the fume-heavy coolness of the dark warehouse while the clear spring sun beats off the pure white walls opposite and illuminates the golden liquid in the sampling column can't help but heighten the experience. Oliver and I swap superlatives, but I'm not sure that Stuart hasn't made a mistake here; I'd have led with whatever comes next and finished with this, because this is simply wonderful; one of the best whiskies I've ever tasted.

I am, however, wrong, and Stuart knows exactly what he's doing.

The second whisky is 28 years old, is down to about 46 proof and is from a fino sherry cask (most sherry casks used for whisky have held oloroso). This stuff is just colossal. One taste (albeit a taste that takes a few minutes, from first amazed sniff to last lingering sensation at the back of the throat) and it goes straight to the top of the list. Very peaty, smoky and salty, but that's just the start; there's a rich creaminess here too, powerfully but sharply sweet in a way that would swamp a less muscularly peated dram but which here is part of a kind of dynamic of phenolic smoke and something like musky perfume. It's a changing dynamic, too, like having some immensely complicated integrated equation of taste working itself out in your mouth, developing as it's held there to swirl from wood-smoke to sea-spray to sherry and back again; one moment it tastes like barbecued licorice, next it's changing to honey-glazed fruit (though at the time my principal impression was, Wow!).

I look at my empty glass, then at Oliver the Editor.

"This is the best whisky I have ever tasted," I tell him.

"You mean we've found the perfect dram?" He looks worried. "This could be a short book."

I smile at Stuart and nod at the cask. "Is it possible to buy any of —?"

Stuart is already shaking his head. "All already spoken for, I'm afraid."

I nod sadly and tell Oliver, "I think the search has to continue."

"Your readers will appreciate the efforts and sacrifices you're so determined to make for them."

For a moment I think I detect a hint of irony, but surely not.

CHAPTER
FOUR

To Jura

Jura. An unbagged island. Always wanted to go there, never been. Jura lies aslant between Islay and Argyll, and is very sparsely populated — well, by homo sapiens, anyway; there are only about 200 human residents. There are, however, zillions of red deer, though from what I could gather these don't seem to have developed the same skills regarding ambushing innocent Land Rovers as their demoniac cousins on Islay, presumably through lack of practice and opportunity. Jura's a steeply, roundedly mountainous, deeply rugged island that looks like it's almost been torn in two by the Atlantic gales. (Actually, for the purposes of the geographical and historical background in my novel *The Crow Road*, it *was* torn in half; I'd decided I wanted to locate the fictional town of Gallanach near Crinan, on the mainland. I needed the place to have a deep-water port with easy access to the Atlantic and I didn't want to edit out the Corryvrecken so I blithely cut Jura in two. You get to do this sort of thing when you're a writer.)

Jura is a short ferry ride from Port Askaig on Islay's east coast, close to the Caol Ila distillery, so — as we're here, the weather's fine and there's a whisky book to be researched — it has to be done. The perfect trip will include a visit to the distillery, a look at the house where George Orwell wrote *1984*, and then a hike to the northern tip of the island to see the tidal race there between Jura and Scarba, that wide, roaring whirlpool called the Corryvrecken where Orwell once nearly drowned.

We managed the first two of these, missing the Gulf of Corryvrecken because we need to make the last ferry.

Meanwhile we've visited Caol Ila, the slightly less remotely sited but even more precipitously shore-pitched neighbour of Bunnahabhain, a couple of miles up the coast. Standing between the big, modern still house and the sea, the view is stunning whichever way you look: to Jura, its mountains mounded high and hazed across the waves, or back at the great coppery bulks of the four great stills, gleaming behind giant windows in the maritime light of an unseasonably warm spring; Ann practically has to be prised out of the visitors' waiting room, mesmerised by the vista.

Yet again, this is a whisky that could well be a total star by now if it had had a bit of marketing oomph behind it, and maybe a bit more consistency in its younger bottlings. It's oily and seaweedy — hardly a surprise, so close to the water — toasty and brisk. Caol Ila is probably the least familiar, least lauded Islay, but find a good one and it'll stand up to almost anything. Arguably the very distinctive toastedness of Caol Ila has mitigated against it being well known as a single malt

81

just because it is so in demand as a constituent in blends. (A couple of months later Jackie, one of the tour guides at one of Caol Ila's sister distilleries, Blair Atholl, assures me it's especially good with a cigar. So there.)

The Isle of Jura distillery at Craighouse is a friendly place — most of the small or out-of-the-way distilleries are. All the same, I start with slightly iffy memories of Jura malt because I once bought a bottle when I was coming back to Dear Old Blighty from France on a truck ferry after a couple of months spent hitch-hiking round Europe, back in the early seventies.

It was not a very good bottle of whisky. Drinkable, but poorer than most blends, which is a pretty damning thing to say of a single malt.

Happily only the waisted bottle shape remains the same and the malt itself is peaty-flowery, salty (again) and smooth. The bottle of the new Superstition expression we buy is all of these plus smoky.

Willy's Definitive Dram Definition.

Willy, one of the guys at the distillery, comes up with what Oliver and I agree is the best definition of what a "dram" actually is: "A measure of whisky that is pleasing to both guest and host."

Favourite memory of the Jura distillery? They had a wooden ball on the end of a bit of string which could be swung against the neck of one of the stills, a bit like you'd swing a bottle of champagne against the stem of a ship being launched, though less destructively, obviously. This was a leftover from the Islay (well, Islay/Jura in this case) Whisky Festival of the year before, when the guys thought it would be fun to show people how, in the old days, a distiller would work out how far up the still the mixture was bubbling. Nowadays stills have wee vertical windows like glazed medieval arrow slits set into them, so you can just look and see whether the stuff's boiling away nicely, not boiling hard enough (more heat required) or about to boil over and make a mess of the heat exchanger (less heat needed), but back in the old days, before this hi-tech glass nonsense, they'd just swing a wee wooden ball against the copper and work out from the dullness or otherwise of the resulting *Dong* whether their liquid was simmering anaemically, frothing nicely or about to blow the place up.

There is even a suggestion that all this whacking away at the copper stills with wooden balls might have led to the stills starting to get a bit dented, taking on the appearance of coppery golf balls, and that this might contribute to the character of the resulting whisky. Hmm, I say. (There is real, probably daft, pointlessly conservative and very superstitious stuff going on here; some distillers really do insist that when coppersmiths replace an old still — they only last about fifteen years or so with all that heating and bubbling, even with repairs and riveted-on patches — they deliberately make exact replicas of the old stills, down to the dents they received accidentally, and even down

83

to the patches and repairs themselves . . . But hold on; what about the way the whisky they made tasted *before* they had the patches? And are these patches cumulative? Do they all add? Will future copies of these stills be so accreted with patches summed from all their many generations of ancestors that they look like patchwork quilts but in copper?)

Oh well; who knows and never mind. Following a very pleasant look round the distillery, the hotel across the road and the wee village of Craighouse — all resplendent in the sunshine — we stock up on a few snacking supplies at the village shop and head off to see Orwell's old place.

After a little negotiation — there is a locked chain guarding the last few miles of the road, and permission to proceed beyond is far from automatic — we take the rocky road to Barnhill, where George Orwell wrote *1984*. Five deserted, dwelling-free miles of sheer vehicle torture ending in a gentle, shallow glen of rock and heather, stunted trees and newly flowered whin, the rich yellow blossom yet to exhale the buttery coconut scent of early summer. The old, white-painted house forms a shallow U-shape when you include the one-time byres and stables on either side. (The track winds on over the hill to one last house further north, the final outpost of humanity before the Corryvrecken.)

We are greeted by two honkily suspicious geese — possibly the remains of a flock that was here in Orwell's time — and a view down across the unkempt remains of garden and lawn over a slope-damp meadow of reed and coarse grass to the still bare trees above the rocks and the shining curve of bay. The rugged shore of mainland Argyll lies in the distance under the haze, more an implication than a presence.

George Orwell — Eric Blair, as he was born — came here to write, not die. I had the impression, before reading the latest biography, *Orwell*, by D. J. Taylor, that he'd slunk here like some wounded animal dragging itself off to breathe its last, but this was not really what happened, and nor was Orwell as alone as I'd thought, either. Orwell knew he was unwell, even if he was loath to admit to his friends that he might be suffering from tuberculosis, but the diagnosis was made after he'd come back to Jura following an earlier stay at Barnhill and a subsequent return to London.

There was a stigma to tuberculosis at the time; people knew it was infectious, and I'd thought that Orwell had exiled himself to a determined solitude which even then, when Jura had a few more inhabitants and the road was better (. . . surely. I mean, he drove a motorbike down *this*? With lungs close to collapse and haemorrhage?), must have been close to complete. The air was purer than anything in the cities — though, given that Orwell was a chain-smoker, this would not have made that much difference — there was little chance of infecting anybody else with the disease eating away at his lungs, and he would have the peace to write.

Yet he came here with a family of sorts, was involved in the local community and the seasonal tasks of farming life, and had various guests to stay. They were never as many visitors as he and they had hoped and planned for due to the sheer difficulty of getting to

Jura, and especially this part of it, but even so it was a fuller and less doom-shadowed life than I'd imagined. A presentiment of death — and a desire to cling to life — informed Orwell's choice of the place nevertheless; even in those very early post-war, post-atomic days, he was aware of the possibility of a nuclear holocaust, and saw that Jura might offer a greater chance of survival than most places in Britain if the Bomb did drop.

Orwell spent most of his last two years in hospital, and died in London.

Peering through the windows at Barnhill, I wonder if he turned his chair and whatever desk or table he wrote on away from that beguiling, ever-changing view to the south, but Orwell seems like the sort of writer, the sort of man, who might have kept the view there to be looked at, and yet still never let himself be distracted by it. Anyway, apparently by this stage he was so ill he was mostly writing in bed.

We return from Jura to Islay, for an evening of stories and laughter and lots of tears. The tears were mine; Belinda had made this wonderful lasagne and Toby had produced a big bag of green chillis to spice it up, leaving the bag on the table where I could reach it too, so that we sat there, tearing these fiery little chillis up and scattering them across the lasagne before wolfing it down (everybody else was sensible and stuck with the lasagne as it was). The chillis were very strong and I tore up so many I swear my fingers turned green. The resulting dish was utterly delicious, but then — laughing so much at one point I had to wipe the tears away — I used my chilli-tearing fingers to do the wiping, which was a major mistake.

I am convinced that the effect was so intense my eyeballs developed a sense of taste; I could taste green. My eyes streamed, my nose did too, I washed my hands, kept dabbing with a napkin, and thought of dousing my eyes with yoghurt (capsiacin, the hot stuff in chillis, is soluble in fat but not in water, so this might have worked ... *Complicity* readers know this stuff already), but I opted for just keeping on eating even though I could hardly see for the wash of tears, and waiting for the symptoms to pass, which they did after a quarter of an hour or so.

I think it was around here, people having been primed for how daft I can be, that the Toby's Party/The Balcony Scene story got told.

The Toby's Party/The Balcony Scene story.

End of August, 1987. Brighton, on the south coast of England. The World Science Fiction Convention. Entitled ConSpiracy. This seemed like a neat name for an SF Con until it came time for two of the Guests of Honour, the Strugatsky brothers, Arkady and Boris, to apply for visas to leave what was then the Soviet Union and travel to the UK to attend the Con; its breezy, just-for-a-laugh title did not play well with the humourless pre-modernists, non-ironicists of the KGB or whoever was in charge of issuing visas, because they did not get the joke and did not issue the Strugatskys with visas either. Doris Lessing was another GoH and gamely stood in for the Non-Flying Strugatsky Brothers on some of the programme items they should have featured in. Given that Alfred Bester had also proved unable to attend, the Con was having a jinxed time with its GoHs (Bester, author of at least one of the greatest SF novels ever written, had an even better excuse for not turning up, having recently died. Willed his estate to his bartender. Class).

But a fine Con all the same, with thousands of SF fans from all over the world enjoying a long sunny weekend; enjoying it mostly in the bars or at panel items in windowless function rooms, certainly, but enjoying it all the same. It was only about my second or third Convention and I was having a great time. Toby was my paperback editor at the time, in charge of the crowded and bustling satrapy that was Futura, part of Emperor "Bobbing" Bob Maxwell's vast imperial domain.

Toby had a party in his suite, a fairly palatial set of rooms on the fourth floor of the Metropole Hotel, facing the beach and the sea. Not that it was really a party to Toby, not technically. It was just "a drink for a few friends, dear boy/dear girl". After about six hours, when the few friends numbered in the treble figures and the bar in the sitting room had been restocked three or four times — and I mean a bar, here, not a minibar; each refill required a porter with one of those vertically stacked hand-barrows, fully loaded — Toby almost admitted that it was really a party, but then insisted that — a few freeloaders he didn't recognise apart — this was still just a drink for a few friends. The few drinks continued. I think it's probably the best party I've ever been to.

Dawn. Most people had gone. Maybe a dozen were left, amongst them myself and Rog Peyton and Dave Holmes of Andromeda, Birmingham's main SF bookshop. The three of us were standing on the balcony of Toby's bedroom, talking about whatever, when my attention was drawn by a nearby balcony; that of Toby's sitting room. More specifically, my attention was drawn by the relatively short distance between the balcony we were standing on and the balcony of Toby's sitting room.

"Dave, hold this, would you?" I handed Dave Holmes my glass.

Now. Especially while I lived in London, I used to enjoy the very much non-Olympic sport of Drunken Urban Climbing. For a while I assumed I'd invented this recreation, but on reflection I'm sure I wasn't the first to partake of its heady, dangerous mysteries, foremost amongst which, of course, is how anybody can ever get so drunk without actually being unconscious or dead that they think this might be a good idea in the first place. I'd get drunk and climb things; city things, like buildings. Well, bits of buildings; I'm not claiming I used to shin up Centre Point or scale the Houses of Parliament or anything.

Reversion-to-childhood thing: I was always climbing trees and scrambling up rocks when I was young, and usually going a bit further on and up than my pals. This was not so much the result of a spirit of competition as the consequence of possessing an *oh, shit!* reaction that kicked in after most other people's had. I was always fairly tall and skinny and I convinced myself that because my mum had been a professional ice skater I must have inherited a brilliant sense of balance and this gave me an edge.

Even so, climbing, drunk or sober, should never have held this attraction for me; it nearly killed me when I was a child. The experience ought to have traumatised me out of such larks and left me with a profound fear of heights.

North Queensferry is sited on a stubby little peninsula sticking out from the south coast of Fife; behind the village is/are the Ferry Hill/Ferry Hills (depends which map you consult). When they were building the rail line to link up with the Forth Bridge back in 1890 the engineers decided to put a cutting through the raised ground, but the rock proved unworkably friable; soft sandstone with scaly boulders of only slightly harder sandstone embedded in it, and it kept falling into the cutting. They dug down about 60 feet but after the umpteenth rock slide gave up and built a tunnel underneath instead, taking the same line as the cutting, which thereafter just sat there, this weird, rock-strewn, overgrown canyon a quarter of a mile long through the Ferry Hill(s).

One day, back when I was seven or eight, I was climbing up the west side of the cutting with some of my pals; almost at the top, I grabbed this big boulder sticking out of the cliff face above me and started to pull myself up. The boulder came out of the cliff like a rotten tooth and both the boulder and I started to fall towards the floor of the cutting, about 50 feet below.

I let go of the boulder; it crashed into the rocks beneath. I was caught by a whin bush growing out of a narrow ledge a few feet below where I'd started falling. I got very scratched and there may have been a degree of whimpering involved. My pals formed a human chain and hauled me to safety and by the time I got home my legs had pretty much stopped shaking (naturally, being a considerate little lad and not wanting to upset anybody, I delayed telling my parents what had happened, waiting a decade and a half or so). I submit that any sensible kid would have learned a lesson from that. Patently, I didn't.

When I left my friend Dave McCartney's flat in Belsize Road, where I'd crashed for a few months, and found my own place in London — living first in a flat in Islington Park Street and later with Ann on Graham Road — my favourite route for handy climbing opportunities was along the section of the Grand Union Canal east of the Angel. It was a more interesting way home than the adjoining roads, and if you suddenly realised you needed a pee, well . . .

I think the Drunken Urban Climbing thing all started when there was some work being done under a bridge and the towpath had been closed off with a wall of wooden boards; I was annoyed that my route was blocked, but then just went hand-over-hand along the top of the boards, legs dangling over the canal, until I got to the far end and resumed my walk. Another time I climbed over a wall into a factory yard and up this piece of industrial paraphernalia that looked like something out of an oil refinery and smelled like a tannery; it was about six or seven metres tall and had some sort of series of stepped, shallow open tanks at the top into one of which I inadvertently put a foot while standing up to get a better view. The boot concerned fell apart over the course of the following week and that sock was never quite the same again, but my foot was all right.

I had, perhaps foolishly, confessed this eccentric but relatively harmless pastime to Ann, who proceeded to persuade me — with a degree of forthrightness I had not previously credited her with — that Drunken Urban Climbing was, basically, unbelievably stupid. When I was sober I realised this myself, of course. Anyway, I made a promise to her: no more climbing.

And I kept my promise, I'm proud to say, until, standing on that balcony overlooking the pebbly beach of Brighton as the horizon went from black to grey and that clear summer's night becoming morning, I spotted a loophole.

While Dave Holmes held my drink, I swung my legs over the side of the wrought-iron balcony, reached across for a handhold or two and made the easy traverse to the balcony outside Toby's sitting room. A traverse, you see? Completely horizontal movement. No height gained at all. And therefore, by definition, not climbing! Promise unbroken; huzzah!

Dave was still looking for a place to put down both the drinks he now held, and Rog Peyton had, after staring open-mouthed, not entirely believing what he was seeing, made a grab to stop me, but I was already gone, holding onto the outside of the railing on the other balcony and looking in at the sitting room where I could see John Jarrold sitting on a couch talking with a young lady. The couch was positioned at about 45 degrees to the opened balcony doors, and this is where the slightly stupid bit comes in. I said, "Hey there, Mr Jarrold," and waved.

When I had John's attention I switched hands and waved with my other hand, then did this again, each time leaving a short interval when I had both hands off the railing and was, effectively — feet not quite balanced on the outside edge of the balcony's stonework — starting to fall. Before I caught myself and waved. Wave, switch (start to fall backwards), grasp railing and wave; wave, switch (start to fall backwards), grasp railing and wave; I did this a few times before John, staring at me, worked out what was wrong with the picture he was looking at (meanwhile Rog and Dave H had given up shouting at me and were stumbling through from the bedroom to the sitting room). When John realised that he could see the railings between him and me, he jumped up and ran for the balcony. Realising the fun was over, I'd put both hands on the rails and started to swing a leg over, but he more or less pulled me to safety anyway.

All good clean fun, really, though I did apologise to all concerned if I'd upset anybody in any way. And there it might have ended, but for the fact that by a hideous coincidence, almost at the same time as I was doing my traverse, a robbery was taking place next door in an adjoining suite, one of those being used by the Con administration. Stuff was nicked, the thief was seen briefly — thankfully the clean-shaven swine looked nothing like me, or that might really have confused matters — the police were called, and I thought I'd better wait and mention to the cop — who appeared to be about twelve — that I'd been sort-of-climbing on the face of the hotel at the same time as the robbery had taken place. Witnesses vouched for me not having taken a quick detour to any further-away balconies, having a big bag with Swag written on it or wearing a stripy jumper and a black eye mask, and so it went no further.

I went to bed, creeping in beside Ann without disturbing her. Plenty of time later in the morning, I thought, for her to hear all the grisly details, roll her eyes and add a cast-iron sub-clause to the no-climbing agreement covering so-called traverses involving what I believe climbers airily term "exposure".

I got up before noon (Ann snoozed on), went for a breakfast Bloody Mary, as one does on such occasions, and the first person I met as I turned away from the bar looked surprised and asked, "Oh! They let you out on bail, did they?"

A lesser man might have spluttered his drink. Having more respect for a healthy breakfast, I managed to swallow quickly before saying, "*What?*"

I discovered over the next half hour or so just how quickly rumours mutate and propagate. Only about six or seven hours had passed since the whole sordid balcony episode, and yet already it was common knowledge around the Con that, a) I was an international jewel thief and, b) I'd been seen by various extremely emphatic witnesses who swore blind they'd seen me, dressed in a Spider Man outfit, climbing the hotel from the ground up to the fourth floor . . . Or, c) I'd been clearly observed — by several people of unimpeachable trustworthiness — dressed in distinctive SAS black coveralls abseiling down from the roof of the hotel down to the offending balcony.

It wouldn't have mattered quite so much, but a lot of Americans were leaving the Con for home that day and so took this travesty of the truth back with them. And then Mike Harrison — heroic writer and rock climber — gave me a climbing lesson on one of the low walls overlooking the pavement outside the bar (there were a lot of handholds on the carved stone foliage decorating the plinths). I jumped off from about two feet up and landed awkwardly, doing something painful to my instep; limped the rest of the Con. From two feet up! After my death-defying fourth-floor antics! I ask you!

The ignominy.

Time for a little stock-taking, as we head back home from Islay. It strikes me there are different ways to get to know a country, or any complicated area or space. I feel I know the landscape of Scotland fairly well; I've driven over most of it, flown over a lot of it, walked various bits of it, sailed round and to and from various other areas, stayed in all its cities and many of its towns, climbed a few of its mountains, boated on a couple of its rivers and canoed a bit. I'm moderately well up on its history, though I could, probably should, know a lot more. I think I have a reasonable grasp of the differences between the various regions of Scotland, the variety of attitudes and accents you encounter, shading gradually from one to another, as you travel from one part to another. I've talked to neds and nobles, got sense and gibberish out of each and I've tried, admittedly not with any great degree of intensity, to keep up with Scottish cultural life.

But there's always more. And there's always different. I guess a dedicated mountaineer, a Munro bagger, could have the same mixture of Scottish General Knowledge I've just confessed to above, but have a radically different idea of what Scotland is, what it represents, just because of their sport; they'd think of peaks unclimbed and climbed and the vivid memories of specific routes and peaks; their image of Scotland's geography would be biased towards the West, the centre and North-West (indeed its physical geography would matter more than most other types of geography). I imagine a golfer has a different view entirely, with their internal map of the land's most important areas being almost an opposite of the mountaineer's, skewed to the South, the East and North-East. A union organiser might have a mental chart that differed radically again, prioritising the central industrial belt, or industry-specific sites like ports or electronics factories. Every job, every field of academic study, every interest, gives people a biased internally fabricated model of the country they inhabit, a weighting of meaning that will differ subtly from every other person's and yet bear similarities of layout to those they share those jobs, pastimes or hobbies with.

So whisky. More to the point, the making of it. The marketing of Scotch is everywhere and its distribution worldwide, but its production is legally limited to Scotland, its focus concentrated on this one relatively small country, and, within that small country, on barely a hundred generally modest, usually out-of-the-way sites many of which employ only a dozen or so people.

Of course, there's whiskey from Ireland, bourbon from the States and Japanese whisky which is Scotch-in-all-but-name and they're fine drinks in their own terms (and, as with individual whiskies, some are fine in absolute terms), but this is a book about Scotch, about Scots, about Scotland, and getting to know about the making of whisky, its history, its relation to the land and what it means to people both here and abroad is a way of getting to know more about the country where it's made and the people who make it.

And there's a further quest involved here, too, besides this search for the perfect dram.

I've never tasted it, never been offered it, never really heard anything about it, but I'm convinced that somebody, somewhere, must be making illegal whisky; whisky the way it used to be made, before it became first outlawed and then legalised, before it became taxed, before it became (and this is very much a relative term, given the small scale and considerable art involved in the process) industrialised. There has to be a secret still out there somewhere; probably there are many, surely there have to be several. I'd like to see a still in action but I'd settle for a taste of the product (I mean, providing it isn't likely to blind me or anything). I'd like to talk to the people involved, if I can convince them I'm not going to expose them or report them to Customs and Excise, but it's that taste I'm particularly interested in, because it'll be a taste, to some degree, of the past, a link to the place where the whisky we know now came from.

Apart from anything else, I'd like to know why there's so little illegal whisky in Scotland. In particular, why is it so uncommon compared to its Irish equivalent, poteen? Go to Ireland for long enough — blimey, stay in Scotland for long enough — and you'll be offered poteen sooner or later, by somebody who knows somebody who knows somebody . . . But in over 30 years of sometimes casual, often determined and occasionally assiduous drinking in pretty much every cranny and indeed neuk of Scotland, I can't recall ever being offered hooch which was actually made in the place, and none of my friends have either. This strikes me as odd. Given the nature of some of my friends, it's practically preposterous.

I'm almost tempted to believe that the more likely explanation is that I've been offered whiskeen — or whatever it might be called — dozens of times and accepted it fulsomely on each occasion, only to, for some reason, forget all about it by the following morning, though this is of course a patently absurd suggestion and I'm mildly surprised I've even thought of it. Come to think of it, just ignore it. Actually, I'll probably take this bit out of the first draft. In fact, I know: I'll remove it tomorrow morning when I look back at what I wrote the night before.

Gosh, this "research" stuff is fascinating. Now I know, from reading other books about whisky, that Scotch poteen is called peatreek.

Peatreek. It's an old word, and has already fallen almost completely out of use, but that is the technical term for what I'm looking for. Actually, as a word, I quite like it. In common with a lot of writers and not a few readers, I kind of collect words, and peatreek seems like a good one to have in the collection.

But no sign of the stuff itself. Not so far, anyway. I've made a few inquiries and dropped a few hints, but to date nobody has come up with anything. I didn't really think there'd be too much chance of illegal distilling on Islay just because there's so much of the legal variety — you'd think that anybody with those sorts of skills could make a good, worry-free living working on the right side of the law — and Islay always feels quite civilised compared to some bits of Scotland, the bits I usually associate with whisky production. It really does feel like it's part of Scotland's central belt in places, certainly compared to the other Inner Hebridean islands, let alone the Outer Hebrides.

But then maybe if you're a distiller in your day job and you find the whole process technically fascinating — and don't just want to get away from it of an evening and put your feet up in front of the telly — you *would* try setting up a portable still somewhere in the wilds just to see if it can be done, and whether your skills translate to a smaller scale. After all, Islay is quite rugged in places, with its own relative remotenesses. I took a solitary drive out to the Oa, the nearly circular peninsula sticking out like a growth from Islay's south-east corner, pointing towards Ireland, and it got really rugged and interesting down towards that fabulously fractured coast; all sea stacks, cliffs, ragged gullies and caves fronting the greyly shining sea and fringed by rocks covered with yellowing foam blown off the waves. You could hide a still on the Oa no problem. Goodness knows, the extravagantly cratered single-track road would be enough to put off any Excise man concerned about the springs and shocks on his government-issue car.

And though this is the fourth time I've been to this not exactly vast island, there are still a few roads I haven't driven and lots of trackless hills and lochs scattered about which I've been nowhere near. These hills are walked on, and worked on by shepherds, foresters, estate workers and game keepers, but even so . . .

Whatever, if there is anything going on, nobody — probably very wisely — is talking about it, certainly not to a daft bumptious distillery-bagging scribbler from Fife. Book or not, research or not, I'm just a tourist here, but it's a good place to be a tourist.

Some of the ancient, semi-desolate flavour of this long-lived-in place came out when Ann, Oliver and I took a turn off the main road from the Jura ferry and drove up to a small loch set in the low hills near Ballygrant. Finlaggan is where, on a small island set in the loch and connected to it then by a drowned causeway and now by a new wooden walkway, there was once the political and spiritual headquarters of the Lord of The Isles.

This was from a time when Scotland was supposedly united, yet still contained various chieftainships and clan lands which were something close to little primitive principalities in their own right. Most separate — almost independent, in practice — was the Lordship of The Isles. Back then social, political, economic and military cohesion was most easily guaranteed by the relative ease of access to and from the sea, not the land. One good ship would take you round any coast with material and matériel but getting to anywhere through the forests, crags and bogs meant hacking out a specific path or using the tracks an enemy would know much better than you. So the sea — and Scotland's multitudinous lochs — provided an easier highway, if you had the talent for it.

Finlaggan was the centre of a small maritime empire for a time; you can stand in the old chapel, in the remains of the old houses and fortifications, and look around in the silence at the rushes bowing in the wind and the swans gliding by, and stare down at the old carved stones capping the graves and try to imagine the people who've passed this way.

The gravestones, with their staring images of the long-time dead, are covered with sparklingly clean perspex supported by thick little metal legs, to keep the weather off. They look like very low and slightly surreal coffee tables, and oddly like art.

★ ★ ★

Back home, we watch the continuing war on TV. Still no nukes turning up, still no biological agents, still no chemical weapons. The ugly mutations, the poisons, the corrosiveness are present though, just not where people are looking for them. Gary Younge, an award-winning *Guardian* journalist who's just moved to the States, is on Channel 4 in a short programme about the effects of the war in the US homeland. He reports on a lawyer who wore a T-shirt saying Give Peace a Chance to a shopping mall in mid America. The other side of the man's T-shirt displayed a peace symbol.

He was told by a security guard either to take the T-shirt off or to leave the mall immediately. The lawyer protested that his right to free speech was enshrined in the US Constitution (for all my many issues with present-day America, I've always admired the serious-ness and genuineness with which Americans take, uphold and believe in this right). But no dice these days. The security guard summoned a cop, who promptly arrested the lawyer.

And so we bid farewell to the Land of the Free . . .

CHAPTER
FIVE

The Heart of the Water

Now then. Glenfinnan. There are quite a few places that can justly claim to be the midge capital of Scotland and Glenfinnan is several of them. It also rains a lot. When my friend Les first moved to Fort William to start work as a teacher, it rained every single day for the first six weeks he was there. Not a continual, apocalyptic biblical downpour, obviously — well, not every week — but at least one shower in every 24 hour period, and usually a lot more than that. Even for a man raised in Greenock, that's a lot of rain.

I suppose I ought to explain here, for those of you not well versed in the geographical ranking structure of Scottish Iffy Weather Areas, that Greenock has something of a reputation in the west of Scotland for being a rainy old place (the west of Scotland has something of a reputation in the rest of Scotland for having more than its fair share of precipitation, too, and it is probably fair to say that Scotland itself is perceived as being a tad rainier than the rest of Britain, while Britain as a whole is not necessarily a prime contender for the first word your average foreigner would come up with when asked to free associate with the word "desert", or "arid").

Basically Greenock is the Manchester of Scotland; people make jokes about how much it rains.

There's always somewhere. In Norway it's Bergen. When I first went there, hitch-hiking round Europe back in 1975, I heard my first — and for a long time, only — example of Norwegian humour: An Oslo man goes to Bergen on holiday. It rains without pause for a fortnight. At the end of his holiday, as he's entering the station to take the train back to Oslo — shaking out his brolly, wringing out his tie, whatever — he sees a small boy and says, "Tell, me, small boy, does it always rain in Bergen?" and the small boy says, "I don't know, I'm only five years old." Oh well, maybe you had to be there; if you're wet through and living inside a permanently anchored dark grey rain cloud with only the prospect of a half-year-long winter when the heavy rain turns to heavy snow to look forward to I guess you too would grasp at anything to relieve the gloom.

Even so, six weeks without a totally dry day was probably some sort of record even for Scotland's west coast, and might, just possibly, have excited comment in Fort William, if anybody apart from Les had been counting. Les began to think he might have made a mistake. However, as the year wore on, a subsequent pleasantly hot and sunny summer — well, technically a brief but welcome Indian summer; okay, actually a warmish and not unduly damp weekend some time in late October — alleviated some of this feeling of doom and after a few years watching from a flat in Upper Achintore as the rain clouds drifted slowly up Loch Linnhe, Les and his wife-to-be Aileen decided to look for a house to buy. Aileen, also a teacher, was brought up in Cumbernauld, where it rains so little that the weather is probably only a few places higher on the average inhabitants' List of Conversational Standbys than it would be for your standard Scot.

Naturally, after all that rain, they were looking for a change, and so settled on a place a mere fifteen miles down the road from Fort William but with a profoundly different micro-climate and in a wholly different league when it comes to heavy drizzle, lashing rain, day-long downpours and sudden but prolonged thunderous tumults of water crashing without respite from leaden skies; in Glenfinnan it *really* knows how to rain. People notorious for having had the bad luck to have been born and raised in Fort William during a particularly catastrophic sequence of above-averagely rainy decades of seriously god-awful drenchingness — and hence no strangers to having apparently unending successions of black, moisture-laden cumulonimbi queuing up above their town to deposit megatons of water apparently targeted specifically on that individual's cagoule hood — have been known to blanch and stagger when confronted with the prospect of spending longer in Glenfinnan than the amount of time it takes to drive — splashing — through it.

Glenfinnan has been, for several proud sequences of years, officially the rainiest place in Britain. There is, allegedly, a small village in the Lake District that occasionally beats it in the We're Wetter Than You Are stakes, however this is only believed to happen when the rain-measuring device in this sorry hamlet actually slips into the lake concerned and thus gives a false and indeed unfair reading (or so the proud, damp, inhabitants of Glenfinnan will tell you, loath to surrender a distinction which, while they are unable to work to help achieve, they most certainly suffer for to be allowed to claim).

Having said all that, I've been going to Glenfinnan for nearly twenty years now. I absolutely love the place and an amazingly high number of my memories of it seem to be of stunning, glorious, breathtaking scenery baking under a high sun set in a totally cloudless sky of surpassing blueness.

Yep, beats me too.

But, hey, if it didn't rain in Scotland, we wouldn't have all that water to make whisky with, now would we? In fact, arguably, if all that at least partially rain-engendered Gaelic misery hadn't needed relieving in the first place, whisky would never have been invented at all. Sitting in your cold, sodden hovel, wrapped in the ragged remains of a barely glorified blanket, ankle deep in animal excrement and choking on peat smoke while your wife wails a lament for her sisters who died giving birth and your children cough consumptively as they quietly work out how soon they can run away to the Lowlands or America and leave you with all the work to do is a pretty damn sure-fire way of turning a chap's mind towards some sort of means to alleviate the sheer bloody awfulness of existence, via the ingestion of home-grown mood-altering substances if that's what it takes.

But enough about Glenfinnan's second greatest scourge. The rain's not that terrible, after all; wear a jacket with a hood or carry a brolly and you'll be fine. The real question is, What about those bastarding midges?

The midge: microscopic megascourge.

The highland midge (there are other types, but let's stick to the main culprit) is a tiny little winged insect with the ability, en masse, to ruin evenings, days, weeks and entire holidays for human beings. They are, basically, microscopic vampires; newly impregnated females need a drink of blood to nourish the next generation of midges, and they seem to have a preference for large mammals, especially large mammals with not much hair. Us, in other words.

Really they're feeble, fragile little things, unable to fly faster than about six miles an hour — so a modest breeze sends them to ground, and running away, if you can, is surprisingly effective — plus they're damaged by bright sunlight, so tend to avoid that too. Despite such weaknesses they have a powerful negative effect on the tourist trade of the west of Scotland and on the quality of life of most people who live there. They'd ruin the summer for the rest of Scotland too if they could, but they're only really happy where the land receives more than about 1250 millimetres of rain per year, and in

Scotland that basically means the side that faces out into the prevailing westerly airstream.

They breed best in peaty, acidic soil with lots of standing water, they love still, overcast days and balmy evenings and they tend to appear between the end of May and the start of September. And they are, collectively, voracious. The Highlanders of old had an especially horrendous punishment which consisted of stripping the convicted person naked and leaving them staked out overnight during the midge season. A midge will only take about a ten millionth of a litre with each bite, so even after a few tens of thousands of bites the victim was never going to be bled to death, but they did, allegedly, stand a very good chance of going mad. Anybody who has ever been subject to a sustained midge attack for even a few minutes — especially when they start to get into your eyes and up your nose — will sympathise.

There are, however, two saving graces, one for people who only visit the Highlands for short periods, the other for everybody. The first is that it's the body's own reaction to the midge bite that distresses rather than the bite itself, and that reaction takes two or three days to develop, so if you're only on the west coast for a weekend you may never notice the damn things. The second is that some wonderful person has invented a midge trap that actually appears to work. This device wafts out carbon dioxide — which is what the midge homes in on, thinking it's the exhaled breath of a big, juicy mammal — then a sort of modified vacuum cleaner sucks the little bastards into an extremely fine mesh net. This can clear a significant area of even a really badly midge-infested site and could even, conceivably, just possibly, let people in Highland hotels and back gardens sit outside of an evening. If this all works in the real world and not just under controlled conditions, the inventor deserves to become a multi-millionaire and have statues erected to him or her from Stranraer to Ullapool.

Anyway, Glenfinnan is midge central. We went out one evening years ago and left a light on and a window open at the McFarlanes' house; when we came back there were so many midges on the angles between the walls and the ceiling it was as though somebody had taken a can of black spray paint and sprayed slowly from one corner to the next. We all just stood and stared, aghast, until Aileen — unknowingly anticipating this new midge-hoovering device — got the vacuum cleaner out and removed the little horrors that way.

Actually midges would drive you to strong drink too, for the anaesthetic effect if nothing else. I've even heard of people smearing whisky onto their skin to act as a short-lived deterrent to the little fiends, though it has to be pointed out that a) it had better be a blend, b) this should only be done under conditions of extreme desperation, and c) there's little proof it works.

We're back home, between Islay and Speyside (via Glenfinnan). The war continues. Bush and Blair meet at Camp David to assure everybody it's all going splendidly and those pesky weapons of mass destruction will be found, gee, real soon now.

I find myself looking at Blair and hating his self-righteous, Bush-whipped ass the way I only ever hated Thatcher before. I look at Dubya and just see a sad fuck with scared eyes; a grotesquely under-qualified-for-practically-anything daddy's boy who's had to be greased into every squalid position he's ever held in his miserable existence who might finally be starting to wake up to the idea that if the most powerful nation on Earth — like, ever, dude — can put somebody like *him* in power, all may not be well with the world. Dubya is that worst of all things, at least at this level of power and influence; a cast-iron, 100 per cent, complete and total loser who's somehow lucked out and made it to the very top.

However. Enough. The next leg of the whisky-book-researching tour beckons. There were pals to see, vehicles to be driven, roads to explore, people to meet, distilleries to tour, drink to drink and fun to be had, and bottles of whisky waiting to be bought at each of the distilleries I visited. I must not get upset at the thought of my taxes helping to pay for this war shit. Hell, I'd just try harder when the time came to convince the tax people that the bottles of booze were absolutely necessary for my research into the book's subject, and therefore a legitimate business expense. (I had thought of claiming them as expenses off Random House, but Oliver the Editor had gone a little pale when I'd tested the air in this direction and so I thought I'd probably better try the tax man instead.)

★   ★   ★

For this leg of the malt-researching multi-tour, we were going to take the M5. I have always liked big fast saloons. A BMW 5-series is a moderately big car (not long ago it would have been regarded as a just plain big car), and the quickest type of 5-series is the M5. With the M5 you get all the benefits of the generic 5-series; it's a well-designed, well-built, dynamically well-sorted and very reliable motor with the usual extras people have come to expect in a new car these days, except in the M5 you get all that plus a stonking five-litre, 400-horse-power V8 engine nestled under the bonnet to make life interesting. There are various uprated bits to cope with the extra power, but it's the engine you'll tend to notice. Well, until you need the brakes, which are equally powerful.

The M5 was the first car I'd had the patience to specify, order and then accept delivery of. I suppose I had just become accustomed to buying second-hand, when there's no real wait; a car is either available or not. When I had the money to afford a new car (i.e. too much; if you're a private individual and being sensible with your money arguably you'll always buy second-hand) — and especially when I had the money to afford a new car that was fairly high performance and therefore not usually readily available straight off the forecourt — I'd get frustrated that I was going to have to join a queue and wait for up to a year, and so usually ended up taking a demonstrator model, or a cancelled order for somebody else.

This latter option led to a 911 which had what Ann insists to this day was an orange interior. I still maintain it was terracotta, but the degree of garishness was one small factor in trading that car in for the M5. We ordered it in black with black and blue leather and something called privacy glass rear and side windows. Only the windows were really a mistake; they're a bit darker than we'd anticipated and make the car look like a gangsta's wheels, but never mind; you don't notice them when you're driving it.

The M5 is fast in a generous, raspingly, burblingly bounteous way. It sweeps through corners like a sports car and then surges towards the horizon on a tsunami of torque and a creamy purr of sound.

I am, as you might have gathered, a fan.

Blame caravans. I can still remember the sinking feeling I used to get, years ago, driving in summer along a road I knew fairly well and seeing a caravan in the distance, knowing that there were few or no safe overtaking opportunities ahead and that I was going to be stuck behind this giant off-white rear-end for the next half-hour or so. I got balefully used to this happening, puttering along watching the blinds in a caravan rear window swinging gently to and fro as some struggling Escort in front tried to haul it round a bend. This at least gave me time — oh, lots and lots of time — to meditate on the bizarre and even deceitful nature of caravan nomenclature. Caravans must have some of the most thoroughly inappropriate names on the road. They're called things like *Typhoon* and *Buccaneer*. What they should be called, of course, is stuff like *A Nice Cup Of Tea*, or *Matching Tartan Blanket and Thermos Flask*, or *Nice Out Again, Isn't It? Reginald*

And Me Were Thinking Of Popping Down The Pitch And Putt Later If The Rain Holds Off, Do You Fancy Coming? But no, they get called *Bohemian* or *Ninja Stealth Bomber Hyper Extreme* or something.

Anyway, the point is that I had all this time to contemplate such cerebral matters because the cars I could afford to drive back then were so slow it was only when we got to a long clear straight that it became possible even to think about overtaking the offending cream lumberers.

But no more. Nowadays I whip past their white-with-a-hint-of-beige arses with a throaty rumble of snarling engine note and a nonchalant one-two of the wrists. When I see a caravan ahead now, I think, Ha-ha! Prey!

Having said all that, the M5's got a towing hitch.

It's not for caravans, specifically, however; it's for trailing boats. For this next week of distillery-visiting I was going to enlist the help of my friends Les and Aileen, from Glenfinnan. As it's the start of April, it's also about the time when our boat would anyway be emerging from its winterisation process in a big boat-filled shed in Grangemouth and have to be trailed to Loch Shiel, where it spends its summers, so I'm combining the two tasks.

The boat is an Orkney 5/20; it has a very small cabin you can squeeze about four people into if it's raining (see above), a more generous open deck area, a 30 horsepower motor and a depth gauge/fish finder. Most people probably use boats like this for fishing, not that we do much fishing. We call it The Boat. It was called

The New Boat for a while, while the boat we now talk of as The Old Boat was still just The Boat, but now what was The Boat is The Old Boat and what was The New Boat is just The Boat. Hope that's clear.

The Old Boat was a Drascombe Lugger I bought off a policeman in Glasgow, years ago; it was a more versatile and characterful boat than the Orkney, but it was showing its age; we retired it to Fife when we bought the Orkney a few years ago, then last summer I took it down to Cornwall to one of my cousins with whom, hopefully, it'll start yet another new life.

The great thing about the Lugger is that as well as having a small (very small) engine for puttering around, and being rowable (if a bit heavy for rowing any great distance), it has two masts and three sails. And not just your standard namby-pamby effete white sails, either; these were tan sails, manly sails, butch sails; sails that looked like they'd been dipped in Forth Bridge paint before being hoisted to the winds.

The Lugger isn't fast using any of its three power sources, but it has always felt sturdy and reliable, and it's fun just because boats are fun. It's even moderately safe for single-handed sailing because it's loose footed. This means that there's no dirty great lump of wood hanging out underneath the bottom of the main sail, so it's much harder to knock yourself out than it is on an ordinary sailing boat.

We all had many happy seasons coasting down Loch Shiel under those tan sails, but the Orkney is more practical and gets where it's going a lot quicker. Actually it feels like a speed-boat to Les and me after years of waiting for the Lugger's original 4hp motor to break surface tension and actually move us anywhere, though we still haven't tried the water-skiing experiment yet. The other thing we haven't got round to is Les and Iain's Guide to Sensible Sailing, a video to demystify the confusing world of nautical terminology.

Les and Iain's Guide to Sensible Sailing.

(Sample dialogue)

Les: Now, Iain, I believe some people would call this a sheet, is that correct?

Iain: Well, that's right, Les, they would. However I think you'll find that the correct technical name for what you're holding there is, in fact, a "rope". A sheet is something you put on your bed.

Les: I see. And if I put this "rope" over here, that would be on the port side of the boat, near the bows, yes?

Iain: No, port is a drink. Made in Portugal, by the way, so it's quite easy to remember where it comes from. No, that's what we call the "left" side of the boat, at the "front".

. . . You get the idea. We took it too far, of course. Masts became sticks and sails big flappy things. I mean, really.

It's yet another amazingly good day. One of the compensations of trailing the boat and so having to stick below 50 is that there's more time to look around

115

at the scenery; I drive this route via Lochearnhead and Glencoe a lot but it never ceases to amaze. The air is so clear the sunlight seems bright as mid-summer, but because it's early April the snow still coats the mountain tops, sparkling like icing sugar. The ragged scatter of lochs across Rannoch Moor are deep blue on one side of the road, light blue and glittering on the other, already surrounded by fresh growing grass and rushes and a carpet of tiny, early flowers.

A single day like this isn't so unusual, but this is just the latest dry, warm day in a very dry winter and a positively sunny and almost balmy early spring. It's been a year of unseasonable weather all round, it feels. In late February Ann and I were in Cyprus with her parents, staying in a villa near Pissouri looking out across to the British base at Akrotiri in one direction and the Troódos mountains in the other. We weren't exactly expecting Death Valley heat in February, but apparently the snow we got was unusual, too; the locals were out taking photographs of the stuff because it hadn't snowed in Pissouri for nearly 30 years.

When I arrive at Glenfinnan, there's not a cloud in the sky and Loch Shiel is just lying there, barely ruffled in the faint breeze, disappearing into the pale distance between the surrounding mountains, shimmering.

Loch Shiel: an appreciation, with reservations.

Loch Shiel is a great loch. Well, I like it, anyway. It's never more than a mile wide but it's nineteen miles long. Fairly deep, too, at 120 metres. At its head is the

116

village of Glenfinnan, where our friends the McFarlanes live. Their house looks out to the water and the place where we moor the boat, then along the shore, past the Lodge (the Glenfinnan House Hotel to give it its full title, and effectively the local) to the stone tower that is the monument to the 1745 rebellion. Everybody seems to assume that the figure at the top of the monument is Prince Charlie; it isn't, just a representative Highland chief. Beyond, on a clear day, you can see Ben Nevis. There's a National Trust centre for the monument, the Glenfinnan viaduct — as seen on postcards, shortbread tins and in Harry Potter films throughout the world — another hotel called the Prince's House, a photogenic Catholic church with a bell in the grounds which you're allowed to ring, a pier and a railway station and that's about it. No shops apart from the souvenir shop and café in the Trust. There is a shed that doubles as a Post Office, but only when the wee detachable sign's displayed.

At the other end of the loch there's the even tinier village of Acharacle, and between the two nothing but scenery; loch and mountains the whole way, the hills descending in height as they head south-west. There is a forestry track on the south-east side but it's locked at both ends; only the forestry people and the postie have keys. On the north-west side it's trackless.

There are beaches, fish farm cages and platforms with incongruous wooden sheds perched on them, numerous little islands, submerged rocks to avoid and rivers to explore. At the far end you could conceivably shoot the rapids — if you were in a canoe — and end up in the sea (a century of global warming could well turn Loch Shiel into a sea loch).

Every year Les and I say we'll take the boat back out of the loch and onto the trailer and go to another loch or even down to the sea, and every year we find there's ample to do on Loch Shiel alone without having to go anywhere else. This does mean, though, that we are unable to describe ourselves as a pair of old sea dogs. We've settled for being loch puppies instead.

Back in the early part of the twentieth century, when the local roads were either non-existent or little better than tracks, there was a steamer service linking the far end of the loch with the railway station at Glenfinnan. These days the good ship *Selas* plies the waters during the season, and very relaxing it is too; it's generally insect-free out on the loch and anyway the *Selas*, though it always seems very quiet and even sedate as it putters along, is easily faster than any midge.

I do have slightly mixed feelings about this stretch of water, all the same. When we had the Drascombe rigged we discovered Loch Shiel has extremely capricious winds. Capricious is what Les christened them, anyway. I believe my term was "fucking annoying". You could be tacking happily across the loch in a fine strong breeze one second, only to have it disappear utterly in the next moment, and then, a random and therefore completely unpredictable amount of time later, just as you were beginning to think about firing up the motor, the wind would come back. Usually from exactly the opposite direction from before, necessitating some rapid resetting of sails. We put this meteorological eccentricity down to the numerous tall mountains at the Glenfinnan end of the loch; they get in the way of the wind and make it swirl.

Sometimes the wind wouldn't come back at all and we'd be left sitting there in perfectly calm water, as though we'd been deposited on the world's biggest mirror. This led to behaviour that Les designated — rather unkindly, I thought — as Speculative Sailing.

Speculative Sailing consists of sitting in one's boat in conditions of absolutely zero wind speed, with no appreciable movement whatsoever, save possibly that of the general mass of water in the loch moving from its head towards its distant outflow (worth, oh, a good millimetre per day or so), under a sky that is either cloudless or, if clouded, utterly still. Then, when one's chum (played here by Mr Leslie McFarlane) — understandably bored after an hour or so of languishing becalmed like this going nowhere — suggests starting the damn engine, oneself has to jump up, point three or four miles down the loch and saying something like, "Why, no! Look; there's a wee sort of ruffled looking bit of water way down there. See? There is! No, really! And it's sort of heading this way. Let's just leave it a bit longer . . ."

Pitiable, really.

My other resentment dates from the time of Joanie's party down the loch. This was last summer (2002 as I write this). Donald-John and Joanie, like Les and Aileen, are both teachers who live in Glenfinnan. For Joanie's 50th, Donald-John thought it would be a laugh if the party was held at one of the pebble beaches a few

119

miles down the loch, so people set up a makeshift pier, an oil-drum-size barbie, a couple of shelters in case it rained (it didn't) and we all took boats and drink, food and fold-up camping furniture. Ann and I went with Les, Aileen and their daughter, the lovely Eilidh. A very fine time was had. My principal memory is of Ian McFarlane (no relation) piping energetically while his dad Charlie tramped back along the shore with an unfeasibly large tree trunk perched on his shoulder, bound for the fire. That and Donald-John's T-shirt, which bore the legend "The Liver is *Evil* and Must be *Punished.*"

Later, in the post-party gloaming, on the beach in front of the house, we started to unload the boat. I think I must have overloaded myself with, well, with whisky, obviously, but also with two camping seats, a camping table, a cool box and my camera, because I fell in. The water was only about a foot deep, but this was quite sufficient to ruin my camera, drown my mobile, soak me to the skin and fill my waders. Allegedly I sort of teetered for a second or two, which supposedly made it even funnier. Eilidh was heard laughing from the house. She claims seeing me fall in the water is the funniest thing she's ever seen, but then she's only fifteen, so what does she know.

The camera was eventually repaired, but the mobile was a goner. I wouldn't have minded so much but I'd only replaced it the previous year after an unfortunately similar incident while canoeing with Les on Loch Eilt, just up the road.

So, Loch Shiel and I have issues. But it's still a great loch.

We get the boat safely into the water, the engine starts first time and we zap down the loch a few miles to a pebble beach and back, just to make sure everything is working. There are maybe a dozen other boats on the loch, which is a lot, for Loch Shiel. This, it turns out, is because it's one of the three annual Glenfinnan Fishing Competitions. Then it's time to sit in the garden with a beer (pre-midge season; no worries). After a very fine dinner of venison and a sensible amount of fine red wine — a Red Wine Frenzy is always a danger on such occasions — Les and I have a couple of SMWS whiskies, just to get into training for the week of intensive researching ahead.

The SMWS: home from home.

The SMWS — the Scotch Malt Whisky Society — is an organisation that any serious malt whisky lover should be a member of (I am, thanks to Les, who heard about it through Aileen's uncle Billy, one of the SMWS founder members). In fact you could make an argument for being a member even if you were teetotal but enjoyed an amusing read every three months; the quarterly newsletter and tasting notes are worth the price of membership alone. The SMWS started decades ago as a few friends who clubbed together to buy a barrel of whisky for their own use. They knocked the bung out of the barrel, ran the whisky through a coarse filter — think of a coffee filter — and bottled what came through.

The idea was not so much to cut out the middle man to get the stuff cheaper as it was to get back to something more like whisky as it used to taste. At the time there was very little whisky available at cask strength; too much of even the best whisky had been chill-filtered, watered down and — in some cases — mixed with caramel to produce a darker colour.

None of these processes will absolutely ruin a malt, and the whisky manufacturers would argue that in each case they were simply giving the whisky-buying public what they wanted, but it was certainly the case that this was an imposed taste; if you wanted your whisky without any of these processes having been applied, you had to live near a distillery or a very good off-licence, know somebody in the trade, or resort to buying your own cask.

I was told about the whole chill-filtering, caramel-adding thing by a guy in Cadenhead's whisky shop on the Royal Mile in Edinburgh, not long after I'd moved back to Scotland in 1988. I'd just bought a flat on South Bridge and I was exploring the area when I found this shop that sold nothing but whisky, much of it stuff I hadn't seen in other off-licences or even heard of at all. The guy was almost messianic in his zeal, and I duly left the shop clutching several bottles of cask-strength, completely unadulterated whisky and with a certain degree of righteous ire that our national drink had been interfered with, emasculated and basically laid low by blandly vicious corporate suits with dollar signs in their eyes.

Something of all this duly got into *Complicity*, a novel I wrote a year or two later; Cameron Colley, the journalist who's the central character, works on a story about this and is personally and professionally affronted that his tipple of choice isn't as hairy-chested as he'd always assumed it was.

So what does chill filtering do? It takes out of the whisky certain oils that would otherwise make the stuff go cloudy when it's chilled. The story I heard was that this was the fault of the American market; most people in the States take their whisky with ice, and — because the whisky has been watered down to get it to a consistent strength — this makes the resulting mix look cloudy, like there's something wrong with it, when the oils come out of solution. The remedy is to chill the stuff before it's bottled and run it through a fine filter (at one time the filter was made of asbestos, which wasn't something the industry used to publicise heavily; there's no evidence that anybody ever came to any harm through drinking asbestos-filtered whisky, it's more guilt by association, though you do have to wonder if anybody ever contracted asbestosis from handling the filters themselves). The whisky will now remain clear when ice is added, but the oils that have been removed will no longer be there to be tasted, or contribute to the feel in the mouth.

The watering-down bit is just to get the whisky to a standard strength, and means the manufacturer doesn't have to keep altering the print on the label that tells you how strong the whisky is. It also makes life easier for the tax people, as they do their calculations. This is the least problematic alteration, always assuming that the water that's added is stuff you'd want to drink neat in the first place. Most Scottish water is quite soft and drinkable straight from the tap; if you wanted to be really purist about it you might want to specify that the water added to your whisky should come from the same source as the water that went to make the whisky — via the mash tun, etc. — in the first place, however even the most nit-picking taster is usually happy with water that simply and neutrally dilutes without adding any taste of its own.

Adding caramel is done to make whisky darker. Some whiskies are just supposed to be dark, according to the public's perception and the manufacturer's promotional efforts. If the whisky isn't dark enough, some distillers will add caramel. It's done in relatively tiny amounts, and caramel itself is a pretty innocuous material — just heated sugar, basically — so if it imparts any taste whatsoever it's surely completely swamped by the flavours left over from the barrel's earlier bourbon, sherry or whisky fills.

What it boils down to is that adding caramel is cosmetic, and — if you are any sort of purist — does seem a bit like cheating.

The trouble with whisky as a product is that it's so variable; each barrel will produce a different whisky, and each charge of the still will have created a subtly different spirit in the first place; even the season of the whisky's production has been known to make a difference to the final taste. This is why the blender in a distillery, or at a bottling plant, is so important; even with a single malt they will mix together different barrels to create something as consistent as possible over time compared to earlier examples (the blending of different whiskies from different distilleries to produce blended whisky is an even more complex task — there are blends with dozens of different whiskies involved and up to a hundred-plus is not unknown).

The SMWS's approach is the exact opposite to the distillers', treating each barrel as, effectively, a single expression; making a virtue of the variation between casks instead of treating it as a problem to be overcome. This adds a certain piquancy to the drinking of a bottle of SMWS whisky; they always tell you how many bottles the barrel concerned produced, and once they're all gone, that's it. Even more so than with a fine wine, unless you personally still have some bottles left you will never experience that exact taste again.

The SMWS has grown immensely as an organisation but it's still just an association of members, it's non-profit-making and it doesn't take itself too seriously. The quarterly Tasting Notes can be hilarious; I've read of whisky being compared to the smell of a China-man's pigtail, wet Labradors in a gun room and the scent of finest Lebanese hashish. Maybe keeping your tongue in your cheek allows the bouquet to reveal itself all the more fruitfully.

There's an SMWS out-station now in central London and various other satellite branches throughout the world, but the real HQ is at the Vaults, an ancient building in Leith, the port of Edinburgh. They have a very well-stocked bar, flats to let and very helpful staff. Most of the SMWS's business is mail order, however if you live in the area or are passing through you can pick up your order direct from the Vaults. I'm banned from having TV crews in our house so I've done various televised interviews elsewhere. Usually this means at the Albert Hotel, down the hill in our village (fine view of the Forth Bridge), however I once did one, with Griff Rhys Jones, in the members' bar at the SMWS. This place looks rather like I imagine a gentleman's club in London might look, all wood panelled and full of plush leather sofas and chairs. I still, occasionally, meet people who've seen this interview and think it was filmed in our home and the members' bar is my study. Even more occasionally, I correct them.

Les and I drink our whiskies from SMWS tasting glasses. These are based on Spanish copitas . . .

. . . No, I don't see how we can avoid this. I'm going to have to say something about how whisky should be drunk.

Drinking: you'd think it would be obvious.

Now, real purists will tell you that nosing a whisky and tasting it are quite different things, and require different glasses. This, I submit, is taking things too far for us civilians. Frankly, a fine malt taken from an old enamel tea mug will taste ten times better than an indifferent blend sipped genteelly from the most carefully designed

126

whisky glass (always providing the enamel mug is clean to start with, natch). Take your whisky from a tumbler if you want — though the old-school cut-glass or crystal tumbler is more about making room for the ice than letting the whisky breathe — but a brandy glass is probably as good as anything, and lets you get your nose into the glass for a good sniff.

Proper professional nosers/tasters will tell you the best way to sniff a whisky is to draw in the aroma while keeping your mouth slightly open; apparently this improves the sensation. I haven't noticed the difference yet (I was only told this last month at Macallan) but I'm going to persevere.

So, what to add, if you don't want to drink it neat? Look, if you've bought the damn stuff you can drink it however you like, but adding, say, Cola or lemonade to a fine malt whisky is a bit of a waste. It's rather like buying a Ferrari and never taking it out of first gear; you want to ask the person concerned, Why did you waste your money doing this? Are you just showing off? Look; I have a small belt and a barely used syringe; let's just inject your favourite dram and see what that does . . .

Malt whisky is expensive. It's expensive because it's made in small batches by skilled people and has to sit for years and years and years doing nothing except taking up warehouse space, evaporating slowly and getting tastier. It will not get you any more drunk than a much cheaper similar-strength blend, so what you're paying the extra for is the taste, and that taste's going to be completely overpowered by the sugary fizz you're adding. If, at the end of all this, somebody still wants to drink their malt with ice and soda, well, that's their choice, and every measure and every bottle sold is helping to keep the industry going, people employed and a way of life thriving, no matter.

The way I was taught to take whisky is first to use your eyes to check out the colour. Then swirl the stuff around the glass to see how thick or thin it is, observing its legs (the little rivulets that run down the side of the glass after you've swirled it). Next have a good sniff, open mouthed or whatever. Then take a sip completely neat. How much you sip can depend on how strong the whisky is — cask strength can be very strong, over 100 proof, and hence a bit nippy, straight. In effect your own saliva will dilute the whisky, so the stronger the stuff, the smaller the sip.

According to taste, mix with water. Adding the same again is a standard measure, though a lot of people think this is exactly double what's ideal. In any event, some cask-strengths in particular might need quite a lot of watering down. Then just drink. And savour, if you will; roll the stuff around in your mouth, feel it there and in your throat when you swallow. Don't knock back in a single gulp unless you're at an airport and they've got to the stage of calling you by name and threatening to close the flight, or unless you have just been told you've won the lottery, or are going to become a father (obviously you won't be celebrating being told you're going to be a mother. Not with alcohol, anyway. Have a fag instead).

★   ★   ★

Les and I met in Greenock High School. At the time I was writing these truly awful stories about a character called Dahommey Breshnev (sic, and, yet again, sic). These were bizarre, poor and just plain bad for lots of reasons but principally because I was really into puns at the time and was trying to squeeze as many puns into each story as I could. The stories became pun-driven, pun-led; I made the stories up as I went along and at every junction of the tale, whenever there was a choice about what was going to happen next, I invariably went for the route that seemed to promise the highest number of puns.

And that's one of the good ones.

Here's an example of those puns: one of the characters in a later Dahommey Breshnev story was called Toss Macabre.

Told you.

As the stories went on I tried to compress more and more puns into each one, and it became a matter of authorial honour to have a greater concentration of puns in the story I was working on than I'd achieved in the one before. I'd count all the words in each story, then count all the puns, divide one by the other and so arrive at the story's pun-to-word ratio. This quickly became by far the most important attribute the stories possessed (it was easy to measure, it was precise, it felt almost scientific . . . sometimes I think I might have made a really average bureaucrat). Characterisation,

129

plotting, moral themes, plausibility? These were just words.

And not even very good words, either, by this way of thinking; "plotting" might have a punning link to gardening or something, but "characterisation" is just a dead loss; ditto "moral", though there might be a way to separate the "m" in "moral" from the rest of the word and so ... No, too contrived even for me. "Themes" could stretch to a lame lisp-oriented pun about seams ... "Plausibility"? No, just useless.

(This weakness for puns and juvenile wordplay is something that I am not quite totally over even now, three decades later; there was, in the first draft of Chapter Three in this book, in the sub-section **"Whisky; the how-to bit**." the unfortunate sentence at the end of a paragraph, "Still, waste not wort not." Thank goodness I took it out.)

I am probably not as ashamed as I ought to be that I can still remember how immensely proud I was when — in Dahommey's final short story, *The Apparently Interminable Adventures of* — I got the pun-to-word ratio down to below one in ten.

Deeply sad. I kind of knew it at the time, too, but I didn't care. It was fun.

All I can say in my own defence is that at least I was never stupid enough to imagine for a nanosecond that any of this stuff would impress girls. I enjoyed doing this sort of thing for its own sake, and if a few of my male pals thought them worth a groan or two — for a groan is about as generous and positive a reaction to a pun as you're likely to get — then that was okay too, though still not the reason I was actually doing any of this.

Even so, in a vain and misguided attempt to get more people to read these appalling pieces of nonsense, I'd started illustrating them with collages constructed from photos ripped out of the *Observer* magazine. These were and are by far the best things in the little school-book-based pamphlets that each of the stories appeared in. Some of the collages are almost inventive, and a few arguably witty.

Possibly because of my fiendish wordplaying, more likely because of rude pictures featuring swimwear models, Les asked to see some of my work one day. Unaccountably disinclined to quickly return it and back away smiling reassuringly while not making any sudden movements — and vowing never to acknowledge my existence ever again — Les instead appeared to think they were actually worth looking at, if not worth reading, obviously. I was flattered in the extreme and we became friends.

The day after the successful boat-putting-in, we say goodbye to Eilidh, who is off to Iceland on a school trip. (Actually I said goodbye the night before because she was getting the bus from the school at 6a.m. or something awful like that and after beer, wine and whisky, even taken in relatively modest quantities, six in the morning seemed a bit beyond the call of duty for groggy farewells).

Les and Aileen are such brilliant hosts, and so used to putting up their many friends, they keep a visitors'

131

book. This is generally just an excuse for drunken ramblings, outright lies, boasts about pool, golf, card and other scores, hopeless attempts at contemporary humour and unspecified incomprehensible gibberish, interspersed, very occasionally, with genuine appreciations for the fine hospitality received (usually from people who don't stay there very often and so don't understand that the visitors' book is really supposed to be for drunken ramblings, outright lies, etc.).

Given that writing is my profession, it's a never-ending source of worry for me that my contributions to this ongoing round-robin work are rarely amongst the funniest, and true to form I do my cause no good on this occasion, leaving a comment about Eilidh going to Iceland and failing to come back with the twelve-pack of frozen beef burgers I'd requested. In reality I ask her to bring back a handful of black volcanic sand, and, bless her, a week later, she does.

Sunday we spend down the loch in the boat under the still unseasonable warmth of a cloudless sky, exploring some of the land down by Glenaladale then heading for the far side of the loch and threading the boat between some of the tiny islands just off the south-east shore, reconnoitring at a putter then belting through at full speed, just for the hell of it. I could tell you exactly where it was but it's four hard-to-pronounce Gaelic words in a row and frankly it's in none of our interests for me even to try. At Glenaladale, despite the fact I am 49 and Les very nearly is — Les rarely allows an opportunity to pass when he can remind me I am a whole three months older than he is — we spend a significant amount of time and effort skipping stones, trying to hit large stones with small ones while the former are in flight, throwing stones at logs, using thin or circular stones — spun — in our attempts to produce duck's farts, and sweatily heaving the largest rocks we can manage up to the tops of small cliffs so we can throw them into the water and so produce Really Big Splashes.

(Look, growing up is about this sort of stuff no longer being the *only* way you're allowed to have fun, not about having to give it up altogether.)

CHAPTER
SIX

WhiskyLandWorldVille!

Monday. We're bound for Speyside, booked into a hotel just outside the village of Dulnain, near Grantown-on-Spey. Aileen takes first go at driving the M5.

Aileen is Les's younger and fitter wife. We know this because it was reported as such in the *Lochaber News* following the incident when the boat drifted off from one of the sand beaches far down on the south-west shore of the loch and Les had to swim after it (long story).

Aileen's a popular PE teacher who seems very happy in her job but she should, I'm convinced, have been an agent. Or some sort of negotiator. I've never met anybody better at striking a bargain, making a deal, haggling for a discount — or getting various bits of kit thrown in for free — who wasn't a professional. And I've met a few professionals who lacked her natural gift. Aileen's skills in this area are, amongst those who know her, legendary. No matter how hard-nosed a sales person might think they are, Aileen will find a way round them. She's negotiated deals where I would never have imagined it was remotely possible, like the time when she and Eilidh were in London and Aileen

134

somehow persuaded the people who ran the open-top bus and river-boat trips that they should have a reduced rate for people doing both. Housewife from the sticks gets one over on cynical big bad city tourist operation . . . nope, still beggars belief.

One of her more remarkable deals was, fittingly enough, with the Ben Nevis distillery, just outside Fort William, when she was trying to attract sponsorship for the Glenfinnan Volleyball Team. A friendly chat with the very pleasant and helpful people at the distillery and she walked out with a crate of whisky for the team, plus a load of miniatures. The distillery didn't even want its names on the team T-shirts or anything; they were happy with a mention in the programme.

In 1995, on a very hot, still, magnificently sunny day, a bunch of us were running the ice-cream tent at the Glenfinnan Games. I'm implying that we all helped out; in fact, I'm ashamed to admit, the reality was that — without us really intending this to happen, honest — the women folk ended up doing the actual serving and taking the money while we guys — and supposedly New Men — stayed at the back of the tent in the shade, sitting on the coolboxes, fanning ourselves with games programmes and guzzling the cold beers which had somehow found their way into the coolboxes along with the more commercially relevant tubs of ice cream.

The '95 games were a big occasion because they were marking the 250th anniversary of the raising of the standard at Glenfinnan at the beginning of the 1745 rebellion (the one that started in Glenfinnan, went by way of Derby and was finished on a bleak bit

135

of moorland outside Inverness called Culloden). Usually the Glenfinnan Games attract under a thousand entrants and spectators — which is still not bad for a wee village — but in '95 there were getting on for ten thousand people swarming over the place: loads of locals, myriads of generally slightly bemused tourists, dozens of history junkies and far-flung nationalists who'd jetted in from all over the world for the event, bunches of TV, radio and press people — thanks to the sun, the setting and the crowds, the photographs were front-page splashes in various Scottish newspapers the following day — and an awful lot of those very serious-looking guys who dress up in authentically bulky and brownly dour highland dress, carry formidable-looking claymores, swords and nail-studded shields and who, as a rule, sport Extreme Beards. Beards of such rampant abundance they look entirely capable of concealing within their tangled topography an entire redcoat-murdering ambush party of tooled-up Highlanders.

On games day '95 these guys mostly had very red faces, partly due to sunburn (and possibly partly due to the presence of so many unashamedly English tourists — I don't know) and partly due to the fact that those heavy, dark, historically authentic plaids — which I'm sure really are what my ancestors used to wear, but which I confess always remind me of giant brown nappies — are fine for keeping you warm in the teeth of a swirling Highland downpour of severe lashingness, but are not really optimum apparel for days when the sunlight is beating down like a golden sledgehammer and the tarmac is melting on the roads. They were, accordingly, some of our best customers at the ice-cream tent, which was, by a coincidence, right next to the Drambuie marquee.

Drambuie's link with the event was more than just gratuitous; after the Jacobite defeat at Culloden, Prince Charlie escaped back to Paris via Skye with the help of Flora MacDonald. He died in Rome, 40 years later, after living in Paris and Florence, mostly, and after having made two or three secret visits to London in the 1750s. There were mistresses and wives and he never entirely gave up hoping he might really become Charles the Third of Great Britain; died with his boots off. Not such a bad life, considering. Certainly more agreeable than being torn to bits by grapeshot and musket-fire during the battle itself, or being butchered afterwards while lying wounded, or trying to run away.

Anyway, while on Skye he stayed with the MacKinnon family and drank Drambuie, which, as Walter Schobert points out in his exhaustive *The Whisk(e)y Treasury*, very likely represents the way whisky used to be drunk back then, at least amongst the toffs; that is as a fine malt mixed with honey and herbs. There seems to be some dispute over whether Prince Charlie already had the recipe and gave it to the MacKinnons as a thank you, or they already had the recipe and just — eventually — made canny use of the romantic connection. I prefer the latter, but in any event Drambuie probably had more right to be there at the 250th anniversary bash than anybody else.

Come to think of it, I have my own link with Drambuie; that cancelled-order 911 we had with the orange/terracotta interior had allegedly been ordered by a director of the Drambuie company (hence the, umm, remarkable colour, maybe).

Aileen, who, I think it would be fair to say, has something of a sweet tooth, set up a very welcome and mutually beneficial deal with the girls who were serving in the by now sweltering Drambuie tent; some of our ice cream for some of their liqueur. We chaps particularly appreciated this as we'd just run out of beer.

Like I say; she'd have made a great agent.

We turn left at the Ben Nevis distillery with its highly photogenic Highland cattle. I can remember when Highland cattle — also known as hairy coos — were relatively rare sights unless you were deep in the Highlands or way out in the islands. Now they seem to be everywhere. Apparently a lot of places keep them just because they look so great — they are, effectively, pets — and in some cases because they get tourists to stop to take photographs or video (and so perhaps thereafter take in the attraction that has positioned them so cunningly). If this is cynical, well, it's a relatively innocuous form of cynicism. And Highland cattle just do look wonderful.

As a piece of architecture, Ben Nevis distillery is nothing special; a bit overly industrial, though the lines are softened by lots of barrels in the grounds. Established by the very tall "Long John" MacDonald back in 1825, it was closed for five years in the late nineteen-eighties before being rescued and reopened by the the Japanese Nikka firm (Japanese whisky really falls outside the remit of this book, but I think it's briefly worth making the point that Japanese whisky can be very good indeed, and that Japanese firms which have taken over or bought into the Scottish whisky business have generally treated the industry, the people and the product itself with more respect than a lot of our home-grown entrepreneurs). Hopefully with an experienced firm like Nikka behind it, Ben Nevis will continue to flourish and develop; the 10-year-old I bought is a enjoyably big, chewy thing, like eating a nut-sprinkled chocolate liqueur.

Past the entrance to Inverlochy. The old Inverlochy castle, nearer the town, is that rarity among Scottish castles: a moated one — or in Inverlochy's case a once-moated one, as the moat is just a shallow depression on the castle's three landward sides, the fourth facing the river Lochy. Off the top of our heads, as we're taking a look round the impressive but only recently de-scaffolded ruins, Les and I can only think of two other moated castles in Scotland: Rothesay and Caerlaverock. Old Inverlochy was off-limits because of safety and remedial work for so long that we'd both kind of forgotten about it, but now it's open to the public again and it's a large and impressive site; worth seeing.

The newer Inverlochy Castle, a little further out of town, is a very grand country house hotel indeed. It doesn't actually have that many rooms but that's

139

because they've wisely kept the apartments pretty much as they were when the place was a private house; big. Ann and I once stayed in a room about the size of a tennis court. You had to stand up and take a good look round — or shout — to determine whether you were alone in there or not. We've stayed at Inverlochy a few times; once with Mum and Dad and on a couple of occasions with the McFarlanes. Hearing that the place is occasionally frequented by some very famous film stars, Les and I always make a point of playing a frame or two of snooker, just in case we bump into Sean and Clint and get to thrash them in a doubles game, but it hasn't happened yet.

Usually when the five of us have stayed there we've had a private dining room. No way is this because we are noisy and might upset the other, more respectable guests.

Our most recent stay at Inverlochy was last year, when Bentley, for some bizarre reason, suddenly took it into their heads to let me have one of their extremely expensive motor cars for a couple of days. Even the invitation to drive the thing was classy; a framed piece of art made up to look like the cover of one of my books (back in the black-and-white days), with the word "Bentlicity" emblazoned on it. How could I refuse?

A shiny silver-grey Continental T was duly delivered to our house and Ann and I immediately zapped off to Inverlochy before Bentley could change their minds, inviting Les, Aileen and Eilidh to be our guests.

140

The Continental T is by far the most expensive car I've ever driven (with the possible exception of the Formula One car at Magny-Cours). At not a kick in the arse off a quarter of a million pounds, this was a seriously pricey machine. And more money — a *lot* more money — for less car; the Continental T was the short-wheelbase go-faster coupé of the range, while the longer four-door version, even with the same turbo engine, cost over one hundred grand less. I mean, *what?*

Went like the squits off a Teflon shovel but you always had the feeling you were basically torturing the tyres, forcing them to deal with nearly three tonnes of very accelerative car moving smartly along a twisty road. No sat-nav, bleep parking or room for anyone older than about six in the rear seats, but it did have a two-stage horn — one loudness setting for Town and another more strident one for Country. As a car for saying I Have So Much Money I Just Don't Give A Fuck, this struck me as very much The One.

At Spean Bridge we turn right, heading cross-country for Speyside on the A86. This is another great road (not a Great Wee Road, just a great road). There's a sort of modern Highland open-country A-road standard which consists of long, usually fenced straights punctuated by clear sight-lined, constant radius curves and torque-testing gradients, all of it through impressive scenery, and this baby, from Spean to Kingussie, is an exemplar. It's a classic example of the breed, too, in that in places its spacey, high-speed wonderfulness suddenly runs out to be replaced by that

141

sort of twisty, randomly variable width but effectively one-and-a-half-lane carriageway which is great fun to drive if there's nothing slower in front of you, and exquisitely frustrating if there is.

The A86 has mostly been brilliantly upgraded over the years, but there are still some stretches where you basically need somebody's cooperation if you are going to overtake them. Still; great views of Loch Laggan, Creag Meagaidh and, at Kinloch Laggan, Britain's largest inland beach. I've always found this to be a slightly surreal sight, just because it's so far inland and — at 250 metres — more than a little above sea level. That surreality only comes from knowing where you are, though; we'd been passing that freshwater beach for years before a flippant remark of mine that the tide was out again revealed the fact that Ann had always assumed this *was* a sea loch, and there was nothing remotely unusual about all that sand. Oh well.

A few hundred metres after the slightly surreal beach there's a wee gatehouse by the river that seems to be everybody's favourite example of Scottish Baronial in Miniature, itself just round the corner from the modestly proportioned but highly snap-worthy falls where the river Pattack performs a one-eighty between Inverpattack Lodge and Feagour.

It's all exceptionally photogenic round here. And filmic. This particular bit we're passing is where they do the outdoor stuff for *Monarch of the Glen*, and back in Glenfinnan Les and Aileen sat and watched them shoot bits of the original *Highlander* film right outside their window many years ago. There's been a lot of film and

TV stuff since — my friend Brad's *Rockface* series for example, and the film of my book *Complicity* to name but one not-quite-straight-to-video British film of the last few years — plus, recently, quite a few locals have been taking part in the filming of the second and third *Harry Potter* films.

Last year and this, a hundred-plus children from Lochaber High School were *HP* extras, mainly for the Hogwarts Express scenes (that viaduct again), and Eilidh was one of them — wizard's cloak and all. Les and Aileen also got to be part of the fun, as two of the legally necessary chaperones a film company needs when employing that many children. The only real problem the third *HP* film caused locally was really due to the exceptionally dry winter; the steam train playing the part of the Hogwarts Express locomotive set fire to the hill behind the viaduct. This usually only happens in the summer, when the sporadic clattering of the helicopter scooping water from Loch Shiel to drop on the gaily burning heather, bracken and sun-dried grass on the hillside becomes all just part of the primordial Highland scene.

Eilidh was and is a serious fan of *Harry Potter* and I felt really happy for her getting to be part of the films but I was secretly deeply miffed that I'd finally been out-extraed. Until now I'd been the only one of our group of friends (plus, now, their children) who'd been in a cool film; *Monty Python and the Holy Grail*.

By the sign for a wee place called Fersit, we pass the place where I rolled a 911 a few years ago. This was all my own fault and there was nobody else involved. We'll come to this properly in What Happened to My Car.

We press on, crossing the youthful upper reaches of the river Spey at Laggan. Aileen seems to be enjoying driving the M5.

"I know. Let's do the new funicular that goes up to the top of Cairngorm," I suggest, somewhere around Newtonmore.

"Is this strictly in accordance with the terms of your brief, Mr Banks?" Les asks. Les usually addresses me as "Mr Banks" when there's a hint of criticism involved.

"What do you mean?"

"There's no distillery at the top."

I think about this. "Ah, who cares," I argue.

The funicular railway up to the top of Cairngorm is a hoot. There was a terrible kerfuffle about building it — an even greater kerfuffle than there was over building the gondola system up Aonach Mor, on the north-west shoulder of the Ben Nevis massif. Both are there for skiers and ordinary tourists, plus the gondola is equipped to take mountain bikers and their bikes up the 2000 feet to the top station so they can plummet down the laughably graded track back to the bottom again (watching lunatic mountain-bikers skittering down the rocky excuse for a trail — more like a dried-up 45-degree river bed than any sort of path — is probably the single most vicariously hair-raising thing you can do while in Lochaber — highly recommended).

The Aonach Mor gondola system also happily ferries hillwalkers to the top, whereas the Cairngorm trains won't; various notices in the bottom station tell you that in the summer there is no access from the top station onto the hill itself, and people with serious backpacks will be asked to leave them behind or be refused passage. This was one of the conditions that had to be met before the funicular system got the go-ahead, the idea being that such restrictions would keep non-dedicated trekkers off the summit, where the delicate flora and fauna might suffer from the added numbers of walking boots trampling the heather (people who are absolutely determined to get up there can, of course, just hike from the bottom).

I don't want to see native species die out, or all of Scotland become like the Lake District, but I still can't help feeling the place needs more stuff like this; a few more gondolas, funiculars, mountain-top restaurants and so on. And don't get me started on the lack of decent alpine-style roads on Scotland, or dead-ends that should be joined up . . .

The day we visit Cairngorm there's still enough snow for skiing and boarding, and plenty of people are doing both, so the ways out from the visitor centre onto the hill are open. The weather is positively balmy for Cairngorm, which pretty much has the very worst weather in Britain. We do the standard tourist things; take photos, browse the shop (I add to my growing collection of wooden train whistles and buy a notebook that you can allegedly write on in the rain which I'll almost certainly never use) and have a fairly bog-standard chips-and-beans-with-everything lunch.

145

We stand breathing in the clear mountain air before taking the funicular back to the car. Les looks around as though trying to gauge something. "Altitude?" he asks.

"Eh? What?"

"You mean you didn't bring your altimeter?" Les says innocently. "Dearie me."

"It's in the car," I say, lamely.

Altitude problem.

The altimeter is something of a sore point. I bought it many years ago in Nevisport in Fort William.

I have a weakness for these outdoors-gear shops. I have far too many hiking jackets, pairs of gloves, Swiss Army and other knives, torches, compasses, camping stoves, sets of binoculars and other assorted outdoorsy paraphernalia. I long ago collected all the 50,000-scale maps covering Scotland and now I seem to have started doing the same thing with the orange-cover 25,000 series. Les claims that there must be a bell that goes off when I enter one of these establishments, and possibly a red flashing light as well. Probably in the staff room or manager's office. Maybe even a sign that illuminates: Attention! A fool and his money have just entered the building! Opportunity! Opportunity!

The altimeter is his first and favourite example of my gratuitous overspending. I saw it in the shop and just wanted it. It's a proper piece of precision engineering and it had an orange lanyard and everything. I justified it to myself as a safety measure; out on the hill you might *think* you knew where you were on the map by compass bearings and all that sort of stuff, see, but double checking via the contour lines would *definitely* help confirm that you really were where you thought you were. Sold. However, I didn't want to be too extravagant, so I even looked at the price, first: £39.99. Very reasonable for such a quality piece of kit, I thought. I took it to the counter and the shop assistant rang up £139.99.

I stared at the figures glowing on the till read-out and then at the price sticker on the altimeter itself. Yup, the first numeral on the sticker had printed across the left-hand edge of the little box the price was supposed to be printed inside, and it really was a hundred quid more expensive than I'd thought. I couldn't even get away with just keeping quiet about this piece of gratuitous overspending, because Les was there at the time, at first looking on incredulously and then trying to suppress his laughter. He didn't quite get to the stuffing-the-hanky-into-mouth stage, but it was a close-run thing.

I never did take the damn altimeter hillwalking. It lives in the M5 now, slotted into one of the cup holders. It works off atmospheric pressure and every time I pass the Slochd summit sign on the A9 south of Inverness, or the sign at Rannoch Moor summit (both of which have the courtesy to tell you exactly how high you are, though not in a druggy way, obviously), I dutifully reset it. Apart from that it's of no earthly use to man nor beast, but it still looks kind of cool. I did once take it on the flight from Barra to Glasgow — wee daft plane, unpressurised — and was able to confirm that when the captain said we were cruising at an altitude of 4000 feet — we really were! Handy, or what?

In the afternoon we head into deepest Speyside, via some fun little back roads and the primly quaint but very pleasant town of Grantown-on-Spey, its grey granite buildings positively sparkling in the sunlight. We have to refuel, and Les expresses some horror at how quickly this comes around in the M5.

"I'm getting 22 miles to the gallon!" I protest (Les and I are both of an age where we still think in terms of mpg rather than km per litre). "For a five-litre engine, that's bloody good. Actually it probably means I'm not driving the car hard enough. I've been known to get 350 miles out of a full tank on a long run. In an M5 that's probably some sort of record."

"Yeah, but our A6 gets 800 miles between refills," Les says.

"It's a *diesel!*" I screech. Not unreasonably, I think.

"Yeah. So?"

Dear Enzo preserve us true petrol-heads from the smugness of oil burners. Les likes fast cars as much as I do but I can see he's on the cusp of being turned by that damn five-cylinder diesel. The sooner we get him behind the wheel of the M5 the better.

"Well, anyway," I splutter. "I mean, it's just not fair to compare . . . hold on. Wait a minute. Where's Aileen?"

"Uh-oh. I think I saw a sweet shop back there."

148

G-on-S has a great sweet shop called the Candy Box; one of those time warp places where they measure boiled sweets out of big jars and sell stuff you thought they'd stopped making years ago, as well as having lots of intriguing-looking modern sweets and some terribly tempting Belgian chocolates. Aileen beelines for shops like this the way I go straight to outdoor outlets.

Astoundingly, we don't bump into anybody who knows Les the whole time we're in Grantown. This is genuinely remarkable. I've never known anybody more prone to meeting people he knows where all concerned least expect it. Usually this happens abroad in the middle of nowhere, and I speculate that maybe we're just too close to home. Then Les reminds me that actually he did bump into another Lochaber High School teacher while we were at the top of the funicular.

We eventually drag Aileen out of the sweet shop before she can do a deal on buying the whole stock for less than trade and sweep off along a wee road through the woods towards Glenfarclas distillery, though only after promising her there are bound to be things like whisky-flavoured fudge and similar goodies to be had in the distillery shop.

The three of us plus my notebook take the tour at Glenfarclas. The tour costs £3.50 each, which seems fairly close to standard for distilleries with decent Visitor Centres (though there are exceptions); as a rule you get vouchers with the tickets which entitle you to get almost all the money back if you buy a bottle in the shop afterwards, which is not such a bad deal. It would

149

be nicer — and feel more like proper Highland hospitality — if all distillery tours were free and ended with a complimentary dram, but visitor facilities cost money and the charges don't seem to have put many people off.

Besides, at the end of the Glenfarclas tour you get to see the beautiful wood-panelled room in the Visitor Centre which is constructed from pieces salvaged from the old *Empress of Australia*. The liner was built in 1913 and broken up in 1960, in Ward's ship-breaking yard, by Inverkeithing, a mile or so away from where we live, in sunny North Queensferry. I have to declare a personal connection here; quite a few of my family on my dad's side worked in Ward's over the years.

Whatever, the tour at Glenfarclas is worth doing. It's not a huge distillery but it does have what looks to me like a pretty enormous malt mill, equipped with dirty great magnets to weed any metallic stuff out of the barley, and the big, bulb-shaped stills are the biggest on Speyside. More interesting than all the technical stuff though is how truly autonomous, cohesive and family-run the distillery is.

The Grant family have owned and run Glenfarclas for five generations, with the sixth generation learning the ropes right now. It's a reflection of the fact they have to do all their promotional and other bureaucratic work in-house — rather than leaving such overhead-heavy stuff to be done by a central HQ somewhere else — that while the distillery itself employs only eight people, the office side needs fifteen. Mash tuns, washbacks and stills just fill the warehouses up; it takes dedicated deskwork to keep the whisky moving out of them, onto the market.

A true independent in an industry that has grown increasingly corporate over the centuries, and especially over the last few decades, it would arguably be something to be treasured even if the whisky they made was only good, but it's much better than that. The Glenfarclas 105 (the 105 proof translating to 60 per cent alcohol by volume) has long been one of the best strong whiskies widely available, and it's hard not to make comparisons between its robust, self-confident style and the independence of the firm that makes it. Given that the effectively cask-strength 105 is only about eight to ten years old, this is a sweet, full and amazingly rounded whisky. The bottle I bought was the 21-year-old, which is even more developed, smoother — only to be expected given that it's 43 per cent rather than 60 per cent — and quite spectacular in its complexity, packed with spicy, fruity flavours all wrapped in a subtle smokiness.

In a sense, it ought to make no difference who makes a whisky, or where it's made; all that should matter is the taste, and that's it. Yet, part of the reason for visiting a distillery is that seeing where the stuff is made, meeting the people who make it — and often breathing in the scent of the place where it rests for umpteen years — undeniably adds to the experience in the future, just for the simple reason that that is what we are like; we are connection-making creatures. You might be on the other side of the world, sweating in a climate Scotland hasn't seen since the pre-Cambrian, when most of its land mass was somewhere over the Equator, but the smell of a dram from a distillery you've been to years before will suddenly whisk you back to a collection of black-walled buildings on a chilly hillside in Angus.

It's a subjective encounter, drinking a whisky. You're bringing as much to the event as the drink is; maybe more. Just as touring a distillery adds to the sensation of drinking its products subsequently, bringing in resonances that have nothing directly to do with the smell or taste or feel of the liquid, so knowing you're making a link to a proudly independent family firm, not a vast conglomerate, however well run and relatively benign, allows you to enjoy the dram with just a little extra relish.

In any event, on taste alone, Glenfarclas is one of the Speyside greats, and deserves to be ranked with the more heavily promoted brands.

We stay at Muckrach Lodge. The owners turn out to be called McFarlane too, though they don't seem to be any sort of close relations to Les and Aileen (I mean, not that we'd actually have asked for a discount if they were. I have a brother-in-law who's a Penfold, but do I ever ask for a discount on Penfold's Grange Bin 95?).

Faced with the irresistible attraction of the Muckrach's Full Scottish Breakfast — pretty much the complete whangy; a typical Highland-hospitality-gone-mad wide-spectrum belly-banging megabrek — I go into Hotel Mode, which consists of having one of these family-size

152

breakfasts (well, you tell yourself, you're paying for it so you might as well eat it), a snack for lunch — usually just soup — and then the equally generously proportioned evening meal. The temptation is to have a big lunch as well, because your stomach is getting kind of used to these enormous portions, but this leads to Expanded Waist Syndrome and is a Thoroughly Bad Thing. I suspect a lot of tourists go into Hotel or B&B Mode while they're here.

We get down to some serious research. Speyside is the focus of the Scotch industry, its epicentre, its spiritual headquarters; if the industry was ever going to have a theme park (may the thought perish), this is where it would be. Whisky Land! Whisky World!

Round here they have the Whisky Trail (they have a Castle Trail too, which both Les and I feel we should do one day, but one interest at a time) and round here it seems you can barely drive a mile without seeing a distillery; sometimes the whole thing, strewn across a hillside, sometimes just the pagoda roofs poking up above the trees or the steam-bannered chimneys standing out over the long roofs of a few acres of bonded warehouses. Sometimes all you see is a brown tourist information sign, pointing the way, and sometimes there's just a very discreet sign by the roadside, for trade visitors and contractors, if a distillery is not set up to accommodate tourists. A lot are, though, and personally I find them very civilised places to be.

There is now a kind of Visitor Centre Vernacular, a recognisable, getting-on-for industry-wide style of layout and furnishing that might seem twee if you're one of these minimalist people who like their houses to look like operating theatres, but which kind of suits the nature of the process that goes to make whisky, and which is anyway changing gradually.

There will probably be lots of wood and sometimes quite a lot of exposed stonework, there will be a darkened area where you can sit or stand and watch a visual presentation which will tend to major on sparkling streams gurgling across moody moors and over bulbous boulders, swaying sunlit fields of barley, gleaming great stills, old buildings wreathed in steam and atmospherically lit barrels in dark warehouses. Often there will be an example of an old illicit still, sitting glistening in a coppery sort of way in a corner, usually in a mocked-up bothy setting. Frequently there will be lots of old distillery tools, from when each concern was more self-contained than today: adzes, malt shovels, rummagers and the rest.

Almost always there will be impressively massive old ledgers and enormous leather-bound books that are the genuine articles from a hundred years ago, detailing aspects of the distillery's processes and general book-keeping. In the bit where you do the tasting there will definitely be lots of wood, various seats, benches and tables — almost always in wood — and sometimes there will be couches and chairs, usually in leather.

These are intensely comfortable places to be. Ideally you want to be able to sample the product as well, to have a decent taste or two and not have to worry about driving, but even if you're unable to indulge there are few more pleasant public spaces. For all the slightly formulaic feel of a standard Visitor Centre — and this may well be something that you'll only recognise if, like me, you're doing them by the dozen — there is a sort of honesty about them, just because they are so close to the production process itself.

They are in the end anyway all different, just as the malts themselves are all different. The people who staff them add an extra flavour to the mix as well: the awkward but knowledgeable ones who you can tell really just want to be back doing the technical stuff, opening valves, sniffing the air outside the spirit safe, waiting for the time to take the best cut of the spirit, but who can answer any production question you ask them; the totally enthusiastic types who really want you to know what a great thing they do here and how wonderful their particular whisky is; the usually slightly diffident manager or even owner who's unsure quite how to modulate their enthusiasm and how much depth of knowledge to go into; and the slightly wacko characters who at their best keep you wide-eyed and laughing and at their worst still make you laugh, even if they do seem to be part of some bizarre care-in-the-community light-industrial outsourcing programme. I'm sure I've encountered somebody on a tour or behind the counter in a Visitor Centre who was just plain boring and uninterested, but obviously I've succeeded in forgetting about them.

One of the plusses of going round lots of distilleries is meeting up with people who know each other, or are related to each other. It is a small industry; less than a hundred distilleries, each one often only employing a dozen people in the actual physical process and usually fewer than that in the onsite office. The skills involved are very transferable within the industry as a whole, and because a lot of the distilleries are owned by larger concerns, people are able to move round within that company's sites and see how it's done elsewhere. I lost count of the number of times I bumped into somebody's mum, dad, son, daughter, brother or whatever, once I'd told them that I had been to all these other distilleries. "Och, you'll have talked to so-and-so . . ."

Come to think of it, when you're a writer, especially one who's managing to keep the wolf from the door, there aren't many professions you encounter which make you think, Hmm, actually this must be quite a decent job. I wouldn't mind doing this . . . but working in a distillery is arguably one of them. That's not to suggest that it must all be sweetness and light incessantly, or that in the end you don't have bosses, who may well be as stupid and/or as malicious as bosses everywhere can be, or that your job isn't subject to the vagaries and volatilities of the market and the changing tastes of the international public, but given that most of this applies to most jobs, it could be argued that working in a relatively safe environment in some of the finest scenery in one of the world's more beautiful countries while helping to make something to be proud of, within a tradition stretching back hundreds of years, can be quite rewarding.

Put it this way; I never did meet anybody who couldn't wait to get out of the industry and away. I'm sure they have existed, but maybe they've all already left to become fashion photographers or skateboard wizards or party planners to the superrich or far-eastern golf-course designers or something.

Wandering round Cardhu distillery — heart of Johnnie Walker, Scottish larch washbacks rather than the more usual Oregon pine — watching some ducks silently preening themselves on the neatly clipped grass by the side of the gently steaming pond where the cooling water goes to relax, looking round the smart, cream-coloured buildings, listening to the quiet hissings and distant creaking noises of the place, surrounded by sloped fields and lines of budding trees, a pleasant glow manifesting itself after a modest tasting — Les was driving — Speyside suddenly seemed like one of the best places in the whole damn world.

Stand-out distilleries? Architecture first. The Tormore is my favourite. Bit old fashioned, given that it was built in 1958, but fabulously dramatic; fountains, manicured lawns, topiary, ornamental curling pond (what?) and an enormous great black chimney sticking up at the back that looks like a super-gun barrel (the original idea was to make it look like a giant whisky bottle, which would have been even more insane). Brilliant building, and nicely matched outbuildings. Why this place doesn't have a Visitor Centre and tours is beyond me. The whisky itself has been criticised as being too metallic, though the 15-year-old I tracked down seemed all right to me; moderately voluptuous, in fact.

157

The Chivas Brothers' Allt-A-Bhainne (1975) reminds me of a Catholic seminary for some reason; severe and inward looking, but elegant. I haven't tracked down a single malt from it yet.

Auchroisk distillery (1974) is quite beautiful in a modernist kind of way, all steep roofs and interesting angles. There's a slightly gratuitous-looking sort of ground-floor turrety thing that I'm not so sure about but otherwise visually it's a peach. This is where The Singleton is produced; a very pleasant, smooth, medium-bodied dram, like an allsort that's been briefly dipped in sherry.

I was kind of hoping to find a genuine undiscovered gem in amongst the folds and rolls of Speyside, a hugely flavoursome shy beauty that hardly anybody has heard of, but it was not to be; the stand-out whiskies, on taste, aroma, feel and general all-round wonderfulness were ones that any malt drinker will know well. I have yet to find any Speyside whisky that is less than drinkable and perfectly pleasant, but of all the drams we tasted during that first week on Speyside, two of the best came from Glenlivet and Glenfiddich, and one of them produced an expression that went instantly into my personal top ten. Another exceptional pair were Aberlour and Balvenie, which may not be exactly household names but they're hardly unknowns either.

It's hard to overemphasise how important Glenlivet was not long ago, not just as a whisky but as a defining standard, even as a region. The primacy of the whisky itself remains, but its nomenclative dominance has gone, and probably just as well for all concerned. One of the books I picked up second-hand for the reading part of this book's research was a 1976 paperback of David Daiches' 1969 *Scotch Whisky, Its Past and Present*. Professor Daiches is one of the world's most respected and authoritative figures on whisky, so it's interesting that in the maps at the back of the book, there is, as usual, one map for the whole of Scotland with the various distilleries numbered, and another inset map showing all the Speyside distilleries of the time, except the area isn't called Speyside, it's entitled the Glenlivet Area. If there was ever a better symbol of the importance of the Glenlivet name at the time, I've yet to see it.

Not so long ago you could go into a bar which had a lot of whiskies, ask for a Glenlivet and something like this would happen:

"A Glenlivet? Certainly sir. Which would you like? We have Glenbogus Glenlivet, Glendokery Glenlivet, Glenmunchkin Glenlivet, Glengeneric Glenlivet, Glennowherenear —"

"Do you just have *the* Glenlivet?"

"Hmm." (Bar person strokes chin.) "Not sure I know that one . . ."

Glenlivet was known as a fine whisky when it still had to be smuggled to its markets, and its name was being taken in vain even then. When Scotch started to go legit, Glenlivet's owner, George Smith, was the first person to apply for one of the newfangled licences; this did not, it has to be said, meet with the universal approval of his peers, and necessitated Mr Smith carrying a pair of loaded pistols everywhere. His son

159

was the J. G. Smith whose name appears on the bottles to this day, and who moved the distillery from its earlier even more remote location a mile away on the shoulder of the hill to where it is today.

It's not a very inspiring set of buildings, but the Visitor Centre is one of the best in Scotland, the tour is, amazingly, free, and the whisky is still one of the absolutely definitive Speyside malts; light and fresh but rich at the same time, and with a scent like a summer meadow. The one I went for was a 21-year-old Archive, which was all that plus with a delicious hint of roast chestnut about it; refreshing and warming at the same time. When we finally started sampling this bottle in July, Ann, Dad and I found this expression *far* too easy to drink; one of those worryingly superb almost overly approachable drams that even people who don't usually like whisky are probably going to like to the extent of asking for another. And this, to be brutally frank, is only ever an unambiguously good thing if you are a person of an exceptionally good, kind and generous nature. Which I have ambitions to be — it's what my dad is — but have not yet really achieved.

Whatever; the Glenlivet is whisky to put a smile on your face.

Aberlour is one of those distilleries which exemplify something of a contradiction in whisky-making. It's often the distilleries which physically stand out which are the least bottled as single malts, the vast majority of their production going into blends (95 per cent is the figure you hear bandied about most often), while the distilleries which seem to shy away from attention — which, in other words, blend in to their surroundings — are the ones most likely to be bottled purely as single malts. I guess it's partly age, and size. The last heroic age of distillery-building in the sixties and seventies produced some very striking and prominent buildings which from the start were always going to produce whisky almost exclusively for blends.

Aberlour is at the other end of the spectrum; practically camouflaged amongst the other rather nondescript buildings at one end of Aberlour town. If the buildings are undistinguished, though, the whisky is anything but. This is one of the best Speysides you can buy; enormous — but not unbalancing — amounts of sherry, buckets of fruit, layers and weaves of spiciness, all of it silkily burnished; if Fabergé made whisky, you suspect this is what it would taste like. The a'bunadh — batch No. 8 — I got (no age given but generally reckoned to be a mixture of barrels between eight and fifteen years old) is a stonker; a powerfully, opulently spicy-sweet cocktail of flavours that makes your head reel.

The Balvenie is owned by the same people who own Glenfiddich, next door. This seems almost unfair, but there you go. Standing more or less in the shadow of the ruins of Balvenie Castle, the distillery still has its own maltings, which makes it unique on Speyside. One word starts to tell you about Balvenie, and that's honey. Only starts to, though, because this is one of the most complex, balanced, elegant and harmonious whiskies on Speyside, packed with exquisitely proportioned

161

amounts of gingery sherry-cum-port, fruit and spice, like the best Christmas cake in all the world. If there is one of the fairly-well-knowns that is arguably still undervalued and deserves even greater exposure, praise and appreciation, the Balvenie is it.

Glenfiddich presents as a trim, neat, well-manicured concern with everything positioned nicely in its place; it has its own bottling plant, unusually, and a splendid shop; worth taking photographs of all by itself. It was where we found one bottle priced at five thousand pounds, which Les and I assumed must be some sort of record for a bottle you could buy over the counter at a distillery retail outlet, until we found one nearby priced at ten grand. Kind of suspect they're not the real ones out there on display.

There are a *lot* of stills here; 28 at the last count, with the spirit stills so small they need two per wash still (this small-still thing may be important — we'll come back to this with Macallan, later). They're coal-fired too, which is very traditional, and also unusual these days.

Glenfiddich is the best-selling single malt in the world, and it comes as a surprise to discover that it isn't owned by one of the big multinationals. It's really another family business, owned by William Grant and Sons, and they pretty much pioneered the single-malt revolution in the early sixties. Respect is due for that alone, but the whisky has remained a standard; floral (like most Speysides) with an accent on heather and a depth of honey that can make it seem halfway to a liqueur at times (a trait it shares with the Balvenie).

They've kept innovating, too, which I think is admirable; there are various different finishes, all of them excellent, and one which is, to my taste, simply astounding.

It's the Havana Reserve, a 21-year-old finished in old Cuban rum casks. This is a colossal, fabulously rich, endlessly, smokily sweet and succulent whisky, bursting with flavour, strong on the nose, long in the throat . . . just magnificent. And, as though this wasn't enough, there should be more of it to go around than we have any right to expect, because it's banned from the USA. The States' punitive, mean-spirited and just generally disgraceful trade embargo against Cuba means that this particular Glenfiddich can't be bought between Canada and Mexico. Well, I'm sorry for US single-malt fans, but, frankly, hallelujah; all the more for us. It is my firm intention to buy a crate of this stuff in the next week or two, on my next visit to Speyside, if I can't find it closer to home. I might even buy two crates and give bottles out as Christmas presents.

The quest for the Perfect Dram very much continues and there are some very strong contenders indeed still to come — Macallan, Springbank and Highland Park to name but three — but as I write, this stuff is joint number one with the fino-finished Ardbeg tasted straight out the barrel as Best Dram So Far.

Zapping between the distilleries, we end up spending a lot of time on a wee road that parallels the A95, which has road works at a bridge necessitating these detours.

On this wee road there are signs saying, "Slow. Young pheasants."

These are the subjects of some discussion.

"Do you think they're meant to say 'Slow, young peasants'?"

"Maybe they're directed *at* the pheasants, telling them to be slow."

"What they mean is, don't kill these young birds with your cars; leave them for us to kill with our shotguns. Bit cheeky if you ask me. Typical toff arrogance. If I see one I'm going to aim for it."

"What, a toff or a young pheasant?"

"No comment."

CHAPTER
SEVEN

Break for Curry

Ann has decided to join us. We head south and west back to Glenfinnan — to feed the cat, basically — then loop further south to the lower edge of the Campsies, north of Glasgow, to take in the Glengoyne distillery before following a succession of interesting B-roads over to Fife.

In the meantime we've found time to squeeze in a visit to the Speyside Cooperage, just outside Craigellachie, which is geographically pretty much the centre of the Speyside whisky industry. This is worth seeing; what we basically have here is Barrel City; this is the Wonderful World of Cooperage, a veritable cathedral of Barreldom. You can sit in giant barrels in the grounds, sit around barrels, sit on barrels, sit in barrel-seats, and buy barrel-related products, including — but not limited to — barrels.

There's a tour, and you end up in a sort of gallery over the main floor of the workshop, watching these guys — a *lot* of tartan shirts — wheel barrels around, whack them with hammers, manoeuvre them into big machines that do unspeakable things to them (the barrels, that is), pick up their hammers and bash them

165

some more, and just generally hit, split up, force together, rip apart, remake, compress, rasp, plane, pressurise to near bursting, singe, sear, kick, wallop and carbonise barrels as though they had something against wood in general and barrels in particular. You ever want to get an idea how resilient wood is, you come here.

It sounds noisy, even through the glazing protecting the viewing gallery. Actually, it even looks noisy. Some of the guys wear ear defenders, some don't. I think I would. They have little sort of miniature anvils on metal posts on which they balance the metal hoops that go round the barrels and hammer away at those as well. These bashing-blocks are I-shaped in cross-section, like they're made from lengths of railway line. I find myself wondering whether these were taken from old torn-up railways in the neighbourhood, and whether each guy has to rip a length of line off with his teeth as some sort of cooperage initiation rite.

The display stuff at Strathspey Cooperage is interesting, too; I hadn't realised that the oak (*Quercus alba* from the US making up 97 per cent of the barrels used in Scotland, as opposed to the remaining three per cent of *Quercus robur* from Spain) that goes to make casks has to grow for between 100 and 150 years before it can be harvested, or that when the bourbon barrels shipped in from the States are reassembled, they're bigger; it takes five US barrels to make four hogsheads, each with a capacity of 56 imperial gallons. Hence a lot of the bashing and banging, I suppose.

And it's a legal requirement in the US that bourbon barrels are only used once, not just some purist whim

166

or tradition. I immediately start to formulate a mild conspiracy theory to account for this perversity. I mean, if Scotch benefits from being kept in old bourbon casks, why shouldn't bourbon itself? Why not at least experiment with second- and third-fill bourbon? Treating these labour-intensive barrels as effectively disposable seems just plain wasteful. I bet a smidgen of research would reveal that it's all a bit of, semi-appropriately, pork-barrel politics; this law will have been passed because some timber magnate had entire forests of oak to shift and got the law passed to help make this happen.

I'm wrong. It later turns out that it's a rare, if dubious, instance of a victory for American organised labour; the US unions sponsored the law so that there would be more employment for *their* coopers. I find this quite heartening, though what real difference it makes that the Scotch industry has benefited from a depending-how-you-look-at-it slightly daft law promoted by some probably not terribly left-wing US unions rather than some megalomaniac forestry owner or seedy cartel of timber conglomerates is debatable.

Craigellachie the town is home to the Craigellachie Hotel (well, if you're going to have a Craigellachie Hotel, that would seem the logical place to put it), whose Quaich Bar offers 500 different malts. A couple of execs from the Japanese Hankyu department store who visited the hotel thought the bar was so impressive they had an exact copy constructed in Tokyo for the November 2002 British Fair. They even had one of the bartenders flown out to staff it. So there you are; Scottish bars travel well too.

The fine weather continues. Speyside looks wonderful, and the distant glimpses of the snow still hugging the peaks of the Cairngorms just adds to the beauty of this warm, early spring. The three of us enjoy using the M5 on these Moray roads. The A95, when it opens again, is a good, open, quite fast if moderately busy highway, and the surrounding smaller roads are quieter, twistier and rollingly scenic, diving and looping through forests and small towns, past fields dotted with dozens of tiny lambs.

It occurs to me that maybe when it comes to roads I'm too much of a mountain snob, a remoteness junkie. I suppose I associate the best, most rewarding driving with a degree of verticality, or surrounding emptiness. I kind of dismiss the A9 because it's so busy and relatively boring — and frustrating, with its heavy traffic and still limited bits of dual carriageway forever collapsing back to two-way — and I rarely drive it these days except where I have no choice.

When heading from Fife to Glenfinnan I have a sort of parallel route that avoids the A9 all the way up to Glen Garry, where there is a good long bit of dual carriageway; this alternative route takes a good half-hour longer than using the A9 the whole way, but it's just so much more interesting to drive. Then, every now and again, when I do take the main road — usually because Ann wants to snooze, and can't do that on the twisty roads — I notice the scenery around the A9, maybe just because there's a particularly flattering light, or because there's some moody-looking mist wrapping the forests and hills, or because it's time for the seasonal drama of autumn leaf colours, and I realise that actually it goes through some very impressive landscapes, that if I lived in Holland or East Anglia or even London or the Midlands, I'd regard this scenery as something close to breathtaking. I've just got too used to it, too accustomed to regarding the A9 as an honorary motorway; a conveyor belt that takes you to where the interesting roads and the real driving begins, but pretty much without merit on its own.

Well, I'm spoiled. I know this. My commute consists of walking downstairs of a morning and aside from shopping trips almost all of the driving I do is for fun, because I enjoy it. I love pootling round the local roads of Fife and beyond on my motorbike, but my greatest loves are the Highland roads, and, as a rule, I tend to feel that the further west and north you go the better the roads get, even allowing for the single-track bits.

The drive from Glenfinnan up to Dornie, near Kyle of Lochalsh, where we used to have friends (and a share in a pub — another long story we'll come to later), was and is one of my favourite routes, especially beyond Invergarry. I'd better point out that this Invergarry lies in a Glen Garry that is no relation to the Glen Garry mentioned earlier — Scotland is full of places with the same name that are nowhere near each other.

Scotland: land of contrasts (not).

Scotland is not really that big, but it is quite rugged, especially in the west, where sheer geological happenstance and millions of years of exposure to the Atlantic waves have combined to produce a coastline of extreme tatteredness. This historically made travel — except by sea and loch, as already mentioned — quite difficult. You can imagine that people didn't get out of their own glen very much. And that is the only excuse I can think of for the repetition of Scottish place names, if we aren't to accept that it isn't all down to basic Caledonian laziness and lack of imagination.

I've just looked up a gazetteer of Scotland and the third and fourth entries in the main section are two mountains rejoicing in the name of A'Bhuidheanach. These are not even very far away from each other! (The fifth entry is A'Bhuidheanach Bheag; guess what? Also a mountain.)

Off the top of my head I can think of two Comries, twin Kincardines, a brace of Crathies, a pair of Clovas, a number of Niggs, more Clachans than you can shake a claymore at and five or six Tarbets/Tarberts in Argyll alone. A lot of the time it's because these are simple descriptive names; Clachan means stone house (whoa — imagine the standard of living that made *that* worth pointing out), while Tarbet/Tarbert means portage point; a place where by dragging your boats across a narrow neck of land you could save yourself some sailing time or avoid rough waters. Argyll, through its basic geography — it has more coastline than France,

170

for Pete's sake — is littered with such sites and therefore names.

But all the same.

Anyway, they had to put in a new road between Loch Garry and Glen Moriston back in the fifties when the push to produce lots more hydroelectric power meant more or less doubling the size of Loch Garry, Loch Loyne and Loch Cluanie, drowning the roads which had grown on the old droving routes. The result was one of the best driving roads in Scotland; a glorious, sweeping, swooping ribbon of tarmac with no built-up areas between Invergarry and Shiel Bridge, save for a vanishingly brief exception at the Cluanie Inn itself.

Beyond, into Wester Ross, lies glorious, mountainous, eye-poppingly spectacular scenery and (amongst the sorry nonsense of single-track, so-called A-roads, which any other European country would surely have consigned to historic editions of atlases decades ago) roads of such beauty and grandeur it gladdens the heart just looking at them on the map. Well, if you're a cartophiliac petrol-head like me they have that effect.

Just a shame there are no distilleries up in this whole rugged reach of Scotland, or on any of the Outer Hebrides. None that we know about, anyway.

So have I, over the years — my head well and truly turned by all this spellbinding semi-wilderness and tempestuous vertiginousness — been too quick to dismiss the more refined, gentle attractions of places like Speyside? Maybe so. All the same, I've always had a soft spot for the Borders and for Dumfries and

Galloway, both as places of great, if — compared to the Highlands — rather restrained, rolling, rounded-off beauty and as the homes of some brilliant, often quite empty roads. Speyside feels similar in a lot of ways; busier than Dumfries and Galloway, certainly, but with a similar mix of forests and hills.

Maybe I'm just getting older. Before too long I'll be one of those wee old guys who wears a bunnet in the car; I'll drive with my nose up against the steering wheel while staring at the road from underneath the rim, ambling along in a big fast car I never really use while looking out for a lay-by with a view of the water so we can get out the camping-chairs and me and the missus can have a nice cup of tea. Goodness knows there are zillions of worse fates, but the prospect still fills me with a mild horror. A love of wild scenery, even if it's just to drive through rather than walk in, might stave off senility for a year or two. This is what I tell myself, anyway.

Glengoyne is technically a Highland whisky, at least given the place where it's made, if not necessarily where all of it's matured, though this is anyway one of those occasions when you find yourself puzzling over where the Highland Line does, and ought to run.

The Highlands: their identification and use.

The Highlands are a bit like science fiction; you generally know with some certainty when you're in the relevant area, but as soon as you start trying to define it

172

you end up getting into all sorts of messes. There are places where I feel I can pin the start of the Highlands down to a matter of a few yards, like when taking the road north out of Gilmerton, near Crief, where the country suddenly changes as you pull away from underneath the trees, opening out as the road rises towards the heathered hills like something uncoiling after a long confinement.

On the other hand, there are whole areas of Scotland where the Highlands seem to sort of fade in. That entire corner between Aberdeen and Inverness; I have no real idea where that fertile, well-cultivated, gently buxom farm land ends and the Highlands start. Plus I have my doubts about the Flow Country, and a lot of that south-east-facing coast between Inverness and Wick. Sometimes it feels like we should scrap the idea of the Highlands altogether, but that only ever seems to make sense in moments of frustration at deciding what is and isn't part of the region in the first place.

I suppose to some extent the definition of the Highlands has anyway changed over the years, moving north from places as far south as Stirling as land was improved and fields spread, the clan system withered and — probably most to the point — as the Gaelic language retreated.

Glengoyne isn't the closest distillery to Glasgow — that would be Auchentoshan — but it is easily accessible from the city, it has a pleasant setting at the southern foot of the Campsie Fells and it does welcome visitors. We pull up on another warm day, brave the main road that divides the car park and most of the warehouses from the distillery proper and walk up the little glen at the back of the distillery by the cooling pond where there's a dinky little Visitor Centre and shop, where I buy a bottle of the 17-year-old. We're kind of toured out and so avoid the formal guided thing, though I take a photograph of the stills from the courtyard outside.

The whisky itself, at least in the 17-year-old edition, is big and fruity, unpeated, quite fresh, and sweetly oaked. It's matured in a different type of sherry cask from most whiskies; palo cortado (I'm quite a fan of sherries — well, dry sherries — but I confess this is one I hadn't heard of). The palo cortado probably has a lot to do with its orangey colour and citrus flavour. So, another healthily flowering branch on the great burgeoning tree of Different Whiskies; the more I taste all these novel expressions the more I get the sense that single-malt whisky is developing in a deeply interesting way, pulling in and making convincing use of barrels which have contained all sorts of different kinds of drinks.

The Ferry. We overnight at our house and the four of us head for the Omar Khayyam. This is a lazy choice, in a way; Edinburgh is full of deeply wonderful restaurants, but Ann and I have settled into a routine that involves — if we're looking to lunch — going to Viva Mexico, on Cockburn Street, near Waverley station, or — for dinner — the OK, diagonally across from Haymarket station. It's all because we live so close to the railway at our end and both restaurants are an easy walk/waddle from the relevant station at the other.

It wouldn't be quite so bad if I varied my choice, but I don't even open the menu in the OK; the guys don't need an order book, just a photocopy: two dry sherries, a bottle of the Sunnycliff (a very full-flavoured, vintage-consistent and good value Australian red), Monkfish starter, Chicken Jaipuri (hot) and a Tarka Daal side dish . . . Ann at least varies her order a bit, but mine is practically set in stone. I keep meaning to try some of the other stuff on the menu again — years ago I was positively promiscuous here, before I decided I'd fallen in love with Chicken Jaipuri (hot) — but then I discovered — after tasting an example which one of my brothers-in-law had ordered — that my second favourite dish after Chicken Jaipuri (hot) is Chicken Jaipuri (mild). Bit of a mixture of emotions, there; happiness mingled with a sort of disappointment. Still, somehow I cope.

Well, ya-bloody-hoo. One good thing, one decent image to come out of the war; the sight of Saddam's statue being toppled. But even this is poorly done, messy and staged and unauthentic and incomplete. The pictures show the awful bloody thing starting to tilt, then they cut and when we see it next they have beefier chains on it and it's a US vehicle doing the pulling, not the locals. The statue falls, but does not detach from its plinth, two big metal reinforcing poles inside anchoring it to the concrete. A US flag is put on top before somebody realises this might give out the wrong — for which read accurate — message, and an Iraqi flag is found instead.

There ya go; we support the bastard when it suits us, we arm him to start a war against them there fundamentalists in Iran, sell him chemicals to gas the Kurds in their homes, we even let the son-of-a-bitch missile one of our own ships without getting *too* upset about it, then we give him a good slap for invading another country — that is, after all, our job — incite people to rise against him, get scared in case those durned Iranians might come out winners from that uprising, leave the uprisers hung out to dry and whistle Dixie while they're slaughtered, impose a decade's worth of sanctions that if nothing else make sure there'll be half a million fewer little towel-heads in the world, then decide it's time to avenge daddy, secure the world's second biggest oil reserves and show the world who's boss. And all for the good of the Iraqi people. Jesus H. Christ, when will these people do something for themselves for a change?

Oh, and still no WMDs, used, deployed, anywhere near being deployed or even found stored in some dusty desert bunker.

Another sparklingly beautiful day, the sunlight dancing on the waters of the river Forth and flaring across the vast red pipes of the bridge, the sky pure blue. I shake my head as we pack the car's boot. "This is like living in southern California. The good weather's getting almost boring."

Aileen passes by, toting bags and laughing. "Are you mad?"

"Is this a piece of your brain?" Les asks.

Les and Aileen are sun worshippers; the ideal year for them consists of three holidays in somewhere very hot indeed — the Canaries, Portugal, Greece, Egypt — with a very hot (for Scotland) Glenfinnan summer thrown in. The way their holidays work they can just about manage this. We've been on holiday abroad with them a few times but I'm usually far too hot — red-faced, lathered in sweat, coated in sunblock with the sun protection factor of kitchen foil and wearing a broad-brimmed hat even when I'm in the swimming pool. Meanwhile the McFarlanes are just about comfortable.

It's not my fault; I'm a cold climate person. Anything much above sixteen centigrade and I think I'm in a heatwave. Weather that has everybody else shivering, blowing into their fists, stamping their feet and pulling on extra layers of clothing will see me, in a T shirt or shirt-sleeved, clapping my hands and declaring the temperature "just nice". Les, on the other hand, ideally likes to have worked up a berry-brown suntan before he even leaves for his hols and has, as I can attest, been mistaken for a Greek guy. In Greece. By Greek people. This does not normally happen to Greenock-born Caucasian chaps who live in Lochaber.

We head north again, passing Brechin. This is where Glencadam used to be made, beside Brechin City's football ground. The 15-year-old I have is quite fresh and tastes a bit like full-cream milk poured over

177

strawberries; interesting but not that inspiring. At Montrose we end up by the seaside, by a funny little water park on the esplanade. I am convinced I see a soliton.

The water park is part of a larger fun-and-games area with slides and climbing frames and so on, but you can find that sort of stuff anywhere; what fascinates me is this set of broad, gently sloped, interconnecting concrete channels, with little taps, gates and controllable fountains. To a long-time incorrigible dam builder like me this is something like heaven, albeit a sort of restricted one. There are about a dozen kids splashing around in it, shoving the little dam-gates this way and that, turning taps on and off or ferrying water from one channel to another by bucket, and a couple of young boys — maybe eight or nine years old — who are throwing themselves into the shallow pools and dancing over the fountains spraying water at each other, getting utterly soaked. This looks, the four of us agree, cold. It's sunny, but there's a breeze coming off the North Sea and even I'm glad I put my jacket on before we got out of the car. What a great place though; like having a dam/channel system you'd have to work for days to create, all set up in concrete with water on tap. Whoever designed this was a genius, I tell myself, then I see the soliton and just whoop for joy, because I've never seen one before.

A soliton is a single wave that propagates along a channel over long distances, losing very little energy. It's all to do with the width and depth of the channel and the wavelength and height of the wave itself; if

178

these figures are all in a certain proportion to each other a kind of harmony is established that sets up a soliton, and it'll just sweep calmly along a channel for a long, long time. They were first noticed in Dutch canals, where they could keep going for kilometres. This miniature example (assuming that's what this is and I'm not deceiving myself) eventually hits the shallows at the far end of one of the little concrete channels after ten metres or so, but while it lasts it's beautiful.

I shout, "Woo-hoo!" the way people who are of a certain age and have watched *The Simpsons* and *South Park* too much will tend to.

Everybody else is looking at me like I'm a bit of a mad fellow, but, hey, I'm used to that.

Via St Cyrus to Fochabers; we have a fine lunch at a hotel called The Ramsey Arms, just through the town's impressive arch. I take a photo of the Fettercairn distillery. This is another whisky I've always been — to use John Peel's phrase — somewhat underwhelmed by, though it's not without its fans, and does well as a component of the Whyte and Mackay blends. Maybe it's something to do with the "Old". It's marketed as Old Fettercairn and somehow that first word just annoys me. In what sense "old"? We know the stuff in the bottle can't have been made last week, for goodness' sake. It's most commonly found as a 10-year-old; that isn't old either. The distillery was founded in 1824, but that doesn't make it particularly ancient — lots of distilleries had been founded in the latter years of the previous century, and many of them are still going today . . . so what the hell's old about it?

179

Still, could be worse, I suppose; could be Ye Olde Fettercairn or something.

Heading north again, we pass William Gladstone's old family home at Fasque, just outside Fochabers. As a prime minister, Gladstone probably did more for the whisky industry than any other, repealing the punitive Malt Tax in 1853 and legalising the retail sale of bottled whisky. I recall reading — again in *Michael Broadbent's Vintage Wine* — about a wine cellar in the house that had lain unopened for 45 years until 1972. It was full of wine and port that had just lain there, undisturbed, at a nice, steady eight degrees C since 1927 — with perfectly drinkable vintages stretching back way into the 1800s — and it hadn't been opened in all that time because nobody could find the key. Toffs, eh?

The B974 rises from the fertile coastal plain that is the Howe of the Mearns — Lewis Grassic Gibbon territory — towards the first low, rounded hills of the eastern Grampian Mountains, wriggling up out of the broad wooded glens, stretching across the heathery moors and up to the summit at Cairn O' Mount. This is a brilliant road. Not busy, well maintained, shrugging off the tight, blind, tree-obscured corners lower down to ascend into sinuous progressions of open, sweeping, climbing curves and gently undulating straights. In a car with plenty of power and torque like the M5, even fully loaded, it's bliss. Faced with a tight bend followed by a steep upward gradient, the car just hunkers down, snarls politely and rockets away.

180

We're not actually travelling outrageously quickly, usually staying within ten or so m.p.h. on either side of the speed limit, partly in deference to my three passengers (who, I'm pleased to report, have no complaints) but the sheer pleasure of stringing together the sequences of bends on the way to the car park at the viewpoint is just wonderful. We stop at the top to admire the view and take photos, though the best view is to the south, and it's a bit hazy and into the sun, so not great for photography.

We set off again, heading gradually downhill towards the Glen of the river Dee through a succession of nicely cambered, generously open bends, gradually encountering stands and small forests of old Scots pine, their scaly red roots curling out of the sandy soil like dragons' claws.

This is, very understandably, a popular route with bikers. You can tell that because every few miles, pretty much since Fettercairn, we've been seeing yellow roadside signs telling us things like 34 ACCIDENTS ON THIS ROAD IN THE LAST YEAR, with a little symbol of a motorbike underneath.

I don't recall ever seeing signs like this anywhere in Scotland, so you get the impression that not only is this a very popular road with bikers, but that it really must be one where they have a *hell* of a lot of accidents. This is slightly mystifying; it's twisty, certainly, but so are hundreds of Scottish roads. There are a fair few deciduous trees in the lower reaches to the south that might cause problems in the autumn when they drop their leaves and it gets slippy under-tyre, but not that

181

many, and once you get above the tree line, that's that problem gone. There doesn't seem to be any particular reason for the road to be especially prone to gravel or stones or mud, and it's not as though the views are so gob-smackingly wonderful that you'd end up staring open-mouthed through your visor at them and forget to steer back out of the corner or whatever, so what's the problem? Maybe it's one of those trial things, where they choose one bit of road to try out a new signage system; we've got one of those on the M90 north of the Forth Road Bridge, opposite Dunfermline; thin posts on the far edge of the hard shoulder whose tops flash when there's a problem ahead.

I find myself wondering if the signs are digital and update themselves in real time; if you wrapped your RS-1 round one, would it suddenly click up from 34 to 35 ACCIDENTS ON THIS ROAD IN THE LAST YEAR . . .? Probably not.

Deeside; all very civilised and terribly nice. After the exposed heroics of the broad hilltops, the roads curl themselves up comfortably amongst the farmed, forested folds of the Dee's middle reaches, dappled under the new green leaves of spring. We take the 976 on the south side of the river, heading for Balmoral.

Lochnagar is a fine whisky and a really neat, smart, manicured little distillery, sitting in the grounds of Balmoral Castle like a model of a distillery put there for the royals to play with, a bit like Marie Antoinette had a pretend farm built in the ground of Versailles. I mean, it's not; it's a perfectly serious and professionally run distillery producing a fine whisky, but there's a still a sense of it bearing the same relationship to real distilleries as show gardens at the Chelsea Flower Show do to real gardens. It doesn't actually smell of new paint — you know that thing about the Queen thinking the whole world smells like that — but it's almost too tidy and well formed. A lovely place, though, unless you abhor things being just-so. It lies resplendent under a bright spring sun when we arrive there, and we see some butterflies jolting their unsteady way around the well-kept shrubs, the first of the year.

For some bizarre reason which I realised at the time I was not fully aware, or indeed in control of, we had, over the past few days, started to critique the toilets of the distilleries we visited. Something to do with being in critical mode, I suppose, and this rubbing off on the people I was doing the touring with (a week later my pal Dave would demand a separate critical category for distilleries' car parking spaces. *Car* parking spaces? I mean, really). I'd even drawn up a special table in my rapidly filling notebook for this purpose (under "T", obviously), with columns for Roominess, Nice Pong, Decor, Cleanliness, Worth Leaving a Comment in the Visitors' Book For and Just Generally Brill, and so I can report that the facilities at Royal Lochnagar came out with a cut-to-the-chase Just Generally Brill commendation.

The whisky (ah yes, finally we return to the whisky) is — at least in the 12-year-old version we chose — very redolent of the second-fill sherry casks it spends its time in, while showing malty and slightly smoky notes, with touches of honey. If I lived in Balmoral I think I'd be quite happy to have it piped the mile or so into the castle, to appear from a third tap in every bathroom. Well, maybe not for every guest.

Apparently Queen Victoria used to mix Lochnagar whisky with her claret.

Oh dear.

While we're wandering the grounds, enjoying the sunlight and breathing in the wonderful scents of the gardens and surrounding countryside, Les and I spot a weird-looking pyramid-like structure poking up from the trees on a nearby hill. We never did ask about it, but having now looked at my OS map I strongly suspect it's a personalised royal cairn. There's Princess Beatrice's Cairn (it's probably that one), Princess Helena's Cairn, Princess Alice's Cairn, Prince Albert's Cairn . . . the hill is littered with them. Some family tradition, perhaps. Anyway, so now we know.

Highway the Hard Way: a Road Bore writes.

Urgh. I think I may be drooling. Because now we come to the A939. In the M5. Actually the first bit from Crathie isn't the A939; it's the B976, but it leads there, then on to the notorious Cock Bridge to Tomintoul stretch. This is the bit of road that's always first to get blocked by snow at the start of a Scottish winter. Sometimes they call it the Lecht road, after the summit pass, where the Ski Centre is. Dear goodness flipping michty-me, what a road.

Partly it's the fact it's just such a gloriously clear, brilliantly sunny spring day, and there's so little traffic

184

— most roads are at their best in these circumstances. Partly, though, it's the openness, the fact that you can see so far, with no trees, no foliage, no lumps of landscape in the way to obscure sight lines round corners. This near agoraphobic bright-sky exposure also lets you make certain there are no sheep preparing to wander across the road, or oncoming traffic that might prevent the use of the road's full width. Partly it's the long, rising, undulating, rarely perfectly smooth nature of the road surface itself, and partly it's just a succession of brilliant bends and just pure plain boffo straights or near-straights lancing towards the horizon or propped against the sheeny slope of heather, aimed into a cobalt sky.

This is a truly magnificent, spectacular, spellbinding, addictive road. If I was alone I'd already be very seriously considering turning around somewhere ahead and coming back to do the whole thing again in the opposite direction, and then turning once more, back this way, to resume the route we're on. Les actually says something to this effect and I laugh and agree, but really it's a petrol-head thing and neither of us think it would be fair on Ann and Aileen. Just this one-way scoot is enough.

Again, we're not going anything like scarily fast, so the whole process feels smooth, with no savage braking, mad-boy acceleration or limit-testing cornering, really just a sequence of balanced stances the car takes up, pitching forward or back and from side to side, all of it way, way within its capabilities. It feels strong and safe

185

and secure, as though it knows exactly what it's doing, and is positively flattering my driving.

We reach the Lecht itself, the emptyish-looking pass where the Ski Centre sits; broad expanses of pitted asphalt braided with gravel washed off the slopes, a few cars and trucks, many grey, shed-like buildings of folded steel, and a thin network of ski-tows straggling off up the hill on both sides. It all appears a bit raw and desolate, already out of season at a time of year when, at the the end of a long hard winter, the whole place might still have hundreds of people skiing and boarding. We slow for the deserted-looking complex, treating it as a built-up area, then start the descent. In amongst such skiing territory (albeit Scottish-type skiing, with, as a rule, the concomitant freezing winds, short steep narrow slopes and face-stinging sleet), it's hard not to feel you're settling into a sweet, curvy downhill slalom-like rhythm, carving the tyres from curve to curve. In an old car, or just something with narrower tyres and less grip, you'd actually feel you were using the shoulders of the tyres the way you use skis' edges, canting and cutting into the turns, the chirp and squeal of rubber on tarmac a synonym for the swish and rasp of ski on snow. As it is, the M5's lawn-roller-broad tyres just tear stickily over the road, barely stretched.

The route descends into the trees and a few mid-afternoon shadows. More wonderful driving, the sort that would be the highlight of most days, but not after the Lecht road.

★   ★   ★

We arrive in Grantown-on-Spey — just time to stock up on some sweeties — then we head via Tomatin to Inverness and a bit of shopping.

Tomatin distillery lies just off the A9 — on a stretch of smaller road that used to be the A9 before the road was improved in the seventies — under a bridge that carries the main railway line from Stirling to Inverness. This is the same line that passes close by Dalwhinnie, and like Dalwhinnie this is a high-altitude distillery, lying at over a thousand feet. It's not quite as snow-prone as Dalwhinnie but it must be a good place to make lots of whisky because it's a deceptively huge distillery with 23 stills, though not all tend to work at the same time. The first distillery to be wholly owned by a Japanese company (and another case of the place basically being rescued from overseas), the tour and tasting are free, which, given that it's so close to the main road, should make it better visited than I suspect it is.

The whisky itself is another of those undervalued ingenues that could stand a deal more promotion; full of sweet, roasted nut flavours and smokily spiced. Arguably the trouble is that there's room for only so many distinguished malts even on the by now fairly well developed and knowledgeable world market; if you put a lot of money behind a whisky like Tomatin, you might just take market share away from other whisky without otherwise making much difference (more to the point for any given owner, you might take market share away from one or more of your own whiskies; this is one reason why manufacturers like to promote a selection of their whiskies together, probably the best known dating from when United Distillers — now Diageo — bundled whiskies like Cragganmore and Dalwhinnie together in their Classic Malts collection). I suppose the solution is simply for the single-malt market to get still bigger, so that there's room for even more whiskies at every level.

There's a house on the road up to the distillery itself which has a white mile-post-style sign in the garden that reads THIS WAY IS THAT WAY on one face, and THAT WAY IS THIS WAY on the other. This is not exactly Highland Existentialism, but it beats garden gnomes.

Inversneckie! Inverness was Europe's fastest growing city in 2002, allegedly. Certainly feels like a busier place these days, though it's not all change; the bit by the river hasn't altered much since the Eden Court theatre was built and the new road bridge went up (not to mention the replacement railway bridge, required after the floods washed away most of the old one a few years ago). This is still a city where you occasionally see somebody fishing in the middle of it. The river Ness flows through the centre heading for the sea, shallow enough by the banks for people to stand there, water splashing round their waders, their lines creating great lazy 8-shapes in the air as the rods sweep slowly back and forth.

There's a huge recently expanded shopping complex which we park in and which I get lost in but eventually, after some apparently compulsory clothes shopping, we make our way to Leakey's before it closes. Leakey's is a second-hand book shop housed in an old barn of a church near the centre of town. It's packed with books, prints and maps, has a busy upstairs café and lots of paintings by local artists. In the cold months it's heated by a colossal wood-burning stove the size of a shed which sits square in the middle of the place radiating warmth and making it feel welcoming even in the depths of winter. The place has become something of an Inverness institution and a landmark for bibliofiends and cartofans. The first time I came here I bought so many old maps I could hardly carry them. This time, while I'm checking that there aren't *too* many of my books for sale in the Fiction section, my arms full of more old OS maps, Les finds the Food and Drink section and the old whisky books; I snaffle the lot, bar a couple of doublers, and need help to get them back to the car.

"You actually going to read all this lot, Banksie?" Les asks as we squeeze the motley collection of tightly straining carrier bags into the boot (most cars would have sagged significantly on their springs under the extra weight, but the M5's made of sterner stuff).

I look at him blankly. "*Read* them?" I think about this. "Well, some of them, I suppose." Les looks increasingly sceptical. I think some more. "Well, I'll sort of scan all of them. I mean, I can't claim I'm going to read every single word of every single one, not cover to cover."

What can I say? I've been given an excuse to buy books; this isn't something I am easily capable of ignoring. Even when I was a student and didn't have much money, I'd buy every book on my reading lists as well as all the books I wanted to read for pleasure or because I thought they were actually necessary for my course work, for the simple reason that — like a reference book — a book on a book list didn't need to be read; a book you felt you ought to have but didn't need to read cover-to-cover was like a bonus for me; it meant more books on my shelves without the nagging guilt of not having actually read them all (at the time I refused to let a book defeat me; I even made it all the way through Sam Beckett's *Molloy, Malone Dies, The Unnameable* trilogy. Took me about a month because I kept falling asleep, but I did it. I'm a little more relaxed about this sort of thing now; if a book hasn't grabbed me in the first hundred pages or so, I just let it go).

At the time — and I do not exaggerate — I preferred to economise with my drinking money than cut back on the book-buying budget. Okay, I was an atypical student.

But anyway; of *course* I bought all the whisky books Leakey's had! I can probably, I remind myself, even claim them against tax. But the main point is; *they're books*. And I have a reason to buy them; I am almost beholden to buy them. I owe it to the whisky book to buy them, to my publishers, to my readers! It would be dereliction of duty not to buy them; they were there, they were for sale, I'm writing a book on the subject they're all about; isn't it *obvious* I have to rescue all of them?

190

In the end I do read all of them. Well, almost all of almost all of them; they end up covering a large part of a table to one side of my writing desk with lots of little strips of Post-It notes sticking out of them denoting Interesting Snippety Bits which at the time I'm totally convinced I'll faithfully incorporate into this book, though when it comes to it the vast majority of them get ignored.

We stay at the Bunchrew Hotel, along the Beauly Firth east of Inverness. This is an old bishops' palace set amongst a profusion of huge, mature trees. It stands right by the water at high tide and looks out over towards the Black Isle. It's that shade of traditional pink that apparently used to be produced by mixing whitewash with pig's blood (that's what they used to do in the old days, I have it on good authority) and it has the pointiest pointy turrets you ever did see. Does lots of weddings.

Fine food, equally fine wine, a whisky or two, a good night's sleep and another generous breakfast. We part at Glenfinnan the following afternoon and Ann sleeps most of the way down the A9. All right for her; I have a day to recover from all this good living then I'm back on the road and back to Speyside with my pals Jim and Dave for another week of intensive research.

CHAPTER
EIGHT

Fear and Loathing in Glenlivet

"This could be your best book ever, Banksie," Dave says. "Na," I tell him. "It could just be rubbish."

Dave pauses for a moment. "Yeah, but it could be your best book ever, Banksie."

Speyside part two; this time with Jim (S. Brown, erstwhile computer operator and shift leader, then publican and now help-desk supremo for Inverclyde Council) and Dave (McCartney, also one-time computer operator and shift leader, later manager, then publican, now enjoying a quieter life driving taxis) and the Jaguar.

The Jag: all the fruity flavour of yesteryear.

Full description of the car: a 1965 Jaguar Mark II 3.8 with overdrive. Dark blue with grey hide. Wire wheels. Fully restored. With added Kenlowe fan, central locking, a decent CD multichanger and beefed-up speaker system. Allegedly a Coombs conversion but with no louvred bonnet and — decisively — only two carbs, not three. Looks and sounds wonderful.

The Jaguar has what appears to be a power-assisted fuel gauge. The needle doesn't just gently fall from Full towards Empty; it positively propels itself from one to the other under full acceleration, describing a shallow curve across the sweep of dial like the path of an artillery shell aimed at your wallet. It doesn't help that the car has an embarrassingly small fuel tank, but the main reason the Mk II appears to — and does — drink like a filter-feeder is that it has an old-fashioned straight-six engine and those two temperamental carburettors to provide it with fuel and air.

The Jag is a relatively heavy car by modern standards, though there is an air of delicacy about the almost bubble-like passenger compartment (this is a very curvy car) and some of the controls. The suspension crashes and, from the sounds it makes, would appear to be constructed largely from wood, the engine roars like a camel which has just inadvertently snagged its undercarriage on a barbed-wire fence, it persistently smells of petrol despite the best efforts of various mechanics, it has a very occasional — but no less exciting for that — predisposition to throw itself out of third gear under hard acceleration, generally just when full power is required for a finely judged overtaking manoeuvre, its windscreen wipers are effete to the point of making the Land Rover's look positively powerful, not so much clearing the rain from the windscreen as flapping hysterically over the glass, utterly panicked at the fact there's water falling from the sky onto the car, there's no air-conditioning or electric windows (though there is power-assisted steering and it does have upgraded, servoed brakes), however it is the proud possessor of an electrically operated overdrive, a dash-mounted starter button, a handbrake on the wrong side and, best of all, a foot-controlled dip switch.

I think this is my favourite Jag eccentricity; to dip the lights at night you have to tap with your shoe a stubby metal button mounted on the floor to the left of the clutch. I am just about old enough to remember foot-operated dip switches from when there was nothing especially unusual about such an arrangement, however I still find this hilarious.

Less amusing but more heartening is that when you drive an old car (and in some ways here, the older the better) you drive surrounded by smiles and general good humour. In an old car, unless you drive like an utter imbecile, you can generally forget about road rage. People grin when they see you, they smile, they stop and look and sometimes they wave, and if they make a digital gesture, it's a thumbs-up, not a finger.

Part of this may be that an old car is seen as less of a threat, less of a declared, fully paid-up competitor in the day-to-day competition for road space and the battle to reduce one's own journey time. But part of it, I suppose, is a kind of veneration we feel for the old in general, a feeling that they deserve credit for the fact they've made it to here through all the trials, challenges and vicissitudes that might have ended their existence earlier and so should be indulged and given peace in a gentle retirement. (Arguably nowadays, people feel this more towards old cars than they do to old people, which is sad, even shaming.)

Now that so many roads are so crowded, and speed cameras seem to be everywhere — when there is, in other words, not much point in having a car that goes faster than anybody else's — this is a serious argument for driving a classic vehicle. You really do feel like you're living in a sunnier, more pleasant, more relaxed and stress-free world.

Well, at least you do until they break down, which is one thing that classic cars are also very good at. This is when you realise that for all the blandness, homogeneity and supposed boringness of the modern motor vehicle in general and the family hatchback in particular, they represent a vast improvement in reliability as well as fuel efficiency, compared to their automotive forebears. Even so, modern cars have bits fall off and they grind spluttering to a stop too; it's just that as a rule they do it much less often. Somehow it's easier to forgive an old car for breaking down, plus — if you have any mechanical aptitude at all — it will generally be easier to effect a running repair to a classic.

Modern cars — and especially modern engines — are binary, digital; they tend to work either perfectly or not at all, and you'll only be able to fix one if you happen to have 30 grand's worth of electronic diagnostic equipment with you and a sealed unit to replace whatever black-box gizmo has just gone belly up. Classic cars are analogue; when they go wrong

195

they'll often sort of half-work, at least for a while, enough to get you home if you're lucky, and sometimes all it takes to fix them is a screwdriver or the reconnection of a wire. So while the fact that they break down more often might reintroduce a measure of frustration into the ownership/driving experience, being able to get them going again without possessing a degree in electronics and the facilities of a big city dealership's workshop actually feels quite rewarding; you feel reconnected to the world when this happens, able to make a difference, to identify a problem and sort it rather than just impotently hand it on to somebody who will take it away, deal with it out of sight and return it.

There is also a kind of comfort to be had from having a vehicle that is most happy at legal speeds. It's an unfortunate irony that speeds and levels of road holding previously only attainable in expensive and exotic machinery are now easily reached in the average modestly specified hatchback just at the time that our crowded, high-surveillanced highways have rendered the use of such abilities difficult, dangerous and (sometimes even reasonably) illegal. So a car that feels happiest at velocities of a non-nabbable nature makes perfect sense.

The Jag is like this — it feels fine on the motorway at about 70 and happy enough at 60 on the open road — and so is the Land Rover, just because of its gearing and the fact that it has the aerodynamics of a light industrial unit. (So, too, oddly enough, is our old 911, though this is entirely because it's a soft-top.)

196

The Jag, of course, comes from the time when our speed limits were set. It was, apparently, an E-type Jag being tested on the then unrestricted M1 motorway at 150 m.p.h. that led eventually to the 70 m.p.h. speed limit being set in the first place. Back then people were happily revving Mk IIs up to 120 and above, however — despite the fact that my one's been fully restored and according to our local garage is probably in better nick than the day it rolled out of the factory back in 1965 — I've never had it above 90, and have no intention of going anywhere near that figure again. The Jag feels its age at these speeds; it complains, it roars and wheezes and there are suddenly all sorts of new vibrations coming from practically every part of the car that mitigate against exploring further.

The Jag is just starting to get unhappy at about 75. The M5, on the other hand, treats twice that velocity like this is the sort of speed it'll be happy with all day, thank you. By the time it's doing 150 — just 5 m.p.h. short of its factory-set limiter; an unrestricted M5 allegedly hit over 170 — it's growling a little louder, certainly, and you're aware that you're surrounded by a jet-like rush of slipstreaming air, but the car just settles down, seems to fix the horizon with a steely glare and thunders on, composed and steady. Instead it's the driver who's on edge, not the car; you're constantly just about to switch pedals with your right foot as a truck or slower car pulls out and you have to brake. In fact you're travelling so quickly you have to react pretty quickly the instant you see a distant sign announcing a limit on the autobahn.

That the nearly 40-year-old Jag feels about right at our national speed limits — even given that it was a serious performance car in its day, the sixties equivalent of the M5 — does highlight how daft these limits sometimes feel in a modern car. Not often, perhaps, and with decreasing frequency, but now and again — for example on certain wide, straightish, flatish Highland roads, especially if they're fenced or the country on either side is clear enough for the driver to spot any wildlife approaching the road — 60 feels idiotically slow.

On the other hand, sometimes 60 feels far too fast even when in theory it's what you're allowed to do. Like a lot of drivers I have my own set of speed limits on roads I know well; often they're a bit faster than the legal ones, but sometimes they're a lot slower. One route I take regularly passes through three villages with no posted speed limits but I treat them like 30 or 40 zones according to the conditions, and I suspect that all other drivers who aren't complete nutters do the same thing.

Ultimately cars are useful but dangerous things and we have to decide where we draw the line between allowing them to remain useful and attenuating the threat they pose. Having no speed limits would be one slightly insane solution (you'd just have to charge people with dangerous driving if they caused death, injury or damage, though of course by then it's too late for whoever was killed or injured), but, then, if you're really, *really* serious about reducing those killed and injured on the roads, why not set the national speed limit at three miles per hour? No, seriously. Then if somebody found themselves in the path of a car or a truck or a bus they could just stroll out of the way. You might manage a whole year with no road deaths whatsoever. Obviously the economy would collapse and we'd all effectively become hermits, but then maybe it would lead to the revival of the railways, with branch lines everywhere. Mind you; trains crash too. Maybe they should have a walking-pace speed limit as well . . . And let's not even start on aeroplanes. I suppose balloons and dirigibles — so long as they're helium filled — might be okay.

The three-mile-an-hour national speed limit is arguably an even madder idea than no speed limits at all, but it has a certain logic to it and it forces us to confront the question: how much do we value human lives? What exactly are we prepared to give up to save some?

However, let's not forget that this is all within the context of a society that doesn't get all *that* bothered over the fact that in excess of one hundred and ten thousand Brits die every year from smoking tobacco, or the fact that alcohol abuse kills tens of thousands too. Three thousand people die every single day from malaria, but they're mostly children and in Africa so they don't matter, it would seem. One injustice doesn't excuse another, but let's at least admit that we prioritise and contextualise our outrage at unnecessary death.

One conducts the Jaguar through to Greenock and thence to Dalmuir, in Clydebank. In Greenock one collects one's friend Mr David McCartney. In Clydebank one picks up one's other chum, Mr James S. Brown.

The Jag is a quite different car to drive after the M5, but by Clydebank I've just about acclimatised. Clydebank is a semi-post-industrial district of high- and low-rise schemes and mostly abandoned shipyards which was bombed heavily in the Second World War and has picked up many more scars since. It has its pleasant areas, there's been some redevelopment and Dalmuir itself is quite leafy in places, but the general area has its problem patches too: poverty, poor health and violence, much of it drug-related.

Substances: the usual disclaimer.

[As ever, what we call drug-related violence is really drug-prohibition-related violence, and the drug which is by far the most commonly associated directly with violence is alcohol. In the — hopefully unlikely — event you sincerely believe that our current drug laws are mostly fairly sensible but just not applied with sufficient stringency, please feel free, of course, to ignore this paragraph, as it has some connection to common sense and therefore does not remotely concern you.]

The drive up Loch Lomond side, across Rannoch Moor and through Glencoe is necessarily a little more sedate than it would have been in the BMW, but the Jag can pick up its skirts and make an overtaking dash when it needs to all the same, and the engine sounds

200

great when it's gunned, like a Tyrannosaurus fart sampled and played back at 960 b.p.m. Standard overtaking technique is to drop out of overdrive and plant the right foot. It's an electrically switched overdrive unit so you're not supposed to need to declutch when engaging or disengaging, but I always do, in deference to the Jag's age.

Corners with lots of white paint are usually taken out of overdrive too, just to get the car better balanced on its rear suspension under power (in the M5 you'd just breeze through on a constant throttle opening with nary a thought. This is one of the most noticeable effects of a really fast car asked to tackle ordinary roads at a relative dawdle; the corners seem to disappear and the road effectively becomes one long straight — blimey, at legal speeds the M5 probably thinks there are only about three bends in the whole of Scotland).

The three of us know this route well, but from Loch Lomond onwards it's still breathtaking.

"Nice lake, eh, Banksie?" Jim says.

"Yeah yeah yeah, very fucking funny."

I moved to London from Gourock at the very end of 1979 and started work as Law Costs Draughtsman in April of 1980. For the first few months I stayed at Dave's flat in Belsize Road. He'd been the first of the people I knew in Greenock to move down to London — I was about the third or fourth — but eventually it seemed like almost everybody I'd known back in Inverclyde was living in London. Jim moved down a year or so after me. He ended up working for a firm called Save and Prosper, which I said at the time was a little like King Herod working for Mothercare, but then I can be cruel. Ann and I met at work shortly after I'd joined the firm, then moved in together the following year. In 1983 we went to live in Faversham, in Kent, closer to Ann's parents in Canterbury but still a reasonable commute to London.

I will never be allowed to forget the fact that once, when Ann and I had the house in Faversham and Jim still lived in London, the three of us were on holiday, driving north up the side of Loch Lomond, when Jim suggested stopping to take a photograph of the view looking back the way we'd come, and I said something like, "Yeah, I think there's a lay-by just round this corner, you can get a good view down the lake from there."

"The *what*, Banksie? A good view down the *what*?"

"Oh shit," I said. "I said 'lake', didn't I?"

Ann was laughing quietly.

Jim shook his head, a great big smile on his face. "Oh dear oh dear oh dear. You've been down south *far* too long, El Bonko."

"And you're going to tell everybody, aren't you?"

He shrugged as we pulled into the lay-by. "You've brought it on yourself, pal; I've no sympathy. Anyway, if I'd said something like that, would *you* let *me* off? Eh?"

I thought about this. I sighed. "Fair enough."

We stop for a fag break at Fort William — smoking is banned in the cars. It's another fabulous day and the weather is getting positively warm. We stand in the loch-side car park at the southern end of the town

202

centre and look out at the loch and the hills on the far side.

Dave is the oldest of the three of us; just over 50 now (we work out that 50 is our average age). Like me he's bearded, though even greyer; almost white. Jim looks exactly like Robert De Niro in *Jackie Brown*, something I find startling. Not as startling as he does, though.

"Really?" He looks quite pleased.

"Oh, yeah," I tell him. "Though it has to be said that Robert De Niro looks pretty shit in *Jackie Brown*."

Jim sniffs. "Well, fuck off then."

Dave is our official driver for the week and is even getting paid for the privilege, the vestigial remnant of the garrulous Glaswegian in the original concept for this book (well, it is his profession, and taxi drivers don't get paid holidays). He walks round the car, kicking the Jag's tyres. "You sure this old thing's up to taking us round Speyside for a week?"

"It's the youngest of the four of us, Dave," I tell him, pointedly. "And it hasn't let us down yet, has it?"

"Hmm," Dave concedes, "not yet."

"Exactly, and has anything fallen off?"

"Aye," Jim says. "That dooberry off the rear quarter light."

"That doesn't count! It's just a bit off the locking mechanism!"

"The locking mechanism?" Dave says. "Right. So the car can get broken into easily. Tut-tut, Banksie. Hope the boot locks."

I look at him through narrowed eyes. "Climb in and we'll find out."

"Oh-oh. He's getting tetchy," Jim says to Dave.

"I am not getting tetchy."

"Aye," Dave agrees. "First day and all. Thought we'd go longer than that before he started getting tetchy."

"Look, I'm not —"

"First afternoon, in fact. That's extreme tetchiness. Even by Banksie The King of Tetch standards."

"Will you two stop it? I am not in any way —"

"This could be a long week."

"Look, I am simply not —"

"Aye. Right enough. What with Banksie getting tetchy so quickly."

"I am *not* getting *tetchy!*"

I have to suffer more of this outrageous tetchiness slander in bursts all the way up the road through the Great Glen towards Inverness. This road, the A82, is pretty good; usually fairly busy, but with enough decent straights to allow some overtaking unless there are absurd amounts of oncoming traffic. There is one bit at the side of the imaginatively named Loch Lochy — my, must have been a hard night's brain-wracking in the smoke-filled bothy to come up with *that* one — where there is a cliff on one side of the road and the loch on the other. This is one of the few places where I've always reckoned it's relatively safe to speed — albeit only briefly and always providing the road is empty — just because there is so little likelihood of a sheep or a deer wandering out on front of the car. There are actually two straights, the southern one shorter than the northern, with a hotel on a sort of wiggle in the middle which spoils what would otherwise have been an even more impressive length of road, but it's still a sweet stretch. And still no speed cameras. Amazing.

The Jaguar takes even this section at a steady 60 or so; rolling along happily, its engine issuing a burbling roar as though it's perpetually trying to clear its throat. The Jag is a very relaxing car to drive, even though it takes a little more concentration than a modern vehicle. It's that suited-to-the-legal-limit thing again; you don't feel that you ought to be going faster just because the car can handle it, and because you're in no danger of being snapped by a speed camera or tripping a radar trap, you can stop worrying about that as well. It's almost as though you're driving in an era before there were such annoyances. Time warp driving. (You get that in the M5 too, though only in the sense that it goes so fast there are times when you'd swear you've arrived before you set off.)

When I was a child and we drove this road we really did keep one eye on Loch Ness, just in case we saw the monster. Well, simpler times. Back then you could still just about believe that a few fuzzily photographed floating logs, grainy footage of boats' wakes, one or two fairly obvious faked stills and the testament of a handful of people could add up to evidence that there was some throwback to the age of the dinosaurs haunting the dark depths of the great long loch.

Then people got serious about it and set up viewing platforms with multiple still and film — later, video —

cameras, sonar sensors and underwater microphones, and the sightings stopped.

The Loch Ness monster seems to be one of those quantum creatures, maybe distantly related to Schrodinger's Cat; its existence is only possible when there's nobody there to observe it.

A friend of mine called Ron Binns once wrote a book called *The Loch Ness Mystery Solved*, which basically went through all the evidence clear-eyed and unbiased and came to the fairly inescapable conclusion the whole monster thing was a load of old Highland bollocks, but because this wasn't what people particularly wanted to hear, you'll struggle to find the book in any loch-side tourist shop (though last time I was there they had a copy in Lochaber High School Library, so it might have helped sow the seeds of a healthy scepticism in a few young minds).

Our musical accompaniment for the week in the Jag is largely retro, majoring on people like Graham Parker, John Mellencamp and Steve Gibbons, then at the chalet we listen to music by the at-this-point-not-quite-dead-yet Warren Zevon. I've brought what I thought was the best album of last year, *By The Way* by the Red Hot Chilli Peppers, and albums by Black Rebel Motor Cycle Club and lots of "The" bands, like The White Stripes, The Hives, The Vines and The Strokes. I've also brought some Led Zep, Pixies, Godspeed You Black Emperor! and early Ozrics, but most of these don't get played and the ones that do don't really seem to meet with the positive reception I'd been hoping for.

Back to Inverness. We're only here because the self-catering chalet in Glenlivet we're booked into for the rest of the week can't take us until tomorrow. I thought self-catering would be a better idea for us three guys than a hotel, especially when Jim started talking about the size of the sound system we'd need to take with us, however for this first night we're staying at the Highland Hotel in the centre of Inverness. This used to be the Station Hotel and Ann and I have stayed here a couple of times, once after a train journey from Kyle of Lochalsh and once en route to Thurso by train, heading for Orkney. I'd hoped to park the Jag in the wee square right outside the hotel entrance itself, but it's full and I have to stick it round the corner in a car park at the back of the station. It was that or the nearby multi-storey. Should have gone for the multi-storey.

The hotel, in a fit of wisdom which instantly marks it out as an extraordinarily sensible choice on my part, puts us in a sort of semi-private short corridor off the main part of one floor; there's a set of doors then just our three rooms. I am relieved to see this. Our record in hotels is, ah, variable, you might say. I have never in my life been banned from a bar, pub or hotel, but I suspect I've come close a few times, and the majority of those occasions have involved Jim and Dave. Nothing serious, you understand, just good-natured boisterousness which may involve some exterior climbing, corridor wrestling, suspicious fumes, snorting noises and loud music. Stuck out here on a limb of the hotel, I feel we are much less likely than I'd feared to cause offence to any other guests, the staff or management.

We hit the town. Inverness has many bars. We favour quite a few of them with our custom, then head for the Shapla, Inverness' very favourably sited and most central curry shop. The city has a half-dozen or so sub-continental restaurants, a couple of which I've eaten in and would again and all of which I've heard good reports of, but I still tend to head back to the Shapla because it's handy and it has a wonderful view over the river beside one of the main bridges; this is a great place for people-watching, car- and bike-spotting and just generally taking in the sight of the Ness flowing calmly between the curved banks with their mix of low-rise and generally handsome buildings.

In the past at least, it's just as well the view's been there to distract the diner, because if there's a criticism to be levelled at the Shapla it's that the service can be a little on the relaxed side. Happily the food is worth waiting for, and in these fries-with-that? days a little deliberation over a meal is no bad thing, but I wouldn't try to nip into the place for some quick nosh before catching a film or a play.

We take in the view, take in the curry, and take in another couple of bars afterwards before heading back to the hotel for a last drink before the bar closes — I have a whisky, naturally — and then withdrawing to Jim's room for a smoke (sufficiently drunk, I am by this time cadging cigarettes).

It is decided that more drink is required so we order a bottle of wine on room service. I am in the bathroom — which is quite grand in an old-fashioned, white-tile sort of way — when the wine arrives, and so get to hear rather than see a kind of kinetic pantomime as Jim attempts to take the tray with the opened bottle of Châteauneuf-du-Pape and the glasses from the young night porter and simultaneously pay him (Jim has forgotten that all this is supposed to go on the bill).

The tray (I am later told by Dave) unbalances as Jim attempts the transfer, sending the bottle in one direction, the tray in another and the glasses in a third, while the night porter guy watches the twenty-pound note wave about in front of his face as Jim attempts, at first, to catch all three of the separately directed articles as they begin to perform their distinct parabolas towards the floor.

Instinct, thankfully, causes Jim to prioritise the still almost entirely full bottle as the object most in need of his attention, and he succeeds in block-catching it — the right way up — against the side of the television while hopping round and trying to break the fall of the glasses with one foot (the tray is, sensibly, left to its own devices). One glass breaks; the other two survive, bouncing off the bed and carpet. The night porter finally takes the twenty from Jim's outstretched fingers and, snorting with barely suppressed laughter, informs us he will return with another glass and a brush and pan, for the broken glass.

All of this sounds hilarious from the bathroom; I start laughing quietly to myself and I'm still giggling when the night porter arrives with the brush and pan and replacement glass. I find myself going, "Hoo-hoo-hoo." (pause) "Hoo-hoo-hoo," a lot.

209

I think there must have been some sort of positive feedback thing going on with the echo in the tiled bathroom, because after a while I'm laughing as much at the sound of my own laughter as at the scene I've had to create in my head from the sounds coming through the door.

"You okay in there, Banksie?" Dave asks.

"Hoo-hoo-hoo," I tell him. "Pretty much." I wipe my eyes. "Was that another example of Brownian motion I heard there?"

"Oh yes."

"The fog, Banksie," Jim says. "It was the fog."

"The what?" Dave asks.

"The fog," I tell him. "The Force Of Gravity. Was ever thus. Hoo-hoo-hoo."

"You finished in that fuckin bog, Banksie, or you having a bath or something? I'm dyin for a slash."

"Hoo-hoo-hoo. On my way out. Hoo-hoo-hoo."

The bottle of wine does nothing to make the incident any less funny over the next half hour or so, and I keep bursting into giggles.

"Hoo-hoo-hoo!"

Jim sighs. "Well, at least he's not being tetchy."

"Hoo-hoo-hoo!"

"I don't know." Dave shakes his head.

"Hoo-hoo-hoo!"

"I think I preferred the tetchiness."

I am definitely not laughing the next morning when two bad things happen (before I get into this I better report that the buffet breakfast was very good and I bumped into a friend of Les's who was there for a union conference). The lesser of the two bad things is that the Jag has been comprehensively shat upon by what would appear to have been a well-coordinated flock of very large and thoroughly diarrhoeic seagulls.

The more important bad thing is that Jim is called back to Clydebank due to a family emergency, and has to jump on a train heading south. This all blows up really quickly; before it's really sunk in we're waving him goodbye and watching the train pull out. He's told us he hopes to rejoin us in a couple of days, but it feels like the holiday is half ruined already.

This was supposed to be the great reunion, the third part of the trilogy after two much earlier escapades. Longer ago than any of us likes to think about we drove round the Highlands, camping and Youth Hostelling, then a few years later, when we were all living down South we took a camper van from Faversham up to Scotland and through the Hebrides and the Highlands. There had been talk of a boat trip as the third big hol together, possibly on the Shannon in Ireland, maybe on the Caledonian Canal here in Scotland, but this had been postponed when the whisky-researching wheeze had suggested itself. (Apart from anything else, Jim and I could never agree on who should be captain if we hired a boat; Jim claimed he should be in charge because he's piloted a boat on the Shannon already with Joan and the two boys, whereas I insisted that I ought to be in command because I — thanks to my dad being a first officer in the Admiralty — had nautical blood. My clinching argument, I was quite convinced, was that I still had one of my dad's old peaked caps, complete with anchor and crown and all that sort of official-looking naval stuff, and what's more it even fitted me, but for some reason this never carried the rhetorical or logical weight with Jim which I thought it so obviously merited.)

Now we three are two, and while Dave is one of my very best friends and we've had some great times together — and I'm sure we'll have a laugh over the next few days — it simply won't be the same for either of us without Jim. There just seems to be a special chemistry when the three of us get together.

"Bastard!"

"It's not Jim's fault, Banksie. He —"

"I'm not talking about Jim!" I shout. "I'm talking about whatever incontinent pterodactyl was responsible for *this*!" I gesture at the Jag's roof, bonnet, boot, windscreen and side windows, all of which are fairly comprehensively splattered. There's even some crap on one of the tyres' side walls. It looks like somebody's thrown half a litre of white paint over the car from a second-floor window, then loaded up a handful of brushes with little gobbets of green, grey and yellow matte and flicked these over the resulting ghastliness as well.

Dave inspects the car and nods. "Aye, it is a bit of a mess."

"A bit of a mess?" I yelp. "It's practically a fucking respray! I mean, *look* at it! What do the fuckers *eat* to produce shit like this? Fucking radioactive waste?"

212

"That could be it, Banksie," Dave says. "Maybe it's a giant mutant seagull which flew down all the way from Dounreay just to target your car. Do you want to open the car up now so I can put my bag in, or should I just break in via this faulty rear quarter light?"

"I think the stuff's glowing," I tell him, plipping the car open. "Do you think it's glowing?"

"No. But you'd better get it to a car wash; that seagull shit can damage paint."

"Oh, for fuck's sake!"

Dave dumps his bag on the back seat and looks at me warily. "You're not going to get tetchy, are you?"

"No!"

After all this nonsense — and a visit to Safeway's car wash which still doesn't entirely remove all traces of the radioactive seagull dump — arriving at the Glen Ord distillery just outside Muir of Ord comes as a particular relief and feels like a return to normality. Dave and I do the tour.

Glen Ord isn't a very architecturally attractive distillery — it's abruptly close to the road and dominated by the massive maltings buildings right next door — but it has a good tour with helpful guides and the way the place is laid out helps make the whole process particularly clear. Ord uses barley grown locally on the Black Isle. (Confusingly, the Black Isle is not an island, but rather the fertile peninsula north of Inverness lying between the Beauly/Moray Firths to the south and the Cromarty Firth to the north.)

The maltings provides the barley for other Diageo-owned distilleries in the area and for Talisker, on Skye, though this receives malt with five times the peatiness compared to Ord itself. The peat comes from Drumossie Moor, south of Inverness and the water from the romantically entitled Loch of Smoke (mainly fed by spring water) and Loch of Birds (mainly rain water). Ord is another 95 per cent blend, 5 per cent single-malt whisky, but the latter — most commonly available as a 12-year-old, which is what I buy, presented in an attractively different roughly square-section bottle — is well worth a taste; malty, lightly but distinctly peated and richly sherried. It's one of the sweetest expressions I've tasted, without being cloying. A very pleasant surprise.

Ord is one of those whiskies which has changed a fair bit over the years, and in his astoundingly comprehensive *Complete Book of Whisky*, the patently extremely knowledgeable Jim Murray reckons they've ruined a distinctively earthy dram which was very much of its region to make just another sherried one which could have come from almost anywhere. I can't comment directly, but it would be a shame if this was true, no matter how pleasant and drinkable Ord is. Anyway, if you want to try out some of the older expressions look out for bottles labelled Glenordie, Ordie or even just Ord; this is one of those distilleries which has been a little confused about its identity over the years.

Oh yes, and until 1949 the place was lit by paraffin lamps. Bleedin paraffin lamps. What was that about flash photography again?

On to Glenmorangie, just outside the town of Tain; a nicely turned-out distillery much easier on the eye than Ord. The place is quiet when we get there — in mid April — scaffolding up around the enormously high-necked stills. I've heard about these eccentrics and been looking forward to seeing them in the copper. I get a glimpse inside the still room and, yup, these really are the giraffes of the still world; quite fabulously tall; double-decker bus in height.

Quiet in the technical sense of having its annual refit, the place is still fairly busy with visitors; there's a coach trip doing the rounds as we're wandering about. Dave heads off to take more photos and I walk down under the railway line, past low warehouses. This is the line from Inverness to Thurso and Wick, a continuation of the rail route which skirts Dalwhinnie and Tomatin, and the same line which passes close enough to Bunchrew for you to hear the trains on a quiet morning.

The Dornoch Firth lies quiet and salty-smelling beyond the little tunnel under the railway. Somehow it's a surprise to be reminded that Glenmorangie is a seaside malt, though the scent of it is there in the whisky if you look for it. The coastline — hill and mountain, forest and beach, dune and cliff — tapers off into the calm and milky skies to the north.

I know this whole area fairly well from when I was a Non-Destructive Testing Technician (Trainee) with a division of what was then called British Steel; a bunch of us stayed in a wee village called Portmahomack and worked — if that's not overdignifying my efforts — at the North Sea Production Platform yard at Nigg, a few miles away from here, back in the late seventies. The Non-Destructive Testing we were doing consisted of using X-ray radiography and ultrasonics to check that the steel cylinders which would make up the legs of the production platforms wouldn't collapse in a North Sea storm and kill all on board.

The job was technically interesting and I met a few characters through it, but it was really just a way to make some money between writing books rather than any sort of career. Still, I have good memories of that summer, staying in Portmahomack, drinking and playing dominoes (badly) with my workmates, taking long walks along the deserted coastline, climbing the odd castle and generally soaking up the atmosphere, because the whole area was the major inspiration for the landscape featured in *The Wasp Factory*, and I just have a great fondness for that book and everything associated with it.

Back at the shop, I buy a bottle of the fino finish 18-year-old, partly in memory of that spectacular dram out of the barrel at Ardbeg. This is possibly a case of cross-distillery inspiration, given that Ardbeg is owned by the same people.

Glenmorangie is another best-seller; no other malt sells better in Scotland. This makes perfect sense to me, for all my apparent Islay fixation. Once again, I think it's largely about the sensational skill in the selection and handling of the finishings. Glenmorangie is still mostly matured in oak casks from the Ozarks which have held bourbon for four years, but it bottles at ten, twelve, fifteen, eighteen, 21 and 24 years — plus it has various vintage-dated bottlings. It has Ruby port, dry Oloroso and Fino sherry and Malmsey Madiera finishes (and has had other special finishes, for example in Malaga barrels), plus various other limited editions like the Claret, Tain Hermitage and Côte de Beaune red wine finishes, not to mention the cask-strength unfiltered Traditional. It even has expressions specific to one warehouse; cellar 13, the one nearest the coast.

Heady, almost bewildering stuff. But it's this willingness to experiment that marks Glenmorangie out as one of the most important and innovative whisky makers, and one of the least stuffy, too. The whisky itself might almost get lost inside this all-over-the-place promiscuity if it wasn't a beautifully structured, complex and yet delicate dram in its own right. There's a lightness of touch and yet a strength in depth about Glenmorangie, a sort of finesse in its subtle mixture of flavours that allows it to mix with all these other influences without either bullying them into submission or being over-run by their flavours.

Glenmorangie is unusual in having to deal with atypically — for Scotland — hard water, from the Tarlogie springs. Quite a lot of salt has to be added to make it suitable for whisky production, just as you have to add salt to dishwashers in hard-water areas, and it's an indication of how the balance of control is weighted between production water and the subsequent influence of the barrels and warehousing that nobody has ever accused Glenmorangie of having more than the faintest trace of saltiness to it, unless it's a still fairly

217

subtle flavour imbued from that close-to-the-waves cellar thirteen.

A sequence of smart advertising campaigns — the whole Twelve Men of Tain thing, and the Glen of Tranquillity series — has kept Glenmorangie in the public eye over the years, and its position as one of the market leaders is entirely justified; an unfailingly intriguing and satisfying selection of whiskies. If you were stuck on a desert island and could only drink the output from one distillery, this would have to be prime contender; another might be Bowmore (plus, if you're me, Laphroaig), though, of course we still have Macallan waiting in the wings.

Perfect Dram? Best Distillery? I may have to widen my brief unilaterally.

I should point out that throughout all this — the last few chapters and the last few weeks — I'm still making my inquiries (discreet inquiries, too, at least by my standards) regarding the whole secret still/peatreek thing. I'm afraid, however, that so far I'm not meeting with much success. Actually so far I'm not meeting with any success. Despite this, I remain undismayed. I have a feeling it's one of those matters where you work away for ages with no result, not change, no progress whatsoever and then suddenly everything happens at once and it all comes right and you meet with total success just when you least expect it.

Cheerfully unrealistic optimism can be such a comfort.

★　★　★

South across the Black Isle and the Kessock Bridge — a handsome example of a cable-stayed bridge, with an almost arrogant lack of cross-bracing between the towers — through Grantown — stopping for ice creams, because of the heat — then on to our base for the rest of the week.

We're in chalet three at the Glenlivet Holiday Lodges. Almost disappointingly, the Glenlivet Holiday Lodges really are quite close to Glenlivet, only a couple of miles away from the distillery. There's a wonderful, very peaceful view to the south west towards the Hills of Cromdale, a bar/restaurant called the Poacher's Bar with a pool table, and a variety of forest walks starting pretty much from the door step. The track up to the place from the B9009 is a bit rough but the Jag's old-fashioned, deep-side-walled tyres cope without a grumble. The chalet itself is fine and even has a sauna, not that we use it. Only mobile reception is a problem, and we end up wandering around in the grass outside the chalet waving our phones in the air trying to get a signal. The old red callbox outside the Poacher's Bar gets used quite a lot as I call home and we try to keep in touch with Jim, who, when we do get hold of him, says he hopes to head back north on the Wednesday.

Steaks at the bar, then a circular stroll along a forestry track where the trees have all been harvested, so that we walk surrounded by the bleached wreckage of stumps and shattered branches. Ben Rinnes rises browny-purple in the north, a swept line of ridge leading to a tipped table of summit.

Dave looks at me. "How's your brain these days, Banksie? Does it work? Is it alert? Up for challenges?"

I groan. "Oh, God, you've brought that game with you, haven't you?"

"Aye! But it's easy once you get used to it."

"Is it still in nine dimensions?"

"Yeah, but like I say, it's easy once you get used to it."

The poison pen method has been resorted to (long story). Wine has been taken. Whiskies are before us. Not to mention behind us, around us and indeed inside us. Our fine and filling meal at the Poacher's Bar seems long ago now and we're still drinking and Dave's giving me a brief run-through of the rules to this game he's been working on for the last few years; he's up to about page 21 at the moment (he's brought a printout of the short version of the rules).

I'm sitting at the wooden table in the chalet feeling a little the better for wear, scratching my head and staring down at the nine, square, seven-by-seven laminated cardboard boards that Dave's placed side by side on the table's surface along with all the relevant cards, pieces and assorted gubbins the game obviously requires. This is all very confusing. I'm not at all sure I've taken in anything apart from alcohol and smoke for the last half-hour or so he's been speaking. I become aware he's just asked me a question. He's looking at me expectantly.

"What?" I ask, smiling reassuringly.

"You got all that?" McCartney asks. "You ready to play?"

I haven't the foggiest concept how even to start. "Good grief, yes!" I exclaim, slapping the table enthusiastically. "What are we waiting for?"

Coffee and bacon rolls for breakfast, then into Dufftown (we take a photo at Mortlach distillery), then we take in Glendronach distillery, hidden away off the beaten metalling in a shallow dip between lots of trees and productive-looking fields. We have a natter to a very nice lady called Allison who opens the shop up specially for us. I buy 15-year-old bottlings of Glendronach, Glenburgie, Glentauchers, Glencadam, Miltonduff and Tormore, and a 12-year-old Ardmore. The Glendronach we tried on site (I had but the merest sip, honest) was a rich, sweet concoction, with some peat and smoke and quite a strong sherry finish. Very palatable, and I look forward to making its acquaintance, and that of its companions — all fine, if unexceptional — again when we get to that bit of the cupboard under the stairs in my parents' house, probably some time in the next eighteen months.

We have a bar lunch in Turriff then swing back to Keith and the Strathisla distillery where we have a sort of self-escorted tour with a handy pamphlet and lots of signs and explanatory posters about the place (though at a fiver a head for do-it-yourself, it might seem a bit steep). Still, it's an attractive distillery of well-kept old buildings, nicely presented, and there's a distinct and even opulent Highland country house flavour to the

Visitor Centre lounge. You suspect the five quid goes to paying off the investment needed to create all this.

McCartney suddenly decides he's a fan of the car park; specifically the size of the car parking bays in the car park, which are brightly outlined with smart white paint and Very Wide Indeed; parking spaces you could reverse a Lincoln Continental into with all its doors open and still not hit anything on either side. Well, kinda.

I try to convince him that the weird kink in the Lyne arm of the second spirit still is of more intrinsic interest, but he's still banging on about how all car parks ought to be this well laid out.

We get to Glen Grant, just outside the town of Rothes, before it closes. McCartney grumbles about the car park not being quite so generously laid out as Strathisla, but somehow life goes on. The walk from the car park to the distillery proper is beautiful and peaceful, under tall mixed trees and in the midst of flowers and shrubs. The distillery buildings are a quiet riot of Scottish Baronial, all turrets and crow-stepped gables. We're kind of toured-out so we just buy some 10-year-old in the smart, modern, pale-wood-and-glass shop and head back across its wee bridge and up the side of the trickling stream to the Glen Grant gardens. These are quietly gorgeous.

The gardens are set within a small, sinuous glen behind the distillery. They were stocked largely with plants brought from India and Africa by James Grant the younger, who was a major in the army. They were reopened in 1995 after being restored following decades of neglect, and Seagram, the distillery's owners since 1972, deserve wheelbarrows of praise for what they've had done here (they own Chivas and Strathisla, so maybe some of the Strathisla fivers have gone into all this horticulture).

It's yet another hot day and the slight climb up to a wonderfully gothic circular gazebo on a rise leaves us glad of the shade and a seat, the better to take in the architectural use of antlers and giant pine cones in the building's roof, which is something you don't see every day. If it had been cooler and our bellies hadn't been rumbling in anticipation of the evening meal, I'd have liked to have explored more of the garden, but never mind; definitely worth a visit even if you can't stand whisky.

If you do like whisky then Glen Grant will probably already be familiar; a light, flowery dram available at as little as five years (especially in Italy — what is it about Italians and very young whisky?). The 10-year-old I bought is sort of firm and nutty and dry as a fino sherry. A perfect mid-afternoon whisky, or with chilled water as an aperitif.

We play Dave's game, which, when it started out, was based on one of my SF books, *Excession*, and had the same name. In its latest incarnation it involves this nine-dimensional set of boards and seems to be awfully complicated. I'm drunk and stoned and that surely isn't helping matters, but even in my present state I have the distinct impression that were I sober I'd still be seriously confused, just by the game. The game isn't really in nine dimensions — even McCartney isn't quite that mad — it's in three dimensions with nine vertical levels. Trust me; this is more than enough to make it so deeply, fractally perplexing that it might as well be in nine dimensions.

"So it is surrounded?" I ask.

"Yes."

"But why can't it move out diagonally?"

"On its own board or on higher or lower ones?"

"Both. Troth. All of the above."

"Well, it just can't; that's the rule."

"But things *can* move diagonally in this game?"

"Oh, yeah, of course."

"Right. They just can't escape diagonally?"

"Other things can, just not this. If it could move, that is. Of course it can't, but if it could, then it wouldn't be able to. Not with the pieces like this. Do you see what I mean?"

"Uh-huh." I sit back from the table, thinking. "May I ask a question, David?"

"Yeah, certainly, what?"

"Are you trying to confuse me deliberately or is it just an emergent property of this hideous nonsense you've set before us, you mad bastard?"

It's late on. We are both pretty drunk. Dave raises the bottle of Strathisla towards my half-full glass. "Do you want a wee . . .?"

"Na," I tell him. "I'm all right."

"Yeah." Dave nods. "So am I." He pours a full measure for himself. "But that's beside the point."

CHAPTER
NINE

The Awemsys of Azshashoshz

Somehow we get up to another great day — and more coffee and bacon rolls — at half-nine despite only getting to bed at five. I feel remarkably fine. We sit on the grass munching rolls, looking at the hills and distant mountains and trying to find a cloud anywhere in the sky.

"How's your head?" Dave asks.

"Better than it deserves to be."

"I was thinking about the game after I went to bed last night."

I look at him. "You *were*?" I shake my head. "You're taking this far too seriously."

"I think the nine different boards is maybe a bit too complicated."

"You will recall that Jim and I were both sceptical."

"Yeah, but it was worth trying."

"So, back to the single-board idea?"

Dave nods and draws on the first fag of the day. "Maybe. With adjustments. Needs more work. I'd still like to try the nine-board idea with three players and simpler rules."

"Really?" I stand up. "I shall go and ring Mr Brown and inform him he is required immediately."

Jim says the crisis is over, he's free to leave and he hopes to make it to Aviemore on the early afternoon train. We have a few problems with mobiles and staying in touch — though, standing by a roadside trying to electronically top-up my phone, I get to see the steam train on the Strathspey Railway chuff-chuffing past in the sunlight — but eventually we meet up in time for lunch. We bump into the couple my Mum and Dad bought their house off, who retired nearby. Small country.

We return to the Glenlivet Lodges via Dulnain Bridge, trying to see a red squirrel (Les, Aileen and I saw one the week before). No luck on the squirrel front; we repair to Dufftown to check out the local bars for Sky reception because there's some football game on this evening which might be worth watching (I have no real interest in football, being a Greenock Morton supporter, so I can't remember which game this might have been). Dufftown rather lives up to its name; nothing much going on, shops very quiet and bars which don't seem all that friendly — there's some muttering in one that another bar does have Sky but hasn't paid the appropriate fee for letting the public watch.

Maybe we were just unlucky. And to be fair, the lassie at the town's slightly antique petrol station, with whom we established a close relationship over the week due to the fact the Jag combines the thirst of an elephant with the fuel-carrying capacity of a gnat, seemed very nice.

We decide it's a bit warm for trudging round distilleries and so head back to the Lodges to play pool, lounge in the sun, test out Dave's simplified game (still confusing), play Grass (it's a card game), drink and smoke.

Azshashoshz: that etymology in full.

A few years ago now, a bunch of us were visiting Glenfinnan for Hogmanay. We were staying at what became known as the Shilly Chalet — basically a wee fishermen's hut a ten-minute or so walk from Les and Aileen's house. The previous day we'd met a slightly misguided English guy on the train up to Glenfinnan. I seem to recall he was called Rollo; if he wasn't, well, it was one of those slightly eccentric upper-class names very like it. Wore a rugby shirt; very obviously public school. I'm sure you're getting the picture. Anyway, Rollo — or whoever — had been trying to get to a tiny remote island off a slightly larger but still remote island off a fairly remote bit of the not-really-all-that-nearby mainland.

We'd explained to him that his idea that he could get off in the middle of the night at Lochailort and hitch-hike to this back-of-the-back-of-beyond island was, frankly, daft, so we offered to let him bunk down on the floor of the Shilly Chalet overnight before resuming his journey in daylight, when his chances of arriving at his destination without frostbite or the effects of terminal exhaustion would be far greater. Anyway, Rollo had been waved off on the next leg of his expedition and we'd gone round to the McFarlanes' for a party. We were all very drunk. Amongst our company was Jim, who has on occasion been known to slur his words a little when he's drunk. On this occasion nobody could understand a single word he was saying except, for some bizarre reason, me, and so I was translating.

Jim would say something like, "Ammeen sjussbeinpoligh ffyimesumbayontray coubeatrai duznhaftibeatray coubeonabuzorsumthin antheyhaven gorraplaystayoff ruma bed ffyougotspayone."

And I'd sit there, frowning mightily with the sheer drunken concentration of it, then nod and say, "Jim says, he means, it's just being polite if you meet somebody on a train — doesn't have to be a train, could be a bus or something — and they haven't got a place to stay, to offer them a bed if you have a spare one." (At which point Jim would generally nod in confirmation, or sometimes offer a corrolaric explanation if he thought one was required, though this too, of course, had then to be translated.)

This went on for some time and I felt I was doing really well until Jim launched into this long paragraph of barely comprehensible drivel which ended with a sound I just couldn't make out at all. It was quite an emphatic, climactic sort of sound, or set of sounds, too, and he was obviously very pleased with it as an argument-clinching sentence ender, given the way he nodded and drank from his can with a sort of swagger, so I didn't feel I could just ignore it. Instead I sort of filed it away phonetically, just as I'd heard it, and started paraphrasing the rest of the paragraph anyway, hoping that by the time I got to the end the meaning behind the unidentified sound would become obvious just by my having had more time to think about it and the context therefore, hopefully, having become clear in the interim. This just didn't happen, so when I got to the end of the paragraph I abandoned the Clear English I'd been translating into and just repeated verbatim what I'd heard him say in Jim Source Code, which was, as near as I could make out, "Azshashoshz."

"Azshashoshz." The word just sort of hung there in the air between all of us, like a particularly vile fart nobody's prepared to own up to.

I shrugged and looked round everybody who'd been listening.

They all looked mystified.

Jim looked mystified.

He couldn't remember what it was he'd been trying to say then, at the time, let alone next morning (well, afternoon/evening), and so we never did find out what Azshashoshz actually meant, but it just kind of became a saying amongst us, especially if we hadn't quite heard what somebody had said, or one of our party was starting to slur their words. Sometimes we use it as a toast, our local equivalent of Cheers.

A year or two later when I wanted to dedicate *The Player of Games* to Jim, I just put "for Jim" on the dedication page of the hardback. Jim thought that this

229

wasn't specific enough — unarguably, there are quite a few Jims in the world — and it was his dedication after all, so I changed it for the paperback edition to "For James S. Brown, who once said, 'Azshashoshz' ".

Next day; more sun, more rolls, more early morning coughing.

But today is no ordinary day. Today, as well as continuing the whisky research — naturally — we are men with a mission. For today we have an appointment with destiny, today we take up the challenge of a profound spiritual quest for a nearmythic location, lost in the mists of time and the depths of ancient Morayshire. We are to revisit the site of one of our most emblematic achievements, a lodestone locus of enormous symbolic power in the personal mythology of all three of us.

Today we go in search of the Bombed Fountain of Elgin.

It was our first trip together round the Highlands, back in the late seventies. We were in the Mk 3 Cortina that had been my dad's. It was white with a black vinyl roof, boasted a two-litre engine and seemed really quite quick at the time.

I had by this time long been attracted to the concept of foam-bombing a fountain. The idea of seeing an attractive municipal piazza or corporate car park entrance knee-deep in soapy suds just struck me as deeply worthwhile; it seemed like an important artistic statement and a veritable piece of aesthetically relevant semi-vandalism; art terrorism.

230

I'd got my hands on a big polythene water container from a camping shop which just fitted into an old fake-leather shoulder bag that my mum would otherwise have thrown out. I'd cut a small but carefully positioned flap in the bag so that I could easily reach the little plastic tap at the side of the container and turn it on. The plan was that I'd select a low-rise fountain, one which you could sit on the side of, I'd stock up on lots and lots of Fairy Liquid bottles, empty them into the water container in the shoulder bag, go to the fountain, sit on the side (preferably somewhere near the fountain's pump inlet) and then — while looking like I was pretty much doing nothing at all — reach down and open the tap, letting the glistening green liquid flow into the waters. With any luck the container would be fully empty and I'd be making my escape before the detergent hit the impeller blades.

Cue vast heaving quantities of foam filling the whole square or corporate HQ entrance, filmy billows of it floating away on the breeze, and assorted comical turns by janitors/policemen/council or corporate officials as I stood somewhere in the middle distance, peeking round a corner and tittering at my merry and not at all in the end destructive prank, readers.

My original intended target had been the fountain in Clyde Square in Greenock, outside the Town Hall, but this struck me as a bit too close to home. I needed somewhere, I decided, where I wasn't known (and probably wouldn't be visiting again for a while). The Highland camping trip seemed to present an ideal opportunity for me finally to fulfil my dream. What was more, with Jim and Dave, I'd have accomplices; they could be lookouts and witnesses.

After days of searching we settled on Elgin the way a cloud of locusts settles on a ripe field of corn. We reconnoitred the target; a perfect, low-walled municipal fountain, rectangular in form, with a single medium-height jet and an easily identifiable pump inlet. Having secured the cooperation of Jim and Dave with a minimum of eye-rolling and head-shaking, I prepared to put my long-mulled-over plan into effect.

A busy but peaceful market town of some architectural significance not far from the Moray coast and about 40 miles east of Inverness, Elgin had no idea, as its innocent citizens woke up on that warm summer morning a quarter of a century ago, of the fate which lay in store for it . . .

. . . And it had no idea, the following morning, what had just happened to it, either, because we had obviously been the victims of unscrupulous local traders selling low-grade adulterated detergent, or perhaps an unsporting killjoy of a County Council committee had anticipated my deviously brilliant plan and fitted some sort of foam-defeating filter, or possibly the water used in the fountain was so incredibly hard it would have taken a petrol tanker's worth of highly concentrated industrial-grade detergent to make it foam up satisfactorily, or maybe I didn't use enough Fairy Liquid.

Whatever, the end result was a sort of off-white scum of bubbles an inch or so deep backed into one corner of the fountain by the breeze, the whole sad mess covering an area not much bigger than the surface of your average household bath and rapidly dissipating in the choppy waters amongst the bobbing ice-lolly wrappers and sweety papers.

I still have a photo of this debacle somewhere, but I forgot to look for it before we left for our week on Speyside, which made our whole return-to-the-scene-of-the-crime quest much more difficult than it needed to be.

It's a really hot day. Elgin and Moray didn't have the dry winter most of the west coast had — they had floods here in November 2002. They appear to be making up for it now, however; the town seems covered everywhere in apple and cherry blossom and we three middle-aged men are deeply appreciative of the fact that the young women of the town are taking the opportunity the day's sun and heat presents to dress in a manner it is hard not to characterise as skimpy; this phenomenon makes our wanderings around the place searching in vain for the fountain actually quite bearable. Frustrated, we lunch in a Wetherspoons place — somewhat against our better judgment, but it's there and it's serving food so what the hell — and, after a very much needed ice cream, I spend quite a long time in Gordon & MacPhail's shop in the centre of town, ogling whiskies, noting down some I've never even heard of and buying a few.

G&M have a long and distinguished history as one of the great independent bottlers of single-malt whiskies. At one time grocers like these were the one of the few sources of single malts; along with Cadenheads of

Aberdeen (now of Campbeltown), they kept the flame of single-malt appreciation burning while the rest of the world seemed utterly lost in blends. With lots of useful contacts both locally on Speyside and in the rest of the whisky world, and vast quantities of whisky stored, Gordon & MacPhail are still one of those names you can look for in a specialist shop and know that whatever the name of the whisky in the bottle, the contents should be interesting.

I'm tempted to buy lots of deli stuff too, especially cheeses, but we've still got that damned fountain to find, and while any whisky I buy won't be harmed by high temperatures, either in a plastic bag or sitting in the car, cheeses and meats and so on will just melt and/or bloom with unwelcome bacteria in this heat, so I regretfully leave all the scrumptious-looking stuff in the shop's fridges.

We finally track the fountain down outside the council offices on the far side of the bypass. It's not a fountain any more; they've filled it in and turned it into an admittedly quite impressive flower bed with a strange giant crown thing in the middle which looks like it belongs on a carnival float. We take some photos — filled, once again, 25 years later, with a distinct sense of anticlimax — open up the baking oven that the Jag has become in the sunlit car park, let it cool off and then head for some distilleries on our way to the coast; hopefully both will be cooler than sweltery Elgin, especially if we stay out of the still rooms and keep to the warehouses.

Dallas Dhu and Benromach are two distilleries which are open again after ownership changes, though only one is actually producing. Dallas Dhu, just to the south of Forres, is an oddity; it's a museum to distilling but it doesn't make whisky. Considering that a lot of distilleries feel and look entirely like slightly creaky museums to the distiller's art which, almost coincidentally, happen to make whisky as well, Dallas Dhu's new status must represent an attempt to fill a gap in the tourist market I'd have thought you'd need an electron microscope to spot, but somebody must love it. I think they do good business with coach parties, and certainly the place is very well laid out with extremely helpful and enthusiastic staff. I buy a bottle of 1980 vintage 20-year-old which is very light in colour. The lightness continues in the character of the whisky too, but it turns out to be a beautiful, satiny, flowery dram and it seems a pity that when the existing stocks are exhausted, that'll be it.

Benromach, just outside Forres towards the coast, has been bought by Gordon & MacPhail, the indie bottlers of Elgin; it'll be a while before the whiskies created under their ownership are up for sale — though as it's been opened for five years now, maybe they're already selling big in the Italian market — but in the meantime I buy a bottle of 18-year-old from its previous incarnation. This is a goldeny-brown colour and reminds me of light burr walnut; there's something nut-like and wood-smoke-ish about the taste too, with lots of sherry. One to compare and contrast with the new stuff when it appears.

★ ★ ★

We make for the coast and the dunes at Findhorn; the river forms a small estuary here with lots of sand and trees on the far side of the river from the long stretch of village, which is busy with people enjoying the unexpectedly fine weather. Dinghies and power boats everywhere. More ice cream. I hang around looking at boats and boring the guys with Drascombe and Orkney Boats spotting.

"Hey; think we'll see Mike Scott?"

"No."

Leaving Findhorn, we pass by the perimeter fence of RAF Kinloss. When I was about nine and we were camping nearby my dad got me to stand here at the perimeter fence just yards from the end of the runway when a Shackleton was taking off, thinking I'd be impressed. The Shackleton was a maritime patrol and ASW aircraft based on the old World War Two Lancaster bomber; it had four colossally noisy propeller engines and when it passed over, about twenty feet above, I nearly shat myself.

Dad just smiled when I told him how terrifying the experience had been and I recall being suspicious about this, but he redeemed himself that evening when he arranged for me to be a passenger in a speedboat towing a water-skier. The Shackleton was once memorably described — by someone in one of the crews that had to fly them decades after they should have been superseded — as not so much an aircraft as 30,000 rivets flying in close formation. The old planes are gone now, but as we head towards Forres again we see something even more impressive in a way; enormous straggling, undulating lines and skeins of birds — geese, maybe, though they're too far away to be sure — filling the skies above the distant dunes and forests.

The A940/939 south from Forres to Grantown largely follows an old military road, and it's just a peach; a beautiful ribbon of tarmac that climbs wriggling out of the sandy-soil-rooted pines near the coast through sunny forested hills towards the open moors by Lochindorb before starting to descend into the trees again, its course shadowed by the remains of an old and now dismantled railway. It must have been a spectacular railway journey. Even the bare bleached bones of this old line are impressive. The bridges, viaducts and tunnel facings have had Scottish Baronial detailing lavished on them; chunkily dressed confections of quality stone crowned with medieval-lite machicolation. Arguably a bit fussy and certainly functionally redundant, but I don't care; it all looks great; a gilt framing for this little masterpiece of a road.

"That's what it is," Dave says from the back seat as we pass near Lochindorb.

"What's what it is?"

"The reason I don't like this bit of Scotland as much as the west."

Jim and I look at each other. Jim shrugs. "Well, it can't be too many distilleries."

"Not enough water," McCartney says emphatically.

I'm confused. "What, with the whisky?"

"No," Dave says. "Not enough lochs."

"Not enough lochs?"

"Aye. This rolling scenery and rivers stuff is fine, but the coast isn't indented enough and there should be more lochs."

"Sea lochs? Inland lochs?"

"Both."

"He's got a point," Jim says. "There is a distinct lack of large bodies of open water in this neck of the woods."

"And I'd like more mountains," Dave tells us, patently warming to his theme. "Proper jaggedy ones."

I glance at Jim. "By God, he's a hard man to please."

"McCartney's geographical requirements are notoriously severe."

"Anything else you'd like?" I ask. "Major island groups, an isthmus or two? Volcanoes?"

"Na. Just the lochs and mountains would do."

"Leave it with us, Dave," Jim says.

"Absolutely. We'll see what we can do."

McCartney looks satisfied. "Aye, well. In your own time."

Back to the Poacher's Bar for the warm evening; more pool, food and drink. But only after a visit to the chalet, and our rapidly increasing stocks of fine whisky. As a result of this I'm in a sort of pleasantly befuddled, slightly giggly mood. I go out to the old-fashioned phonebox to phone home but there's no answer. Instead of putting the phone down I kind of get fixated on the wee *bee-bop* (pause) *bee-bop* tone the phone makes just to tell you it is a pay phone. After a while it starts to sound like it's actually saying, *fuck off* (pause) *fuck off* and I start to laugh. This gets quite bad, and I have to put the phone down, take a few deep breaths and dry my eyes before going back into the bar for another game of pool. Which I only lose, I'm convinced, because I keep getting little quakey aftershocks of giggles, usually just as I'm taking a shot.

We have fun in the bar. This is our natural habitat, on this side of the bar. The time — the many years — when we were involved with the Clachan Bar in Dornie seems like a long and terrible aberration. Jim ran the place, then Dave — with Dave's girlfriend Jenny coming through from Aberdeen whenever she could — and even Ann and I took over for a week to give Dave and Jenny some time off. There were high points, but basically it was one long disaster. Somehow between us all we succeeded in investing over a quarter of a million pounds in the place and then selling it for 50 grand. No amount of creative accounting on Earth is going to turn that into anything other than a financial catastrophe. Oh well; we're all still alive and mostly talking to each other.

We retire to the chalet to test the bamboozling nine-layer game again, drink more wine and whisky, imbibe ourselves silly and play Scrabble.

At some point in the evening Jim comes up with another Mystery Word; an Azshashoshz of our days.

"Awemsys."

"Awemsys?"

"Did he just say awemsys?"

"Yes. He just said awemsys. You did, didn't you?"

"What?"

"Just say awemsys."

"Oh aye, yeah, that was me."

"So?"

"So what?"

"So what does it mean?"

"Yeah, what *does* it mean?"

"I don't know."

"You said it; you must know what you were trying to say."

"I forget."

"You *forget*?"

"Yeah, I forget."

"Well, try to remember."

"Remember what?"

"Don't try to be funny."

The tragic thing is, at one point later on in the wee small hours Dave and I *do* remember what Jim was saying (despite the fact that what he meant to say actually sounded nothing like awemsys), and get that Ah-*hah* moment, and agree we've cracked it. *That* was what awemsys was supposed to mean; of course!

. . . Except by the next morning we've forgotten it again.

Head crash: talking on empty.

(The following was discovered on my laptop's hard disk. I'm fairly certain this is what was said but I wouldn't be so confident about ascribing identities. Anyway, I think it sort of mumbles for itself.)

Robin Genius is a genius.
   What?
   Robin Genius is a genius.
   Robin Genius is a genius?
   Yes. Robin Genius is a genius! Why? What's the problem?
   Robin Genius is a genius?
   Aye!
   You meant Robin Williams, didn't you?
   Don't be too sure. He might mean Robbie Williams.
   Now you're being even more ridiculous than him.
   How am I being ridiculous?
   You meant Robin Williams, didn't you? That he's a genius.
   That's what I said. Robin Genius is a genius.
   He said it again.
   You said it again.
   Robin Williams is a genius?
   No!
   Yes!
   What?
   Eh?
   What do you mean, No?
   What do *you* mean, *Yes*?
   I meant, no, that's not what he said. That was what he thought he'd said, but it wasn't what he actually said. Not the first couple of times. That's what I meant. What did you mean?

I meant, yes, he finally got it right.

What the fuck are you two gibbering about?

You, ya numpty. (disparagingly:) Robin fuckin Genius.

Robin who?

Oh, don't start again.

What's he on, anyway?

The same as us. (sound of bottle being tapped)

I was afraid of that.

You guys are starting to talk shite. I'd better open another bottle and pour us all a drink.

We're starting to —?

Ssh! Let the man concentrate.

. . . anyway, he's been rubbish since he went to Hollywood.

In a way I'd like to report that we spent most evenings engaged in deep discussions about the Iraqi War (Part Deux), its provenance, course, likely repercussions and mooted sequels, but by this time there's little left to say. The war is as good as won, we're told, with just some mopping up to be done while the search goes on for those fiendishly well-hidden WMDs.

The three of us know each other so well there's not much chance any one of us going to surprise the other two by saying something like, "Oh no, I was all for the war." All there's been are a few, brief, bitter exchanges confirming we each despise the illegitimate, warmongering scumbag bastard who's in ultimate charge of our armed forces, and that we don't have a lot of time for Tony Blair either.

We play Dave's game instead, where the takings and the victories are bloodless, and where, as in most games, there are no civilians.

McCartney: the case for madness.

It took us years to convince Dave he was crazy. Even the driving under the truck thing didn't count according to him. To this day he claims that driving underneath a 40-tonne truck in a tiny little Fiat X1/9 sports car just to avoid having to abandon an overtaking manoeuvre halfway through was an entirely sensible thing to do. I could rest my case there, but McCartney won't let me.

The Fiat X1/9 — the baby Ferrari as it was called at the time — was a beautifully balanced if rather underpowered little car with a targa top you could take off and stow in the boot. Dave foolishly let me have a shot of the car one night in darkest Fleet Street, in the old days when they still printed papers there; I had a great time whizzing through the narrow streets, dodging giant lorries loaded with ten-tonne rolls of newsprint.

Dave was driving the car in north London one bright, sunny day in the early eighties, behind a big articulated truck. He started to overtake, then — when he was about midway along the side of the artic — saw a traffic island ahead blocking his route. Now, he had the top off, so he could see that from the top of the Fiat's A-pillar — in other words the top of the windscreen — to the bottom of the truck's platform there was a gap of a few inches, and, the X1/9 being quite a small, short car, there was plenty of room between the tractor unit hauling the thing and the double set of axles at the rear. Back then there were no safety barrier rails hanging underneath long trucks to stop cars submarining underneath in a side-on crash and so decapitating their occupants, so Dave just swung the car half-underneath the truck (his side was still in the sunlight), waited for the traffic island to disappear astern, then swung back out again and completed the overtake.

Is there anybody out there reading this who fails to understand what an act of utter insanity this really was? It surely can't just be me. I've tackled McCartney on this a dozen times or more and every time Dave protests loudly that it was a perfectly safe and even sensible thing to do. He's a persuasive arguer as well, the swine, and a few times I've almost found myself agreeing with him, but never quite.

"McCartney, *I'm* fucking crazy, but I'd never do that!"

"Well, that's just you being blinkered. It was the rational response at the time."

"What are you talking about?"

"I could see really clearly there was loads of room, because the roof was off. I probably wouldn't have done it if there had been somebody else in the passenger's seat; they might have got upset, but there wasn't. So I did."

"What if the truck driver had seen you?"

"Maybe he did."

244

"How could he have? If he had he'd have done what any rational person would have done and braked on instinct, panicking because he's just seen a nutter drive under his truck! You'd have ploughed into the tractor unit's rear tyres, bounced off again and then the rear trailer axles would have rolled right over you! You'd have been paste!"

"Aye, but it didn't happen, did it?"

"But it could have!"

"But it didn't. I don't know what you're getting so upset about."

"I'm not upset! I just think you're crazy but you won't admit it."

"It wasn't crazy; it was a perfectly good bit of overtaking with a sort of wiggle in the middle. You'd have done the same."

"That's my point! I wouldn't!"

"How do you know?"

"Because it's a patently insane and crazy thing to do!"

"Why?"

"Dave; *you drove under a truck.*"

"Well, put like that . . ."

And so on.

What ought to have finally persuaded Dave he was insane was when he, Jim and Dave's then girlfriend Jenny bought that damn pub in the Highlands despite the fact nobody concerned had any experience running any sort of licensed premises, or even a shop. This seemed like a good idea at the time, but wasn't. I remember sitting in Dave's house in Uxbridge along with Jim, trying to convince them they were both mad — in fact that all three of them were mad — but they weren't having it.

Ah, Dornie. It's hard not to like a place set in the midst of glorious mountain scenery with one of the world's most picturesque castles barely a stone's throw away, but in the case of Dornie it was worth making the effort. There were some good, friendly people there, in the village and the area, but working behind the bar at the Clachan was enough to convince you the village was home to a disproportionate number of chip-shouldered, hypocritical, right-wing sexist shites.

They'd put down their copy of the *Sun* long enough to tell you in some detail what they'd like to do to these hippies who smoked dope and dropped E, then they'd order their eighth or ninth whisky of the day and plenty of change for the cigarette machine. Later they'd drive off. Or, sometimes, the wife or the daughter would arrive by car and try to drag them out of the bar to take them home for their tea.

These guys could even turn what ought to be an act of generosity into one of aggression. I came to think of it as Aggressive Dramming. Aggressive Dramming usually took place when you'd told a bunch of these people you weren't drinking, or at least weren't drinking much — maybe because you were going to be driving later — but then found the bar in front of you filling up with unasked-for whiskies whenever you turned your back. Insisting, even with a smile, that you really had meant what you said and therefore wouldn't be drinking the whiskies tended to be met with scowls and accusations of being a Poof (in a seriously homophobic, non-ironic manner). A surlier bunch of rednecks you couldn't wish to avoid.

There were occasional fights. I think I feel the same way about men who start pub brawls as I do about countries that start wars.

Anyway, if Dave, Jim and Jenny were mad, so was I, because later on I put money into the pub.

It was in Uxbridge one night that Dave and I got to talking about why, despite me starting to make mildly serious money from my books, I had no intention of buying a Ferrari.

"Because I'd just get all over-enthusiastic with it and wrap the fucker round a bit of Highland scenery and kill myself," I told him, sort of semi-presciently.

Dave looked thoughtful. He nodded slowly. "That would be a terrible, terrible waste," he said solemnly (and like an idiot, I started to make a bashful, self-deprecating gesture of acknowledgement), before he added, "of a beautiful car."

Ditto Brown: telling who your real friends are.

Summer 1981; one night. Jim and I walking back up Adelaide Road en route to McCartney's flat after an evening listening to bands at Dingwall's, Camden Lock. The south side of Adelaide Road consists, for one long stretch, of a brick wall — maybe nine or ten feet or so high — with a steep embankment behind it sloping

247

down to the main railway line leading to Euston. I was still in my Drunken Urban Climbing period, and had shinned up a bus stop sign to get onto the top of the wall so I could walk along the top. Jim was keeping pace on the pavement below. He shouted up;

"Banksie?"

"What?"

"Do you trust me?"

"Of course I trust you."

"You sure?"

"Positive."

"Okay. Throw yourself off the wall and I'll catch you."

"What?"

"Throw yourself off the wall and I promise I'll catch you."

"Are you insane; we'll probably both break our necks."

"No, we won't. Come on!"

"You're fucking mad."

"I can do it. I know I can. You'll come to no harm. Trust me."

"James, we're both very drunk indeed. This is a bad idea."

"Ach, just dae it anyway."

I considered. "As ever your impeccable logic has proved too much for me, my fine friend. I'll do it." I stopped and got ready to jump down onto Jim.

He moved out into the street a little. "Na, wait."

"What?"

"You've got to jump off backwards."

"*What?*"

"It's too easy if you jump off forwards; you'll see that I'm there to catch you."

"Ah," I said, seeing what he meant. "You're right." I thought. "Could I not just keep my eyes closed?"

"Don't be daft, you're bound to open them; only natural. It's a lot simpler if you just turn round and jump off the wall backwards."

"Oh, well, what the hell. Okay." I turned round, then shouted over my shoulder. "Ready?"

"No. Hold on a minute. There's a bus coming." We waited until the bus had passed. I waved at people on the top deck, then turned round again.

"Ready?"

"Ready!"

I threw myself backwards off the wall.

Jim caught me — well, broke my fall — and we ended up sprawled in the middle of the road.

"You okay?" Jim wheezed.

I rolled over and stood up. "Seem to be. You?" I put out a hand and helped him up.

"Fine," he said, limping to the pavement with a pained look on his face. Then he grinned at me triumphantly. "See?"

I shook my head. "You're aff your fuckin heid, pal."

We walked on, only stopping at one of the high flats further up Adelaide Road to try to get out onto the roof to look at the view of London By Night. We hauled ourselves up through a hatch into the lift machinery space, but that was as far as we got; the outside door was locked.

(I asked Jim to look over this story to make sure I wasn't getting anything wrong and he said that for him the funniest bit was right at the start, when we'd been walking up the road. He must have been looking at something across the street or otherwise have become distracted because he didn't notice me shinning up the bus stop and climbing to the top of the wall in the first place; he thought I was still walking along beside him and when he turned to talk to me couldn't understand where I'd gone. I seemed to have disappeared. He stood there confused for a few moments, looking all around, then shouted "Banksie?" I said, "Hello," — wittily, obviously — from above head height and that was when he realised where I was. Jim also claims the wall was only eight feet high, but — ha! — he wasn't the one standing up there.)

"Banksie, what's this thing here that says 'Palm'?"

"Oh, that's for the Palm Tungsten handheld thingy I got for going on the Trans-Siberian. I should have returned it and got my money back after we junked the passports but I kind of took to it. Especially the wee fold-out keyboard thing; that's just totally brilliant. I mean, I've never actually used it, but . . . Anyway, that folder on the laptop called Palm is for the software that lets the laptop and the Palm talk to each other."

"Awright. Not porn, then."

"Eh?"

"Not porn."

"Of course not porn; I don't *have* any fucking porn."

"What, really?"

"Really."

"You serious?"

"Yes, I'm serious."

"Awright. I just thought when it said 'Palm' it might mean . . ."

"What?"

"Nothing."

Next day is Friday and we have to leave; originally we'd meant to have the whole week but Jim has to be back home for the weekend so we settle up and head south through another Whew-it's-a-scorcher-sez-the-Scum-stylee day.

However we get to see wolves, which is entirely the coolest thing about this day. They're at the Highland Wildlife Park, between Aviemore and Kingussie, along with enormous black Highland cattle, European bison, Przewalski's horse and just about every animal presently or ever associated with Scotland. The wolves have their own big enclosure so they don't eat the other animals, and they pad quietly along their bit of green hillside like grey ghosts, stealthily impressive. We investigate the smaller forest enclosure where various birds and polecats, wildcats and pine martens hang out, some of the latter in caged areas linked by a complicated system of aerial runs made of wood and wire mesh, reminding me oddly of a train set. Mostly the animals are pretty quiet, but they look dozily content on this hot day.

The golden eagle does not look happy; it has a fair-size rocky bit of hillside fenced off for its use but it keeps launching itself at the hessian side netting as though trying to escape, and its enclosure just isn't big enough, not by about a mountain range or so. I'd rather see some well-shot high definition film of an animal like this than have to watch it suffer in what must seem to it like a punishment cell. Actually I'd rather see a grainy black and white photo than this; it's the only off-note in the park, which otherwise seems well set out for the comfort of the animals. Well, having said that, the café isn't great either, but we have a snack that is at least edible and head for our homes through what feels like summer heat.

Even the Jag is sounding like it's got all cranky in the high temperatures, idling at 1500 revs and running on after the ignition's been switched off, coughing and popping before spluttering to a stop. I contemplate trying to fiddle with its carbs, maybe adjust the slow running jets, but I'm worried I'll just make matters worse, so just let it rev away; I'll book it in for a service tomorrow.

We take a certified long-distance multiple GWR; the great A9 short cut, leaving the main road just before the end of its longest dual carriageway section to head over the hills for Trinafour, Tummel Bridge, Schiehallion and the Appin of Dull (for about three decades I've meant to stop and take a photograph of me standing to the side of the sign that says "Dull"; finally I get to). Past Castle Menzies and through Weem for Aberfeldy. Near the Castle is the House of Menzies, which is a sort of combined art gallery, coffee shop and upmarket off-licence formed out of some attractively preserved farm buildings. I have spent far too much money here in the past, taking away a crate at a time of interesting New World wines and the odd rare whisky. Somehow I manage to resist its siren call this time.

Aberfeldy is approached over an old light-controlled one-way humpback bridge. Another of General Wade's. General Wade was the geezer charged with building roads over large parts of the Highlands after the '45 rebellion, to make quelling any future uprisings easier. Visible from the summit of Wade's structure is an elegant looking footbridge which is made of plastic. I seem to recall this was hailed on a long-ago edition of *Tomorrow's World* as the future of small bridge-building, though that may have been a little optimistic. Aberfeldy's a neat little town with good places to eat, several huntin' shootin' fishin' campin' hillwalkin' type shops (the kind Les claims have lights above the door just for me), a good butcher's and an outfitters with an intriguing upstairs bit that sells antiques and lace, though the opening hours seem a little erratic.

The road rises steeply out of the town, winding up towards the long undulating straights which carry us across the moors for Amulree and the Sma' Glen before we rejoin what feels like the world of ordinary roads again at Gilmerton. When I was working up at Nigg and coming back to Gourock at weekends — in the seventies when the A9 still went through a lot of the towns it now bypasses — this short cut genuinely did save time. Nowadays the A9, for all its faults, is a lot quicker, and this route just presents a more interesting way to go, not a faster one. Heading for Fife I'd normally aim for Gleneagles from Muthill (I've never stopped to check, but I'd lay odds the locals pronounce it Moothill or something similar, rather than the obvious way), however today we take the original shortcut route, on a wee daft road pointing straight at Braco. Then it's cross-country round the back of the Fintry Hills for Dalmuir to drop Jim and onwards across the Erskine bridge to Greenock to deposit Dave.

"I wasn't really tetchy, was I?" I ask as Dave retrieves his bag from the boot.

"I've seen you worse. Like the time you straight-armed the controls off that Pelican crossing in Glasgow."

"So," I say brightly, "not that tetchy."

"Definitely not *that* tetchy."

I decide I'll settle for this, bid Mr McC. a hearty farewell, climb into my comically over-revving Jag and hightail it back to sunny Fife.

CHAPTER
TEN

Welcome to the Land of Heederum-Hawderum

Porsche time. Indeed, 911 time. We have a light blue 964 model Carrera 4 Cabriolet on a K plate, so it's about ten years old right now. The "4" means it's four-wheel drive. This is not so you can take it off road, it's to give the little blighter more grip in the wet and try to tame the notoriously tail-happy behaviour 911s have exhibited since the sixties because they have the engine in the wrong place, i.e. hanging out astern of the rear wheels.

It's a creaky, rattly, bangy kind of place to be, the 911, when the top's down. Actually it's a fairly noisy old thing even when the top is up, when, in addition, it feels dark and claustrophobic, but then it's almost never used with the hood closed unless we've gone out in sunlight and encountered unexpected rain. The 911 is another unexpectedly relaxing and limit-friendly car to drive, because — while it will very happily scream along at three-figure speeds with the hood stowed, and give every impression of enjoying it — it feels just as content at much lower speeds.

Happy cars: in defence of anthropomorphism.

This is all, obviously, about our perceptions, about human comfort, in the end; when we talk about a car enjoying a certain speed all we mean is that we feel happy with the sensations we experience while in the car at that velocity, based on our earlier experiences of being in cars. To the extent that a car exhibits (in the widest sense) behaviour, this is what makes us treat it as alive even though we know perfectly well that it isn't. The conceit of ascribing emotional states to cars or other vehicles is simply shorthand for expressing our knowledge of the parameters within which the vehicle is designed to perform and its current relationship to — and position within — those parameters.

A degree of mechanical sympathy is necessary here; an even moderately good driver should experience a degree of discomfort if they hear an engine being overrevved, and, equally, when a person feels that a car is humming along, engine singing, their sensation that the car is "happy" probably reflects as accurately as possible a state in which the vehicle is performing just as its human designers intended it to in those conditions.

So, in the 911, with the top down, wind roar and hair-mussing tend to increase beyond the acceptable at very much more than a mile per minute, and certainly when sustaining such speeds for long periods, and it's that feeling of being battered by the slipstream that tends to rein in any accelerator-flattening proclivities while you're exposed to the elements.

And exposed to the elements is how you jolly-well should be driving it, of course, unless it's absolutely bucketing with rain (though, thanks to the effects of that same slipstream, you can drive with the top down in quite heavy rain and still keep dry. Until, of course, you stop, say at traffic lights. Then you get soaked). Nevertheless, it has to be said the number of people driving soft tops with the hood raised on beautiful sunny days is one of road life's more perplexing enigmas.

And it doesn't have to be a scorcher, either. Some of the most fun to be had with a convertible is in the winter, when you get a fine, clear, crisp sunny day. You'll need outdoor clothing, and a hat and gloves probably, even with the heating turned up, but the sheer joy of zipping through the winter countryside with a blue sky above and somewhere or nowhere in particular to go is entirely worth the effort, even if you do sometimes get the odd funny look.

There is an even more esoteric kind of joy to be had driving in the country with the top down at night, though this is best in the summer. Then it's the smells you notice. Your nose gets more of a workout in a soft top than it would in a closed car anyway, but something about a summer evening darkening into night seems to bring out the scents of the surrounding land with particular intensity.

Perhaps equally esoterically, in a 911 you come to appreciate things you'd never think of appreciating, like

257

driving past walls, under bridges and through tunnels. These hard surfaces all reflect engine noise (it's behind you, remember, so you're always leaving the sound behind, never driving through it as you would in a front-engine car) and the engine noise a 911 makes is definitely something worth hearing; a bassily metallic clatter like a sextet of barely muffled pneumatic drills.

For my next trip I will require the help of a member of the choochter race . . . Ken MacLeod is a proper Islander, from Lewis, in the Outer Hebrides — also collectively known as the Long Island, which sounds more romantic (and a large part of the character of these isles is created by the tension between their undeniably romantic appearance and the effort and practical compromises required to live there all year long).

Ken's family come from Skye and Lochcarron, on the mainland. He was brought up on Lewis — with lots of brothers and sisters — until his father, who was a minister in the Free Presbyterian Kirk, moved to Greenock in the sixties. This was a considerably more traumatic relocation than mine from Fife to Gourock at about the same time. We just moved from one coast to another, about 70 miles across Scotland's central industrial belt. For the MacLeods, especially the young ones, leaving the wild, bare purities of Lewis's Atlantic coast for Greenock with its smoke and bustle, its teeming tenements and crane-stacked shipyards must have seemed like moving to a different country, almost another planet.

We met in Greenock High School. Ken was joint editor of the school magazine and had heard I wrote stories (through Les, I've always suspected). *My* version is that I was at school enjoying a free period, lying on the grass slope overlooking the school playing fields watching the sixth-year girls playing tennis, when MacLeod suddenly appeared in front of me, his feet encased by big tackety boots and his thick tweed trousers held up by a leather belt that looked like it had come off a diving suit. I put my shades down, raised my eyebrows and said, "Hmm?"

"I hear you write stories," he said in a sing-song voice.

"Yeah, I suppose," I said, very coolly (while thinking, What's that bastard McFarlane dropped me in now?).

"Would you like to write one for the school magazine?"

"Yeah, sure, man," I said. I put my shades down and leant to one side, trying to see round him or at least give the impression that the sixth-year girls required my full attention.

I did write the story but it had mild swearing in it and Ken's co-editor, a teacher, wanted the swearing taken out, so it never appeared in the magazine. I was still in my full-on pun period, so this was no great loss.

(Ken's version of how we met is entirely different and possesses the additional merit of being true. However I don't come out of it nearly so coolly so I haven't thought to trouble you with it here.)

Ken and I became good friends, discovering a mutual love of both science fiction and writing. We developed a relationship that revolved around swapping short stories and ideas for novels, and which included me, on a Friday morning, telling Ken about the previous evening's *Monty Python*, because Ken's home had no television. The small Calvinist sect Ken's dad was a minister within was and is eye-wateringly strict. I've unconsciously caricatured its outlook in the past as a blanket belief that theatre, cinema and television were all regarded as evil in themselves, but it's not as simple as that.

It boils down to a Puritan objection to drama, which is associated in the Free Presbyterian mind with lasciviousness, and it's lasciviousness which is A Really Bad Thing (this goes back to the fairly bawdy theatre that existed in Britain between the reigns of James VI and Charles II). Exceptions are made for the classics, though whether this includes Shakespeare on a close reading — the phrase "country matters" and the like — appears to be moot. Factual stuff of a non-prurient nature is okay, though given that you don't see many documentaries on stage and precious few on general release in the cinema, both media are largely shunned. Radio is mostly all right but television is suspect (I can't help wondering if TV is slightly more okay in theory nowadays given that a quick blip on the remote is all it takes to remove something unsavoury from the screen; at the time we're talking about here the only way to change channels was to leap across the room and twist the tuning dial or stab at a mechanical preset button or the off-switch — much slower. On the other hand there was no Channel Five back then either).

260

Books are fine — indeed respected — and even novels are okay, strictly providing there's no smut (that House of Stuart again; racy novels of the 1600s; tsk). Singing in church is permitted, but must be unaccompanied. The Sabbath is observed with some severity; no going for a walk unless it's to and from church (and no taking the scenic route) and no reading unless it's religious in nature.

I always felt kind of sorry for the MacLeod family, and especially for Ken because as the eldest he seemed to have had the most authoritarian upbringing of all, but for all the — by modern standards almost laughably grim — strictness imposed by the Reverend and Mrs MacLeod, they were a loving and protective family, and — unless they're really some secret siblinghood of mad axe murderers or something — Ken and all his brothers and sisters seem to have grown up to be well-adjusted, well-educated, functional and productive members of society, with flourishing families of their own.

More than I can claim, I guess.

Anyway, with no telly, and it being perfectly obvious to me and my pals that *Python* was the best thing on TV at the time and hence the only thing worth talking about the following morning, it seemed only fair to keep Ken in the loop by recounting as much as possible of each programme to him before register class (I wasn't the only person doing this — Les and others did too, though I maintain I was the most enthusiastic). I doubt my memory would be up to it these days, but at the time I used to quite enjoy the process.

Ken and I have taken entirely different routes to getting published; I wrote six books and a million words of purple prose, picked up rejection slips from every reputable publisher in London and — very gradually — learned some important things the hard way (such as: It's often what you leave out that's most effective, and: You rarely need that many adjectives, Iain), while Ken talked about writing a novel for twenty years and always seemed like he was just about to start, but never did — so that his friends started to despair that he ever would — then sat down, wrote a book called *The Star Fraction* and got it published by the first publisher he sent it to.

I pick Ken up from South Queensferry on yet another brilliantly sunny morning; perfect convertible weather. Ken and Carol live on Society Road, which is part of the approach to Hopetoun House, Scotland's grandest stately home. I feel like I know Hopetoun fairly well by now; I've recorded a TV programme there, done the tour a couple of times (fine view of the bridges from the roof), taken photos of Ken in the grounds (in my Kim Sabinan, ace photographer, persona) and — when we were taking in the gardens with Les and Aileen one sunny day in 2002 — got to watch the Worshipful Company of Archers on one of their ceremonial practice shoots.

This was great fun; all these toffs in tartan trews and bonnets with feathers in them whanging arrows from man-tall long-bows over the giant fountain towards straw targets hundreds of yards away. The McFarlanes and I thought it would have been more sporting if they'd left the fountain working and had to shoot over the top of it, but that's by the by. And a particularly tall and impressive fountain it is too, if I may say so, and obviously I speak as one who's cased a few.

One of the archers came over to where we were sitting on a grassy bank watching all this to explain to us what was going on, which was very kind of him and I suspect quite decent and understanding too, given that we were probably letting down the general tone of things by applauding what appeared to us to be especially good shots.

From Society Road it's conveyor belt to the end of the M9 south of Dunblane, then the small but perfectly formed B824 to Doune. (This is where the Python boys filmed the Rude Frenchman/Trojan Rabbit scenes in *Holy Grail*.) Through Callander to Strathyre where the road opens out properly and then the usual A85/A82 to Fort Bill. The weather is just stunning, the mountains' summits are still brushed with snow and the hills and trees and lochs just shine with light. Ken drinks in the view and smokes the occasional cigarette — I got special dispensation from Ann for this so long as the top is down.

We talk about ideas for future novels and about the different histories of spirit-making in Scotland and Ireland, wondering why Scotch is so well developed as an international drink and Irish whiskey much less so. We speculate that maybe it's something to do with the reliance of the Irish on potatoes while the Scots had all this barley which they might as well use, effectively preserve and maybe make some hard cash from, by turning into spirit. The local ambient temperature might have something to do with it, too; you need cold water — and it's a case of pretty much the colder the better as long as it's not actually ice — to cool the spirit vapour as it exits the still, and Ireland's relatively balmier climate might make efficient home or farm distilling just that little bit less effective than in Scotland.

I mention how expensive Scotch was in Cyprus compared to the local brandy and we end up reminiscing about Rotten Drinks We've Had Abroad, Ken's being a Turkish gin which he describes as not just rough, but inclined to hang around your sinuses like a drunk ghost in a damp castle.

I've loaded a bunch of CDs for the journey but at no point in the two days do we even turn the player on; there's neither point nor need when the top's down, and that's the way it stays for the whole trip save for overnight at Portree.

We stop for lunch at the Prince's House in Glenfinnan. It seems odd being in Glenfinnan and not seeing the McFarlanes, but they're still at the school and we have a ferry to catch. The Prince's House is the other hotel in Glenfinnan, right on the main road near the station. Our usual watering hole in the village is the Glenfinnan House Hotel, down by the loch and just a couple of minutes along the shore from Les and Aileen's. This place is known in the village as the Lodge, but you have to be careful; many years ago I was trying to contact the hotel and unthinkingly rang the number for Glenfinnan Lodge given in the phone book, only to get whoever was in the estate shooting lodge at the time. I rang back just to be sure and he was not a happy toff.

We used to come up to the Prince's House fairly often until some new owners, wanting to go upmarket, removed the pool table and just generally brought about an ambience in the place that wasn't as local-friendly as it might have been. A real era ended for us when the Lodge took out its pool table too. Chimney-farting antics aside, we had some great times there and the pool table going was a real blow. These days as a rule we sit around Les and Aileen's dinner table and drink wine rather than go to the Lodge for beer. It's fun, and home apart there's almost nowhere I feel happier, but I still miss the pool table. Place is a laundry room or something now. Very sad.

(If Les was reading this right now he'd be indignantly making the point that these days I do have my own pool table, over in my parents' house, but that isn't the same either.)

The Prince's House has another set of owners now; it's a bit quiet when we stop but the soup and sandwiches are good and we head off into the sunlight again. The road to Mallaig is a GWR which is gradually becoming just a great road. It's another split-personality work; fabulously long, open straights sweeping past breathtaking views suddenly plunging into tiny twisty sections wriggling through the trees or rolling abruptly into the straggling villages on the tattered rockscape of coast. This is *Local Hero* territory; they shot a lot of exterior scenes out this way, and the bits in the office of the head man Happer — played by Burt Lancaster — were apparently filmed inside Ben Nevis distillery while it was mothballed. Fort Bill standing in for downtown Dallas. Now there's a thought that wouldn't strike you every day.

Most of the time the railway from Fort William to Mallaig is nearby, swerving from one side of the road to the other over a succession of concrete echoes of the Glenfinnan viaduct. There used to be a short cut through Arisaig where you could go straight on while the main road dipped left to the sea and round the front of the village, but that seems to be turning into a proper micro-bypass. At Morar, too, they're still working on the road, straightening and widening.

Finally we arrive in Mallaig for the ferry to Skye.

Nowadays, of course, you can take the bridge to Skye, at Kyle of Lochalsh, but I try to avoid taking this route if remotely possible. The Skye Bridge is grossly expensive to cross and is a glaring example of Why Private Finance Initiatives Are Shite. To use the Skye Bridge is to shovel money into the coffers of the Bank of America, which owns it and will be allowed to collect the grotesquely inflated tolls until 2022.

It wouldn't be quite so bad if there was any sign of this supposedly so damn spiffing competition capitalists keep whining about, but Caledonian MacBrayne, the still-just-about-nationalised-but-just-you-wait ferry company which operated ferries across the narrows between Lochalsh and Kyleakin, was told by the government it wouldn't be allowed to do so any more once the bridge opened, to force people to use the thing no matter how high the tolls were. And, as usual with PFIs, the taxpayer takes the risk and the shareholders pocket the profit. The Bank of America didn't even put up that much money to build the bridge in the first place; £6 million to the taxpayer's £15 million.

Locals on Skye and on the mainland — and various others with a love of the place and some sort of belief in putting people before profits — have fought a long and honourable campaign against the way the bridge is run since before it opened, and there is now just a chance that the bridge might be brought into public ownership, as the Scottish Parliament is considering buying the bridge. Doubtless the Bank of America's shareholders will walk off with a tidy profit, but at least we'll be rid of them.

In the meantime, in the holiday season, there's the not-yet-fucked-up-by-privatisation Cal Mac ferry from Mallaig to Armadale and the brilliant wee ferry between Kylerhea and Glenelg (which, to be fair, has never been anything other than privately owned, and works just fine). Both are worth making a detour for, lie at the ends of some great roads and are set in breathtaking, sigh-drawing scenery. The *Pioneer* takes us over to Skye in about twenty minutes, over a calm sea beneath a shining blue sky, attended by slow-flying gulls. To port, the single ramp of Eigg and the rounded mass of Rum bulk through a light sea haze; to starboard lies Knoydart. The peak of Ladhar Bheinn stands like a brown-black wing of rock stroked with white at the tip. We sip coffee and watch the gulls, gliding straight-winged a few metres off, soot-dark heads swivelling this

267

way and that as they scan for scraps and bits of thrown
food.

As we bump off the ferry at Armadale — the 911's
tyres making a rirring sound on the ramp's metal ridges
— a lone piper strikes up; a lanky kid struggling with
what may or not be the *Skye Boat Song*. Oh well, a
tourist thing. Ken and I look at each other.

Ken grins. "Welcome to the land of heederum-
hawderum."

The first part of the road from Armadale to the main
route between Kyle and Portree, Skye's capital, is either
single track or that awkward one-and-a-half-lane size;
the 911 is great on these roads mainly because it's so
small. It isn't furiously fast — the M5 makes it feel slow
— but it's quick enough, and it's wieldy. Being based
on so old a design — the body shell is much as it was
when originally designed in 1964 — the 911 is short,
and narrow.

It's the lack of width that pays off on Highland and
Island roads; you can squeeze past oncoming vehicles
on the one-and-a-half-lane bits without worrying
overmuch about scraping or losing bits of bodywork,
take blind bends that little bit quicker knowing that
even encountering an oncoming truck shouldn't mean
an emergency stop because you'll have the room to play
with, and any manoeuvres within passing places are a
lot easier. The four-wheel drive makes putting one or
two wheels off-tarmac in a passing place a much less
nervy experience too, and sometimes you can get round
another car between passing places — it's almost like

268

the 911 is drawing itself in and holding its breath for you.

The upper reaches of the A851 are newly widened but still curvy; bliss in the 911, especially in this weather. The main road is the A87 and it's a peach too; not too heavily trafficked and basically a glorious, gratuitous succession of gob-smacking views over hill and sea, huge straights, long, spooling curves, torque-hungry gradients and just enough slow bits through villages to trickle through while allowing one's passengers a better look at the view.

As we drive, it occurs to me that Skye, bridge or no bridge, still feels like an island. I look at the road, then at the relatively modest speed we're doing and think that on exactly the same road on the mainland, I'd probably be going faster. I've noticed this before; islands slow you down. I think it's something to do with knowing that, on an island, nowhere's too far away from where you are now, so what's the rush? Maybe, also, it's because by their nature islands are usually your destination on a holiday, and so you're not in any hurry to get anywhere else.

Having said that, we go straight through Broadford — Skye's second town after Portree — even though it's looking fairly groovy these days. Cool-looking craft shops and the like will have to wait for another visit; we are men on a mission and there's research to be done. At Sligachan we head west for Carbost, and the Talisker distillery. The hills rise rotundly all around, with the great jagged forest of peaks that is the Black Cuillins rearing over everything a few miles to the south. The

Cuillins are probably the most intense piece of large-scale verticality in Britain; a dark snaggle-ridged near-circle of rearing fractured geography bursting out of land and sea like a vast staggered series of frozen rock explosions.

Basking, I think, is the only word for Carbost on a day like this. The white of the distillery's walls reflects the sunlight like a ship's sail against the blue of sky and loch. We do the tour. Talisker should really be called Carbost because that's the name of the village; Talisker Bay lies over the hill five miles away. But what the hey. They use Black Isle barley here, malted at Glen Ord. There's a fair amount of peatiness (25 p.p.m. for those of you who were paying far too much attention back in Chapter 3; five times more than is in Glen Ord itself, though a lot less than the big peaty bruisers of Islay), however the water used is very peaty too, and it's reckoned this contributes to a marked degree of peatiness in the nose. The use of traditional outdoor worm tubs rather than the more modern column condensers sited inside next to the stills is reckoned to produce a more flavoursome result.

Talisker has produced whisky since 1831, with a break for World War Two and some rebuilding after a fire in 1960 (somebody left the access door on a still open, the low wines over-flowed and ignited on the coal fire underneath. But at least nobody was taking flash photos at the same time). In the very old days the local laird wouldn't allow a pier to be built, so the barrels had to be floated out to boats waiting in the loch — a spirit of selfish, short-sighted obstructionism that many modern Highland landowners seem only too happy to continue.

The weather is the threat to this year's production. Walking over the bridge in the car park we cross the stream that feeds the distillery, and it's barely a trickle down a channel obviously designed to take a flood; the dry winter and warm spring mean the hills above the distillery are nearly dry.

Talisker is a prodigious whisky, and one of the few that — I've heard it closely argued — never benefits from being watered down. It's like the Black Cuillin range itself; unique, fiercely intrusive, savagely spectacular, not for the faint-hearted but wildly rewarding for those prepared to tackle it. Representing the Islands in Diageo's Classic Malts range has given it some of the wider recognition it deserves, though you can imagine that some people, just taking a casual tasting, might find its uncompromising power off-putting. It's another Drambuie/Jacobite link, as it was Talisker, unsurprisingly, which was used in the original home-made version of the liqueur, available in the Broadford Hotel.

A rich orangey-red colour, Talisker exudes a lazy pungent, smoky peatiness backed up by a sudden landslide of flavours which wouldn't be out of place in a curry; spicy, peppery, nutty, salty, fruity, sweet and sour. Rolling in some time after this onslaught, the finish is like a blast of smoked seaweed wrapped around crushed peppercorns. Inhaled. A bit of a tube-clearer.

It's usually watered down to the unusual strength of 45.8 abv (and some caramel colouring is added), however the bottle I buy is a 60 per cent abv and only available at the distillery (it's hard for me to resist exclusives like this). This is one of the first bottles we open when we start our next round of tasting back in Fife, and it's the first to be finished. Talisker is the favourite whisky of a quite amazing number of people and I completely understand why; there really are few better.

We head for Portree by the B885, a GWR that leads over the hills from Bracadale, rippling thinly over the peat and diving through the forest before curving round and down into the town.

"And I'll have the Cuillin Skink too; never could resist a pun, and you rarely see them on a menu."

The waiter looks blank. "Sorry?"

"Cullen Skink," I say, pointing at the menu. "It says 'Cuillin Skink' here. Just saying I appreciate the joke."

"Umm," the guy says, frowning, "it's not a joke, actually, sir. That is how it's spelled."

"No, it isn't. There's no 'I' in Cullen Skink."

The waiter looks at the menu. "No, it's Cuillin Skink."

"I know that's what it says there," I tell him patiently, "but the dish is pronounced 'Kullin Skink', not 'Coolin Skink', and there's no 'i' in it. Look, it's an old East Coast dish and I know how it's spelled. My aunt Peg makes the best Cullen Skink I've ever tasted and I've seen it on dozens of different menus always spelled the same way. Trust me; I'm a Fifer." (I confess that's a line I've long wanted to use.)

"Okay, sir," the waiter says, but I can tell he's not convinced. "And will you be having any wine with your dinner?"

I just smile. "Yes, please . . ."

We're in the Cuillin Hills Hotel, Portree. This is a very pleasant hotel with beautifully kept gardens, good food, and — aside from those of the waiting staff on matters of pronunciation — brilliant views. We sit outside at a table on the lawn after dinner, drinking Talisker and soaking up the view of the broad bay and the moored boats, watching the lights of the town coming on while the dark distant mass of the Cuillins stands silhouetted against the golden-blue glow of the southern sky.

The Cuillins are, as we sit here and look at them, for sale. John MacLeod, the MacLeod of MacLeod, the 29th chieftain of the clan and the gent who owns the MacLeod ancestral home of Dunvegan Castle and large tracts of land on the island, including the Cuillins, has put the mountains up for sale. Ten million quid and they're yours. No takers yet, and obviously what the vast majority of people locally and with any interest in the island would like would be for the Scottish National Trust or a similar body to buy them. But that's a hell of a lot of money for something you can't actually *do* anything with (you suspect that Westminster would have a hard time forcing Edinburgh to let somebody start, say, a quarry).

We shall see. These are interesting and progressive times in Scottish land ownership. Thanks to the fact we have our own Parliament again, the last feudal country in Europe is finally showing signs of joining, well, the nineteenth century; the people who live on and make their living from the land are finally being given the right to own it. This has to be a good idea. Even if you were undecided about the merits of this sort of change you could tell it's a good thing just by the sort of people who're vehemently opposed to it: Peter de Savary, Mohammed al Fayed and most of the big private land owners.

It's still only late April, and it gets cold after the sun goes down, leaving the Cuillins stark against the glow, and black as their name, but it's worth staying for the midge-free view and nipping in to get jackets and gloves.

Another belly-banger of a breakfast, then we head north into serious scenery under a glorious blue sky edged with faint streaks of high cloud to the north. We're heading home today but there's plenty of time for some fun driving first. The A885 heads up the Trotternish Peninsula, threading the long wavy step of land between the sea cliffs to the east and the chaotically sundered escarpment complex of towers, tilted ridges, pinnacles, cliffs and ravines rising to the west.

Descending fractionally after the first gentle ascent out of Portree, the view opens out to display the great spearhead rock that is the Old Man of Storr standing precariously proud of the broken wave of rock behind, all of it poised over a slope of brindled forest and the twinned lochs Fada and Leathan. The sea cliffs to our right are best seen from the air or sea; a monumental fringe of ragged verticals and extreme slopes, riven with boulder-jumbled clefts, dotted with natural arches, pocked with caves and studded with rocks and a very few tiny islands. The best place to see the cliffs from land is at the car park where the short stream from Loch Mealt plunges over the rim rock towards the sea. The only slightly fancifully named Kilt Rock to the north displays its pleats of Middle Jurassic sedimentary rock to the wide expanse of breeze-ruffled sea leading to the hills of Wester Ross.

At Brogaig a perfect prince among GWRs heads due west out of that part of the long, straggled settlement that is Staffin and darts straight towards the cliffs of the Quiraing, curling its way across the rising slope of moor past rock formations with names like The Table, The Needle and The Prison before throwing itself upwards into the chaos of rock like a salmon leaping a torrent, zig-zagging up the broken face of the tumbled cliffs with a briefly tortuous Alpinicity only outshone by the Bealach-na Bo road to Applecross. Even that famous road struggles to match the sheer spectacle at the summit pass here; the view falls away in green folds of grass intagliated with burns and long lightning-path fissures in the peat, punctuated by unkiltered broken castles of rock and blue roundels of lochs before pausing at the dotted houses near the main road and then reaching out to the shining pale void of distant sea and the hazy frame of mainland mountains far beyond.

Blimey, I love this road and this view. The only time I had to use the Skye Bridge was when I was giving

275

Dave a lift to the court in Portree one winter to renew the pub's licence. The ferries don't run then, so I'd had no choice about using the bridge. It did mean that while McCartney went besuited to renew the Clachan's licence, I got to drive up here in the Drambuie 911 beneath a fine clear winter's sky, encountering drifts and streaks of snow towards the summit and a breath-sucking, eye-wateringly cold north-easterly wind when I got out at the top to take in the view. Probably shirt-sleeves wasn't that sensible either, even for me.

The time I saw the Pass of the Cattle at its best was, oddly enough, when there was a lot of cloud. I'd come to Dornie for a couple of days, arriving in the late evening. I'd persuaded Dave we should head as quickly as possible for Applecross and try to catch the sunset, but then — as we drove out of Ken's old stamping ground of Lochcarron — the cloud started to thicken to the west above us, and by the time we were swinging up the long loops of the road to the Bealach-na Bo we were inside the cloud, a grey mist everywhere, lights on and visibility down to under a hundred yards. For all its mountains, Scotland is a low country by Alpine standards, and when you hit cloud like this it's usually an utterly forlorn hope that you'll ever come out above it again into sunlight, but we reckoned there was just a chance, by the time we got to the long flat summit, that we'd strike lucky.

We cut back into the light on the last hairpin, rising above a sea of cloud that stretched towards the west and the half-set sun. Submerged beneath the horizon-wide expanse of white, almost all of Skye was invisible. Only the Cuillins rose above the ridged ocean of mists like a fabulous serrate island of darkness, stark, severe and serene.

"Your dad used to walk all this way?" We were heading south now, having zapped up to the ancient MacLeod stronghold of Dunvegan castle on Skye's north-west coast. MacLeod country indeed; the two hills known as MacLeod's Tables rose like decapitated miniature Fujis to our left. We were close to Roag, where Ken's father, Lachlan, had been brought up, looking for the house Ken remembered visiting a couple of times. We'd passed the building where Ken's dad had gone to school some way back and Ken reckoned there was still a bit to go to the house.

"Aye," Ken said, grinning. "In bare feet. And carrying a turnip for his lunch."

"Ah," I said, laughing. "An' *we* used to live in shoebox in't middle o' road an' eat hot gravel, but tell that to young folk today and do they believe you?"

Ken shook his head. "No, seriously."

"You're kidding," I said, glancing at Ken to see whether he was or not. "He really didn't have any shoes?"

"Shoes were for Sunday, for church."

"Dear God. What happened in the winter?"

"It got colder," Ken said, straight faced.

"And a fucking *turnip*?" I couldn't help laughing. "For lunch? Come on, that's got to be a joke, Ken."

"It wasn't his own lunch," Ken explained patiently. "It was for the pot. All the pupils brought something to make a stew and he usually contributed a turnip." He shrugged.

I shook my head. "Good grief." I thought I'd had it tough because we had slates and chalk for the first year at North Queensferry Primary School, back in 1959 (slates and chalk and a wee sponge, for clearing the slate. If you were good you were allowed a damp sponge because you could be trusted not to throw it at anybody. My sponge, I am ashamed to say, was dry after day one).

We find the house where Ken's dad lived when he was a boy; Ken takes a photo and we continue south along the A863 — Talisker distillery and Carbost visible across the loch — then retrace our route of yesterday along the grandly scenic coastal road, heading on to the turn-off for the narrow, twisty roller-coaster of a single-track road down to the small but perfectly formed ferry at Kylerhea.

The good ship *Glenachulish* is a micro car ferry; you could squeeze maybe half a dozen vehicles onto it. If two of them were motor bikes. It used to be the Ballachulish ferry until 1975 when the bridge was opened there. When it glides up to the slipway at Kylerhea the two guys operating it use leg power to turn the whole car deck round to face the right way so the cars can exit ahead; we clatter on along with one other vehicle. There's a dog that seems to be part of the crew too. It looks a lot like one of those slightly mad black-and-white collies that hides by farm gateways in the outer isles and jumps out to chase unsuspecting tourists and their cars, but proves friendly, before

278

exhausting itself being patted and going for a lie down in the shade of the loading ramp. It barely gets its head down when we bump gently against the slipway on the far side and its time for the hound to resume its duties, carefully watching the unloading and loading.

The Kyle here is very narrow indeed and the tide can surge through like a broad rushing river. My dad has tales of his old Admiralty boat, the *Mandarin*, making full speed ahead in the straits but nevertheless — the timing not being quite right and the ship encountering the still increasing force of the tide — finding herself going slowly backwards.

In the old days they swam their cattle over here before setting off on the long journey south via the droving roads to the cattle markets in Falkirk. You imagine they paid close attention to the state of the tide.

As the ferry ties up and nestles closer to the slipway, I watch the mooring rope as it straightens, tightening, quivering briefly with tension that wrings the water from it, drops spotting the ramp's pale slope of concrete.

From Glen Elg — ignoring the GWR round the coast to Arnisdale and Corran, and the route to the fine broch in Gleann Beag — the road twists and turns energetically up to the Bealach Ratagan — Ratagan Pass — to reveal one of the finest views in Scotland: Loch Duich and the Five Sisters of Kintail. As if hypnotised with the scenery, the road goes a bit mad after this, looping and writhing and swooping through the forest in a series of wild curves and heroically pitched gradients down towards the loch and the main road at Shiel Bridge. It's a tight, constrained wee drive; fun but a bit slow (it's more challenging as a hill climb going the opposite direction). The A87 from Shiel Bridge to Invergarry on the other hand is, as mentioned in Chapter 7, just superb.

It's the usual route after that on the way south to South and then North Queensferry, via Spean Bridge and Dalwhinnie, then the Trinafour cut-off and — appropriately, given that we've been to Ken's nominal ancestral home at Dunvegan this morning — Castle Menzies near Weem, which is mine. That is, if you believe at all in all this clan stuff.

On the A86, passing the Fersit sign, I point out where the P-reg 911 came to grief. No, let's be honest; where I brought it to grief.

What Happened to My Car.

High summer, 1998. You could tell that it was the weekend for the annual T in the Park music festival just up the road from us at Balado because it was bucketing with rain. We were the proud owners of two 911s at the time; the old blue K-reg we still have, and a dark blue Carrera 4 coupé which was Ann's car. I was going up to Glenfinnan for the weekend and asked to take the coupé because the soft top has a bad and very un-Teutonic habit of leaking if left out in heavy rain. Ann was happy for me to take the coupé and the car and I had a grand old time even though it was raining so hard I almost thought I was in Glenfinnan already.

280

Everything went fine until that bit of road approaching the sign for Fersit.

I'd been pressing the car fairly hard over the last few miles and couple of dozen bends or so, whenever I could see I had a whole clear road ahead to play with, and the car hadn't shown any sign of going skittery at the back or anywhere else, but I just overcooked it totally on that curve; the rain was the heaviest it had been during the whole journey so far and there was a lot of standing water where the verges were struggling to clear the rain fast enough off the tarmac. A slight change of surface where one bit of road met another as I set the car up for the bend, and the back of the car spun away, sending the rear arcing round to my right.

What was really annoying was that I thought I'd caught it, twice; I opposite-locked, thought I'd got it straight, but then it went the other way, heading for the gentle slope of grass and heather on my own side of the road. I corrected again, still not braking, but the rear went whipping back to the direction it had first thought of and almost immediately we left the road and whumped up onto the very slightly uphill side of the road, connecting with a small raised ridge hanging a couple of metres over the tarmac. There was a very loud bang indeed and the airbag detonated. I think I must have closed my eyes at this point because when I got this terrific whack on the head it took me a moment or two to realise I'd rolled the car and I was now upside down, skidding along the road on the 911's roof. I'd have been hanging by my seat belt if the roof hadn't caved in to press on my head and the top of the driver's seat, so keeping me wedged in.

The bang on my head transmitted itself down my spine and I felt something sort of click in the middle of my back. (This didn't hurt at the time but gave me painfully sleepless nights a fortnight or so later when we were in South Africa, holidaying and doing publicity; I found the only way to alleviate the pain sufficiently to get to sleep was to lie in the bath.)

Round about here, sliding along the road upside down, I put my hands over my head (or under my head, if you want to be technical about it, given that I was inverted at this point). It did occur to me even at the time that this was a fairly pointless action, but I couldn't really come up with much else to do. I remember thinking, quite clearly, Oh, bugger; I could die here, and being kind of annoyed with myself; somehow there still hadn't been time to feel properly afraid. The sliding went on, then there was another not quite so dramatic impact, and then another thud, this time from beneath, and then silence.

I had, I realised, *smelled* the whole accident. There had been a damp, fresh, new-mown grass and earth odour as I'd slammed into the bank at the side of the road, then a sharp smell of something like flint, like rock when you strike it with another rock, then a scent of chalk, then burning, charring paint and hot oil.

I opened my eyes and looked around.

Well, I certainly appeared to be alive. The car was the right way up, sitting on what was left of its wheels just off my own side of the road on a patch of fairly level grass by a shallow slope of heather and fern. Definitely not poised rocking over a high cliff in an *Italian Job* kind of way. I moved my extremities, waggling fingers and toes, and everything seemed to be working. I couldn't feel much pain; back and head a bit sore, ears ringing, and I guessed I was slightly in shock so might not be entirely aware of any other injuries I might have, but really this was quite a good result after thinking only a second or two ago that I might be about to die. And no fire; the car did not appear to be showing any signs of going up in flames. That had to be a good thing.

On the downside, I recall thinking, it is still raining.

There was a white car stopped almost opposite me on the far side of the road with two people in it; they must have seen the last part of the accident as the car sailed upside down across the road in front of them and then flipped the right way up just across from them. The driver's side window was lowered and two pale young anxious faces, one male and one female, peered at me through the rain. I undid my seat belt, kicked at my door — it opened with only a minimum of complaint — got shakily to my feet on the grass, made a show of brushing myself down and said, "Aren't airbags wonderful?"

My only excuse for this pathetic piece of sub-Bondian attempted drollery, miserably inadequate though it may be, is that I must indeed have been a bit in shock.

The pale young couple were from New Zealand. There was no mobile coverage on that stretch of road so they very kindly took me to the Stronlossit Hotel in Roybridge, left me their address in case I needed them as witnesses (though all they had really witnessed were the final stages of the result of my spectacular stupidity) then went on their way.

I phoned Ann and then the cops.

"Hello. I've just had an accident on the A86 by the junction with the wee road to Fersit."

The guy at the other end took my name and details and established that I basically had a few minor cuts and bruises and that there were no other vehicles or persons involved. Then he asked, "Was there damage to any road furniture, Mr Banks?"

In my slightly dizzy state, this question caused the sudden, bizarre image to come to mind of a remote Highland road buffeted by driving rain, with a nice easy chair and a standard lamp with tassels on the shade sitting in the middle of the tarmac.

"Pardon?"

"Were any signs or crash barriers affected, sir? Any fences, that sort of thing?"

"Nothing. All the damage was to my car. Oh, and a dirty great rock about the size of a washing machine; think I hit that when I first left the road. It sort of tumbled into the ditch."

(I had the firm intention of having a brass plaque made to stick on this rock, commemorating the death of the P-reg 911, but before I got round to this the council cleared and re-formed all the ditches on that stretch of road, and my boulder disappeared.)

"But there's nothing blocking the road, or any damage to anything else at the roadside?"

"Nope."

"Well, you're actually through to the Inverness control centre here, Mr Banks, because the officer who'd normally deal with this sort of thing in Fort William is away. If you're sure you're all right we'll just leave it at that. Have you called anybody to remove the car from the roadside?"

"I'm going to call the AA next."

"Well, that should be all right then. I don't think we need take any further action."

"You mean you're not sending anybody out?"

"I don't think it's necessary if everything's as you say."

"Oh," I said. "Okay then. Right. Bye then."

I felt cheated. I called the AA. They said it'd be about an hour before they could get to me, and so, standing in the bar at the Stronlossit a little later, talking to the sympathetic young barman, I ordered a large glass of Laphroaig and a cigar. Might as well celebrate my narrow escape, I thought. I had the cigar between my fingers and the glass at my lips when the door opened and an AA man looked in. "There a Mr Banks here?"

I looked at the barman; he looked at me. I sighed and pushed the whisky over to him and left the cigar beside it. "Here; be my guest."

The AA guy found he couldn't tow the 911 on its undamaged wheels because it didn't have any and so had to call a local breakdown company with a ramped flatbed truck and a winch. I got a lift into Fort William and then a taxi to Glenfinnan, carrying the stuff I'd rescued from the car. I finally did get a whisky, sitting in Les and Aileen's house while Les answered a call from Ann, making sure I was still okay.

". . . aye, he mentioned he took a bump to the head," Les said, standing in the hall looking in at me. There was a pause while he listened to whatever Ann was saying in response to this, then he told her, "No, he's telling the truth; no bleeding or anything." A further pause while Ann spoke, obviously asking another question, then Les nodded, looked at me in a serious, measured sort of way and said into the phone, "Well, no more oddly than usual."

CHAPTER ELEVEN

The Smell of a Full Scottish Breakfast in the Morning

The following week we have a slightly delayed birthday celebration for my dad's 85th. My dad is the most easy-going man I know and professes himself quite happy with either no celebration at all or the prospect of just going down the hill in the village to the Ferrybridge for a meal there. This is not to be sniffed at because they do very good food there these days and the wine list has got really interesting over the last year or so; they've got Chateau Musar on there for one thing, a wine I find it hard to see past (or, following a third bottle, after).

However, a fine and rich tradition has evolved in this family of remorselessly exploiting the birthdays of our elder-folk as excuses for slap-up nosh-fests, and Dad is rapidly persuaded that what he really wants is for Ann and me to take him and Mum to the Champanay Inn across the river in Linlithgow, for enormous steaks and, oh, maybe a bottle or two of something nice from a sunny continent of an antipodean persuasion.

We used to celebrate Mum and Dad's birthdays at the deeply wonderful Peat Inn, not too far away from us, near St Andrew's, but my mum's a bit frail these days and doesn't like to stay away overnight anymore, so — being a lot closer — it looks like the Champanay has kind of inherited the dubious honour of hosting parental hoo-has. The fact they have Grange on the wine list certainly doesn't count against the place either. Like the Peat Inn, the Champanay is a restaurant with rooms. The relatively recent accommodation section is built on top of the wine cellar, which I got to visit once and is what my idea of Heaven would look like if it didn't have windows. And if I wasn't an atheist.

The Champanay's main dining room is housed in an impressively appointed octagonal mill house. Like the less formal Chop and Ale house next door, it majors on steaks that are hung for three weeks in an ionised chill room. In the main bit there's a proper restaurant pool with darkly lurking lobsters of various sizes, their claws peace-bonded by rubber bands. Altogether not a place for vegetarians of a delicate disposition.

We eat wonderfully (apart from me; I habitually use my fork upside down for peas, but there you are) and drink accordingly. We have Cullen Skink — spelled correctly — cream of parsley soup, scallops and cold smoked salmon to start, washed down with some Chassagne Montrachet, then rib-eye steaks, fried cod and more scallops for main courses, with a bottle of '91

Grange and a delicious '90 Nederburg Eminence to finish.

Now then. Grange.

How much? Nested digressions around Aussie wine.

Penfold's Grange Bin 95, as it used to be called, is red wine made from the shiraz or syrah grape — in the past usually with variable though generally small amounts of cabernet sauvignon added — from southern Australia, specifically from near Adelaide. This is my favourite wine, and trust me I've tried a few. Ann's favourite is the even more gulpingly expensive Pétrus from Bordeaux, but I just don't get it with Pétrus, or any of the other fine French wines I've sampled over the years in my valiant attempts to find one that surpasses Grange. They may well all be great, but Grange is, for me, just in another league; I am simply in love with its fruitily unplumbable depths. That subjectivity thing, I guess.

Ann and I first tasted the stuff in a brilliant little restaurant called Floodlite in Masham, Yorkshire. Masham is the spiritual home of Theakston's Old Peculier, the lunatic broth of Yorkshire, the famed and — at the time — idiotically strong real ale of sweet, chewy darkness and sudsy strength. Ann and I's first date, back in London in 1980, involved Old Peculier. We went after work from Denton Hall and Burgin's offices on High Holborn to the Sun on Lamb's Conduit Street. I'd heard it was a good real-ale pub and had wanted to check it out for a while. I was confident this attractive blonde secretary I'd invited for a drink would be on the Bacardi and Cokes, but at least I could have a decent pint.

"Oh, they do Old Peculier," I said as we approached the bar and I saw the sign on the tap. "I know what I'm having."

"So do I," said Ann.

"So, what'll it be?"

"A pint of Old Peculier," she said, indignant at not having been understood.

"What, really?"

"Oh yes."

"Brilliant."

It was not brilliant, it was embarrassing. We drank and drank and I ran out of money and had to borrow a fiver off Ann, which has never been a cool thing to do on a first date. Plus she drank me under the table. We had a pint of Sam Smith's down on the Strand and I saw her onto a bus home, then I somehow got myself back to McCartney's flat, where I was staying while I looked for a place of my own. I lay on the floor and told a bemused Dave I had just met this wonderful girl who liked a drink as much as me! Hurrah!

Some of this was Les McFarlane's fault (I imagine you'd already guessed that). He'd been to Tadcaster in Yorkshire on a field trip with his Economics class from Paisley College some years earlier and had come back enthusing about this wonderful beer called Theakston's Old Peculier. We discovered that you could buy this strange, darkly powerful ale of insanity in Glasgow, and became its apostles. A bunch of us had gone on a pilgrimage to Masham, taking in York and Castle Howard en route. Later a contingent of us London-living Scots would meet Les and a few other Scotland-based pals halfway, in York, again to sample the delights of Masham's finest product.

Well, things change; we went back to Lamb's Conduit Street a few years ago on one of our infrequent trips to London, but the Sun was no longer the mazily eccentric real-ale nirvana it had been back in the early eighties; just another pleasant, open, sensibly laid out café-like bar with too many alcopops and flavoured vodkas. And OP isn't what it was either, changed long ago into a less powerful formulation and made in Carlisle, not Masham; still a fine beer, but not the mad, bad, brilliant stuff of near hallucinogenic power it once was. One of the Theakston family fell out with the others and started brewing another beer, back in Masham. You could tell he'd fallen out with the rest of the family because he called this new real ale Black Sheep (itself a fine pint, but no Old P.).

Masham, on the other hand, seems only to have changed for the better. The first couple of times I went it felt a bit too quiet and sleepy; now it appears more lively, without being exactly frenetic (though it positively bustles on market day). Set in beautiful rolling Yorkshire scenery Masham is full of Good Things, like the White Bear Inn (which appears to have some connection to Jethro Tull, a band I still have a real soft spot for), several other great pubs, the old brewery, the King's Head Hotel, not one but two brilliant delicatessen/sweet shops, some interesting craft outlets,

291

the wide central square where the market still takes place, and the Floodlite restaurant. Which brings us back to that first bottle of Grange.

In 1995 I decided Ann and I ought to start a new tradition of going to Masham every April, as close as possible to the anniversary of that first date, to drink at least one pint of Old Peculier. The first time we went we stayed at the King's Head Hotel and on the second night ate out at the Floodlite, which was one of those instant finds, where you immediately know you've stumbled on to something special; just amazingly good food. Plus it had a bottle of Ozzie plonk on the wine list for 75 quid. I'd decided a few years earlier that I was a real fan of the way Australian wine tasted in general compared to most French reds, plus I'd just had a royalty cheque and was therefore feeling relatively flush, so, though I'd never heard of this Penfolds Grange Bin 95, I stopped and thought about it.

I remember thinking that 75 was an awful lot of money to spend on a red that wasn't a Bordeaux, but I felt kind of encouraged by the quality of the food in Floodlite and the fact that everything else on the menu and the wine list seemed reasonably priced; maybe this 1989 Bin 95 stuff was entirely worth the money. So we ordered a bottle. It became my favourite wine from the first mouthful.

I started looking out for it. I began, when we were going posh, to choose restaurants largely according to whether they had Grange on the wine list or not (so that, in London, Quo Vadis and then the Oak Room became favoured hang-outs in succession). I even started making notes about Grange; where we tasted it, what vintage it was and how much it cost. I never quite got round to the more esoteric business of rating it for taste, though I think I was on the brink of that before deciding it was all starting to get out of hand. It's thanks to this now discontinued practice that I know the next two bottles we tasted after the Floodlite were an '87 at Sharrow Bay in the Lake District and a 1990 at Inverlochy Castle, outside Fort William.

So I'd like to thank Les, Yorkshire, Masham, the Theakston family, the Floodlite restaurant, the Sun on Lamb's Conduit Street, London, in its early-eighties real-ale period, my automobile's feng shui consultant, both my eyebrow stylists, my dog's therapist . . .

On our return from the Champanay, heading back the few miles to the Forth Road Bridge in a people carrier taxi, we suddenly plough through a drift of whiteness in a little dip in the road. The fields for about 50 meters on either side shine in the moonlight, covered with — we work out after some confusion — hailstones. Otherwise the night is quite mild and the countryside as dark as it ought to be at this time of night and year. We have to check with the taxi driver that we're really seeing what we seem to be. More weird weather.

Back home, Ann, Dad and I attack the stash of single malts under the stairs. I believe it's this night that sees the end of the 60 per cent Talisker.

I think it's how it would have wanted to go.

★　★　★

293

A week later, after an afternoon's retail therapy in Inverness, Ann and I make for the pointy pink confection that is the Bunchrew Hotel. We bump into a guy we met on Islay years ago, when we went to Crowcon, a microcon of people who'd got together over the net on a newsgroup discussing my books (hence the "Crow" bit). One of the group happened to live on Islay and have a connection with Ardbeg distillery, which is why I'd already been there before the research for this book.

Another fine meal — I can feel my belt crying out for a new hole to be cut even as I look at the sweet menu — and we finally have a French wine that does taste quite like the glorious Grange! Les has been banging on for years about how Grange used to be called Grange Hermitage because it was the taste of Hermitage that Penfold's was trying to emulate, and I've been trying to track down an Hermitage that fits the bill all this time. At last; a Jaboulet Hermitage '93.

During the meal we get talking with a very nice couple from Florida called John and Tina. In the bar I try to persuade John that his Macallan will taste better with just water rather than the soda he's adding, using a Macallan Gran Reserva to do the proving. He's polite but obviously unconvinced. Ah well. Happily we manage to stay off politics; crudely statistically there's less than a one in four chance any randomly encountered American will actually have voted for Dubya, but you never know, and in a convivial atmosphere it's usually best to avoid unpleasantness. And they do refer to the word Goddamn as "Gee Dee", which is sort of charming while being infinitely worrying at the same time. I promise to send an SF book to Tina, and they insist if we're ever in Florida we must visit them. I manage to keep my trap shut about the passport thing.

Meanwhile, in Iraq, after eleven protesters are shot and killed by the US forces in the town of Falluja, the townspeople stage a protest over the killings. So the Americans kill two of those protesters too.

Meanwhile two British Moslem guys who've flown out to Israel become our first home-grown suicide bombers.

Amazingly, still no Weapons of Mass Destruction . . .

The Bunchrew suffers an atypical power cut just in time for breakfast the following morning so we head off into one more gloriously clear and sunny day, heading north towards Wick via Beauly, Muir of Ord and Brora, where we stop to have a look round Clynelish distillery.

I know this road well; the first bit from the days of driving to and from Nigg Bay and Portmahomack, and the sections north of Tain from driving to Thurso for the ferry to Orkney, where Ann's eldest sister Jenny and her husband James live. There are a lot of good long straights up to Tain but the road as ever is fairly busy in both directions and it isn't until after Tain that the traffic thins and the road offers up its wonderfulness.

These days, passing the Cromarty Firth, I count the drilling rigs sitting out on the water. This is a Bill Drummond thing. Bill Drummond was one of the band called KLF back in the eighties and also part of the K Foundation, the guys who burned a million quid on Islay (it would have been hopelessly uncool, while I was on Islay the month before, to have sought out the place where they performed the burning, so I didn't). Drummond's a fascinating character and my pal Gary Lloyd has been something of a fan for a long time. He gave me a present of one of Drummond's books, *How To Be An Artist*, which involves the man, back in 1998, driving his Land Rover Defender (ha!) from southern England to Dounreay nuclear power station, on the north coast of Scotland, stopping every now and again to take pictures of a sign that says "FOR SALE, A Smell of Sulphur in the Wind. Richard Long. $20,000" (long story — read the book). In this he mentions counting the rigs on the Cromarty Firth as he passes by on the A9. So I do this as well, such conduct counting as a sufficiently mild symptom of fan-boy homage behaviour not to be too embarrassing to mention in a book like this one, obviously.

When we first started making this journey, once past Tain you still had to go round the Dornoch Firth, only crossing the river at Bonar Bridge, but nowadays a long low bridge sweeps over the sand and waves from just past the Glenmorangie distillery. The local communities were very proud about getting this new bridge; they sponsored a series of events to celebrate its opening, one of which I was involved in (if I recall correctly I was invited because I wrote a book called *The Bridge*. I wonder if I wrote a novel called *The New Ferrari . . .* ? Na, forget it). The road contains a good mix of straights

296

and twists thereafter before the town of Golspie, followed a few miles later by Brora. Just outside Golspie is Dunrobin Castle, a slightly bizarre if undeniably dramatic construction with an arguably inappropriate amount of Loire châteaux about it, even for the locally mild climate of this eastern coast. The place also has unfortunate associations with the worst excesses of the Clearances, when the crofters — the small-scale farmers of the Highlands and Islands — were driven off their lands at gunpoint and their homes torched to make way for sheep and cattle. So, like Culloden, it remains a place I'm waiting to be in the right mood to visit.

Clynelish is, anyway, sort of a start.

The original Clynelish distillery was built in 1819 at the instigation of the Marquis of Stafford, who was later to become the First Duke of Sutherland. There was a lot of illicit distilling in the area and the Marquis apparently felt that it was much to be preferred that he invest in a licence and satisfy the local demand — and make a tidy profit out of it — rather than have the local crofters flout the law of the land and scrape together a few extra pennies. 1819 was a busy year for the Sutherlands; while the distillery was going up, so were 250 crofts, in flames, the better to persuade their inhabitants of the desirousness of cattle-farming as opposed to, say, feeding their families.

Clynelish has a wide, open view towards the sea. The new buildings are somewhere between inelegant and plain ugly, but it's a cared-for-looking sort of place with

297

well-tended grounds — dotted with wildly flowering cherry trees at this time of year.

It's really two distilleries. The old Clynelish distillery was renamed Brora when the new plant was completed in 1968 and it produced one of the great lost giants of the world of single malts; a peatily intense beauty combining some of the best characteristics of a Highland and an Island whisky. Brora was shut down in 1983 and the whisky is becoming harder to find these days. I found a Rare Malts 24-year-old from 1977 at the distillery shop, clocking in at a fairly throat-catching 56.1 abv. It truly is a cracker; seaweedy, smoky, redolent of dock-sides thick with coiled, tarry rope and containing a spice rack full of hot, intense flavours. It would not be technically impossible to start production again at Brora, but it appears it's unlikely. A shame.

Clynelish itself, the product of the modern distillery and its very large stills, is certainly nothing to be ashamed of; the 14-year-old — which seems to be pretty much the standard age for this whisky to be bottled at — is a similarly briny, tarry, almost oily dram, also strong on pepper and mustard flavours though much less peaty compared to Brora and anyway somehow greener smelling and tasting; certainly sufficiently distinct from its mothballed neighbour for Diageo to be able to market both if they wanted to and thought the demand might be there.

The A9 tends to get better the further north it heads. Beyond Brora is some wonderful, free-feeling road set in extravagantly open, wide-screen scenery; even if you weren't on a probably doomed quest for some unspeakably supreme whisky, you'd still have the exhilarating feeling — twisting along this rising, rushing braid of tarmac — of whirling towards the end of the world. To the left, north and west, are the hills and lone, distant mountains, the few forests and many moors. The sea is always there to the right, glittering, studded in the distance with rigs and production platforms, its ever-changing surface textured and grained with the competing influences of tide and wind, fraying to surf at the stony margins of the winding hem of coast. The single-line rail route from Inverness to Thurso and Wick twines beside the road as far as Helmsdale, usually between the road and the coast, often coming close enough for trains to shield passing cars from spray when the weather's foul and the waves break mountainously on the rocks and shingle beyond.

Entirely the worst weather for this journey, however, is when the fog rolls in. You have to go slow, you can hardly overtake, and worst of all there's not even any scenery to look at to compensate. So far over the years we've been very lucky, never encountering more than patchy mist, and today it's just fabulous; bright bright bright with a few scattered fluffy clouds. The M5 eats miles on a road like this; even staying at licence-friendly speeds there's an easy rhythm to the road the car slots into like a Scalextric racer, barely slowing from such modest speeds for bends, and dispatching the occasional instances of slower traffic with ease. Part of the fun of a truly good drive in a fast car on the real-life roads is not going too fast; the faster you go the more comparatively slower stuff you have to overtake, and at a certain cumulative point overtaking can stop being fun and just become a chore.

The driver's own abilities being taken as some sort of constant, the sweet spot on a non-trivial drive is finding the right speed for the mixture of variables involved: legality and safety, the abilities of the car, the physicalities of the road, the weather and light, and the balance of similarly directioned and oncoming traffic. The drive to Wick feels like a good 'un and my passenger seems happy, which is generally the single most important and telling thing to get right when you're not driving alone.

We stop at the Pentland Arms Hotel in Lybster. Another definite find. Lunch at Jo's Kitchen there more than makes up for any breakfast deficit; I go for a baked potato and salad with the firm intention of leaving plenty of room for whatever might be on the Bunchrew's menu tonight but the spud that arrives is the size of a rugby ball and surrounded with half a field's worth of salad; I immediately resolve not to eat it all but it tastes far too good and besides, I wouldn't want to upset the chef. I get lost trying to find the Gents and wander past some very nice-looking bedrooms on the first floor, gleaming in the sunlight as they're cleaned and tidied. The short drive from Lybster to Wick is pleasant and relaxed, not quick, with lots of long settlements and little farms dotted along the way.

Wick is where mainland Scotland just about runs out. Poised on the fringe of the long flat Flow Country facing the often not so flat sea, near the corner where the North Atlantic Ocean and the North Sea bump into each other and tend to kick up a fuss about it, it's way out of the way from almost everywhere apart from Thurso, which is a place you could say exactly the same things about except substituting "Thurso" for "Wick" and vice versa. I like both places; there's a clean airiness about both, plus what at least from the outside looks like old fashioned civic pride about these limpetly extraneous, independent-feeling communities. Wick still has a mixture of fishing and agriculture to work with and Thurso, while worryingly close to Dounreay in every sense, feels like a miniature Norse capital of this remote corner of the British Isles; a preparation for the sheer difference that is Orkney.

The distillery at Wick is out towards the sea from the relative shelter of the town centre, through a quiet grid of streets and a tree-shaded square. Old Pulteney — ah, that questionable "Old" again — is a small distillery, neatly slotted into the edge of the town, drawing its water from Loch Hempriggs. It's not the only distillery that used to be some sort of mill — a meal mill in this case, where oats were ground to a powder — but it does have the longest lade in Scotland (a lade is just the old technical term for a channel bringing water to a mill).

It feels like the sort of place that doesn't get that many visitors and perhaps because of that the welcome is relaxed and genuine. The distillery has a slightly compressed, higglety-pigglety air about it, largely as a result of being based on a conversion — the washback

301

is in the still house and the squeezed-in-looking underback looks like a giant brass shell case. The stills are just plain weird; the wash still has a giant boiling ball above the main bowl, a squat neck which looks like an only slightly elongated copper bucket and a Lyne arm that emerges, pointing slightly downward, from barely more than halfway up this sawn-off looking structure (and it did have to be truncated when it was installed, to fit in under the low roof). The spirit still has a bizarre up-and-over piece of plumbing connecting it to a dustbin-sized copper purifier that essentially means the whisky is distilled two and a half times, then the pipes exit to an old-fashioned outside worm tub set up, sitting steaming gently at one end of that extremely long lade.

A dark feline slinks round a piece of pipe work just ahead of me as I'm shown round by Gordon, one of the managers.

"Distillery cat?" I ask.

"Aye, that's it."

"What's it called?"

"Oh, just The Cat," he says, nodding.

Fair enough. Given that Les and I have had two boats now both called The Boat and when I was a child all two of my hamsters were called Hammy, I'm in no position to cavil.

Gordon takes a hosepipe filling a barrel at one point and lets the clear raw spirit pour over his hands for a second, then pats his palms together and sniffs the result, inviting me to do the same. Washing your hands in spirit; cool, in every sense. The smell is not unpleasant; very chemically, astringent, a little sweet.

The finished whisky, after it's been properly matured, is briny, fresh as you like and only slightly peaty. There's no phenolising of the barley, so the peat flavour that is there must come from the water. Old Pulteney is a quick maturer, often bottled at eight years old, and the 12-year-old I got was sea-air bracing with touches of a clean, sharp sweetness. I don't recall ever having tried this whisky before but I'm extremely glad I have now. What with this, Ord, Clynelish, Brora and Glenmorangie I seem to be developing a real taste for these far north-easters.

The drive back is notable for an unimpeded full-bore climb out of the depths at Berriedale Braes — when a slope has one of those deep gravel run-offs for suddenly brake-free heavies you know it's a serious gradient — a pit stop at the Morangie House Hotel in Tain, a quick photo at Balblair distillery (I have yet to track down a bottle of this stuff) and a slight but entirely worthwhile detour via the highly splendid A836, a lightly trafficked route since the Dornoch Bridge was opened and just one of the most fun roads in this part of Scotland; effectively an A-road that's become a fast, sky-exposed GWR simply by being bypassed.

The next morning it's a kipper for breakfast, which, compared to your average Full Scottish is positively healthy (compared to the dread beguilements of the Buffet-the-waistline-slayer option it's *incredibly* healthy). It's another beauty of a day, a circumstance that feels only fitting given that we have the very pleasant prospect ahead of us of a drive home with a stop off for an extended tasting tour at what is for many people the distillery which produces entirely the best whisky in the whole wide world; Macallan.

Macallan. I almost changed my name for this whisky. Well, sort of. Back in 1985–86, after I'd had a couple of mainstream novels published, I'd decided to go back to my first love and try to get some of my science fiction published too. At the time my hardback publishers, Macmillan, didn't really publish SF so I was expecting to go elsewhere with it. Using a different name for the SF novels seemed like a good idea, just so that people didn't get confused. I came up with the name John B. Macallan. These were my two favourite whiskies at the time; Johnny Walker Black Label was my favourite blend and Macallan was my favourite single malt.

Two things meant this didn't happen. One was that my editor, the estimable Mr James Hale, kept having to ask, What was that *nom-de-plume* again? Jim Beam Morangie, was that it?

Given that James was not entirely unfamiliar with Scotland's finest product, this was not a sign that I had picked a particularly memorable name. The other thing was that Macmillan decided to publish my SF after all. So I dropped the idea of naming myself after two whiskies and settled for putting the "M" back in my name. It had been there on the title page of *The Wasp Factory* when I'd submitted it to Macmillan in 1983 but we'd removed it because James thought it looked a bit fussy and was worried people might make a

304

subconscious connection with Rosie M. Banks, a character in Wodehouse's novels who happens to be a very bad romantic novelist. While I'd been at Stirling University I had used the names Iain Banks, Iain M. Banks, Iain Menzies Banks and even Iain Menzies-Banks as part of a vicious let's-fuck-with-the-establishment-man campaign to make the administration think there was more than one of me (there is no evidence whatever to suggest this had any subversive effect at all, other than causing me to be known by the admin people as That Git Who Can't Decide What His Name Is).

Anyway, I was quite happy dropping the M, until I was upbraided by a couple of uncles for denying my birthright or something. I'd have put it straight back in there for my second novel, but that really might have confused things. The SF books seemed like the M's rightful home, I reasoned. After all, hadn't Brian Aldiss become Brian W. Aldiss when writing his non-SF books? Made perfect sense. Somebody once called it a transparent attempt on the World's Most Penetrable Pseudonym record, but at least it kept my uncles happy. It did have the unfortunate effect of meaning I had to keep answering the question What does the M stand for? And sticking with plain Iain Banks for the SF would have made it clear that I was just as proud of those novels as I was of the mainstream books, rather than, as some people appeared to assume, obviously inserting the M to show that these were sub-standard entertainments, mere slumming-it indulgences compared to my serious, weighty non-genre works. (Ha!)

Maybe I should have stuck with John B. Macallan.

James Hale was a good friend and a brilliant editor. Back in 1983 it was James's future wife, Hilary, who pulled *The Wasp Factory* off the slush pile — that's the unflattering though usually symbolically depressingly accurate term publishers use to describe the unsolicited manuscripts they're sent — and took it to James, who was then fiction editor at Macmillan. It was James who decided to publish the book, to publish me. It wasn't as though my manuscript was so self-evidently stunning that the first editor to look at it was always going to grab it instantly, either, because Macmillan was the sixth publisher I'd sent it to, and others had thought about it but decided to pass.

James saw something in it though, and took the risk of publishing this weird story by a complete unknown, and I will forever be in his debt for that. I owe him just as much thanks for an opposite kind of favour too, because I once submitted a book to him which I wasn't sure about and he told me it wasn't good enough and he wasn't prepared to publish it.

I met up with him at his and Hilary's house at Peckam Rye a few days later; he was trying to repair the marble-topped table he'd broken when he'd realised the manuscript just wasn't good enough (thumped it with his fist — only time I ever heard of James inflicting physical damage on human, beast or inanimate object). He confirmed he couldn't take the book, but he also

306

told me that there would be at least half a dozen publishers in London who'd jump at the chance of taking it on if I wanted to submit it elsewhere, and he wouldn't stand in my way if I wanted to do so — those other publishers would know the book wasn't very good, too, but I was a youngish and moderately hot property at the time and they'd publish the book just to get me on board and hope the next one might mark a return to form. This would be a strategic mistake for me to make, because a weak book remains a weak book, but James could understand any writer's reluctance to throw away months of work.

I took James' advice, salvaged the few good bits, threw the rest of the clunker away and wrote *The Bridge* instead. Arguably still my best book, so *boy* was that guy right.

Irreplaceable, unforgettable, James died just before this book, *Raw Spirit*, was finished.

It was with James one day that we both discovered just how subjective an experience whisky appreciation is. Our usual way of working, both while he was employed by Macmillan and afterwards when he went freelance, was that I'd go to the house in Peckam and we'd work through the manuscript of my latest book, sitting side by side at a table. Usually this would take most of a working day; once or twice it took two days. We always argued like hell but we *almost* always agreed in the end (and James was almost always right). I never had anything less than a great time and my principal memories of those one- or two-day sessions feature lots of uproarious laughter from the pair of us.

We were going through this whole process one day not long after James' 40th birthday and — as was usual — we helped the creative process along with a heart starter; a little whisky each. James had been given a bottle of Laphroaig for his birthday by one of his friends; a 40-year-old, appropriately. I was pretty much just used to the 10-year-old and I'd never seen a 40 year-old Laphroaig (disappointingly, it looked like the plain label design hadn't changed much in the intervening years). I felt quite privileged that James had chosen this as our mind-lubricating dram of the day. We both sipped it, savoured it, and agreed it was something very special indeed. We kept on taking small sips as we went through the book.

There was a point where we wanted to change something and I couldn't think quite how to do it or didn't think the offending bit needed changing in the first place, so James sat staring at the manuscript trying to work out how he would suggest re-doing the relevant words. Released from concentrating on the book, my gaze fell on the bottle sitting on the far edge of the table, near the wall. Maybe the light was falling on it in just such a way as to make the chicanery obvious — I don't know — but for whatever reason, I looked more and more closely at the "40" bit of the "40 years old" legend on the bottle's label. I picked the bottle up, I squinted at it while James mulled over whatever he was mulling over and then I said, "James, this isn't a bottle of 40-year-old at all. It's a bottle of 10-year-old which some devious cheapskate scumbag has altered by adding a sort of small upside-down '7' shape to the '1' to make it look like a '4'. With a thin black marker pen, by the look of it." I held the bottle up to the light. "See?"

James's eyes widened alarmingly as he stared at it. Eventually he said, "*Bastard!*"

The point is, until that point we really had thought that what we were drinking was something above and beyond your normal 10-year old Laphroaig. Just thinking it was old and rare and special had helped make it so in our minds. Either our noses weren't up to the job in the first place, or our brains were ignoring what our noses were telling us. Either way, a humbling, salutary experience. I never liked to ask whether James mentioned all this to whatever so-called friend had set out to hoodwink him, but I think a stern talking-to would have been in order.

However. To the Macallan distillery, back on Speyside, over-looking the river itself from a ridge on the north-west bank a mile or so from Craigellachie. The photogenic bit that you see on the cartons is Easter Elchies house, which — along with a long, low, tastefully executed extension alongside — houses offices and doubles as a corporate entertainment venue. The distillery itself is to the right as you approach it down the drive. The Visitor Centre is to the left and is quite new, with lots of pale wood furniture in interestingly sculpted, organic-looking shapes. We're booked in for the extended tour, which features a range of whiskies to taste at the end in a special tasting room next to the professional tasters' facility, but first there's the usual walk round the plant, notable for the proliferation of relatively small stills in a big, wide-windowed space which feels oddly like a ship's engine room ("oddly" because ships' engine rooms are not normally notorious for having enormous windows looking out to valleys in Speyside).

"We've been thinking of a plot for your next book," one of our hosts tells me genially as we look round.

"Really?" I say.

In the circumstances, "Really" is Authorial for "Oh-oh."

"We thought, you could have a body turn up in a mash tun and your Inspector What's-his-name would have to investigate."

"Inspector Rebus?"

"That's him!"

"Ah. That's Ian Rankin. My name's Iain Banks."

"Oops."

"That's okay." I smile widely to show that it really is okay (some writers can get amazingly petulant over this sort of thing). "A few years ago it was always Irvine Welsh I got mistaken for. I'm used to it."

Writers: What Not to Say.

Right. Clichéd subjects/questions writers encounter all the time. There are two in particular. The less common one is, If I give you this brilliant plot, you could write it and we could split the loot. What do you think? (Not that the people at Macallan were after riches or fame, they were just trying to be helpful and make me feel welcome.) But you do get the full commercial proposition now and again. I dare say if I lived in London and went to lots of dinner parties this would happen to me a lot more often than it does.

It has to be said that this is not usually a good thing to say to a writer. Often we have lots of plots and ideas of our own lying around and just lack the time to write them. Adding one of yours to the mess that's long-since boiled all over a distant back burner isn't really going to do either of us any good.

Even if you do have a sure-fire idea, it's very rare indeed for a writer to share the credit for a book like that. Frankly we are much more likely to let you tell us the idea and then just steal it. Unless you've got lots of witnesses and/or are a senior partner in a legal firm specialising in litigation and intellectual property law, that'll be that. If you seriously think that a writer's going to sign some sort of legally binding agreement *before* being told an idea for a plot, well, you're welcome to try.

Stealing stuff is what writers have been doing probably since before writing was even invented — if you include as honorary writers the prehistoric story tellers who earned their share of meat by telling stories round the camp fire at night rather than going out and helping to catch it. One of our more shameless defences is that Shakespeare nicked ideas, themes and indeed whole plots from other writers, so if it was good enough for him, it's good enough for us. (It does no good to point out that it's different for Shakespeare because he

311

was a genius — that's a highly morally dubious defence in the first place, and, besides, all writers secretly think they're geniuses too so they'd only take that as further encouragement.)

To the people who insist they really do have a great idea but they just can't write, I'd say that given some of the books I've read, or at least started to read, it would appear that not being able to write is absolutely no obstacle whatsoever to writing a book and securing a publishing contract. Though becoming famous in some other field first may help.

The other, much more common inquiry is, Where do you get your ideas from?

Leaving aside the obvious, "Class A drugs, actually," or, "A wee man in Auchtermuchty," I've sometimes wondered what sort of answer people really expect to this. What class of possible reply are people anticipating, or are they completely in the dark regarding the creative process?

The answer, by the way, is startlingly simple; writers get their ideas from the same place as everybody else. When asked The Question by an individual, it's perfectly okay to look them in the eye and say, "Well, the same place as you do." This usually leads to people saying they don't have ideas.

But everyone does. Everybody has ideas. If you've ever had a sexual fantasy that wasn't a perfect copy of somebody else's — you've had an idea. If you've ever thought about what you'd do if you won the Lottery — you've had an idea. If you've ever passed some time pondering the exact form of words you would use —

having just heard from your bank that the Lottery cheque has cleared — to tell your boss or colleagues how much you have enjoyed working with them over the years — you've had an idea. If you've ever read a book or watched a film and thought, But what if *this* had happened instead of *that* — you've had an idea. If you've ever been walking down the road with lurid red kebab sauce dripping onto your good shoes when you suddenly think of the stingingly witty reply you should have come out with half an hour earlier in the pub, when somebody insulted you or said something you wanted to take issue with but couldn't quite work out what it was you wanted to say at the time — then you've had an idea.

Some of these ideas would qualify as rudimentary plots, some as lines of dialogue, but they are all ideas and everybody has them. If there is some benighted, possibly genetically deficient part of humanity that genuinely doesn't ever have an idea of this nature, ever ever *ever*, then they surely constitute a vanishing tiny minority of our species, and as far as I know I've never met one of them.

The difference is simply that writers do this idea-generating sort of stuff more frequently and more consistently than the sort of person who doesn't realise that they even have ideas of their own, and — perhaps more to the point — we do it deliberately. We mostly start doing it when we're quite young and it becomes a habit; we're always on the lookout for ideas, whether they're generated by our own lives, by the lives of people we know, by the lives of people we don't know

313

— via reports in news media — or by the works of other writers — non-fiction works as well as fiction.

Where do I get my ideas from? Here's an example:

In 1978 I went on holiday to the States. I had an uncle in Washington DC and an aunt in Los Angeles and to get from one to the other I decided to try one of these drive-away schemes where you drive somebody's car from one coast to the other for them (meanwhile they've flown). I was driving along Interstate 40 through Texas when I came to a part of the highway where the median had been burned.

The median is what a lot of Interstates have instead of central crash-barriers; essentially it's a shallow V of ground, maybe a hundred feet broad, between the two carriageways. If something goes pear-shaped on one carriageway and a vehicle — especially one of those colossal American trucks — starts heading towards the other carriageway, it doesn't smash through a crash barrier into the oncoming traffic or even bounce off it to hurtle across its own side of the road, it just trundles down towards the bottom of the gently sloped median. This is actually a really good idea, if you have Texan amounts of land to play with.

Driving at the then legal limit of 55 miles per hour — which I was dutifully doing, though I did seem to be entirely the slowest vehicle on the road — for eight hours a day, for five days, through mostly very flat scenery, can tend to create an almost Zen-like trance state in the driver. I tried to keep myself alert by constantly changing radio stations, attempting to identify passing cars and trucks, and just generally looking around for anything interesting. For an hour or so, the median to my right had been just a near-featureless green blur of grass, like the land on either side of the Interstate. Then suddenly the median was black. Burned black.

I looked in my rear view mirror and saw where a ragged line separated green from black. It looked kind of odd, too, because the land on either side of the Interstate — low hills rising to a blue sky — was still luxuriantly green with long, breeze-ruffled grass.

Probably somebody had thrown a cigarette out of their vehicle window and the wind had fanned the flames along the median (and nothing burning had been picked up by the wind and blown across either carriageway to ignite the grass beyond). It struck me that it must have looked distinctly weird at the time, to have seen a line of advancing fire making its way along the median while the countryside on both sides it was unaffected. If it had happened at night and you'd seen it from some distance away, it would have looked even stranger.

I wondered how I could use this idea, this image. I thought of myself entirely as a science fiction writer at the time and one of the neat things about being an SF writer is that you get to extrapolate. I always interpreted this as *carte blanche* to grossly exaggerate, to take every idea to its non-Earthbound limit, and this was exactly what happened to this idea.

I started thinking about a long line of land sitting in a sea or lake, and the fire spreading from end to end. Or maybe a circular island, a sort of thin doughnut

315

shape; *that* burning. Of course the fire would go out eventually . . . Unless the circular island was so big that the plants left behind after the fire had passed had time to grow back before the fire circled back round again (I'd read about — or seen on *Life on Earth* — plants in Australia that couldn't successfully seed until they'd been through a fire). A never-ending wave of fire . . . *Now* we were getting into decent skiffy-type ideas, I thought. And with SF, you're allowed, even expected to keep upping the scale. So, if you made the island really big . . . it could girdle a planet! You could have a sort of island continent going right round a world, edged with sea to north and south. On Earth it would be like having nothing but ocean except between the tropics. Big enough planet, fast enough growing plants (I remembered reading about some bamboo species which grows so fast you can hear it creaking as it gets taller); it should be possible . . .

A couple of years later, when I was looking for an exotic setting for the climax of a novel called *The Player of Games*, the fire-planet thing was already there, sitting on the shelf just waiting to be used.

Anyway, *that* is where ideas come from.

Macallan has a cat. Unlike the nameless mog of Old Pulteney, this one is blessed with a name. He's called Cyril, and when we see him he's lying stretched out, shaggily luxurious, on a large wooden desk in the pleasantly warm still room, beneath a flat-screen computer display edged in gleaming, polished brass and showing some colourful custom software indicating

316

the state of the local storage vessels, pipe work and valves. It's a wonderful, almost iconic sight worth stopping to stare and grin at (I would have taken a photograph, but that, of course, would inevitably have led to the whole place instantly blowing up and burning down).

Macallan uses Golden Promise barley, a variety which is out of favour with farmers these days because it produces much less yield than more recent, more productive but less tasty forms. As a result, Golden Promise has become hard to get hold of over the years and even Macallan has had to resort to other varieties, using only about 30 per cent Golden Promise since 1994. It'll be interesting to see whether the 10-year-old Macallan bottled in 2004 tastes appreciably different compared to the year before.

The 21 small stills are heated directly with gas, which also alters the taste of the final product compared to stills heated indirectly with steam pipes, introducing a caramelised, slightly burned flavour into the mix.

The main influence on the taste of Macallan, however, is the sherry casks it's exclusively matured in, and the distillery goes to some lengths to control their supply. Macallan buys 70- to 80-year-old Spanish-grown oak, has it made into sherry butts in Jerez and then loans the barrels to various bodegas for three years; one year for the fermentation of the dry oloroso sherry and two for storage. Then the complete butts are shipped intact to Speyside. This is more expensive than breaking them up for shipping, as happens with most American bourbon barrels, but it's reckoned complete casks have a stronger influence on the maturing whisky than re-formed ones. In most Macallan two-thirds of the whisky will be from first-fill casks and one-third from second-fill. Using nothing but sherry, rather than a mixture of mostly bourbon with a dash of sherry, makes the whole process expensive, but without its profound sherry influence Macallan would hardly be Macallan.

Those Italians again; they have their own special edition of the stuff, bottled at seven years old. Look, are we sure these people actually drink such eccentrically young whiskies? They're not using it as fashionably expensive after-shave or something, are they? It isn't being drizzled into the fuel tanks of sundry Vespas and Fiats to produce an increase in power and a pleasant pong in the crowded streets of Rome and Milan, is it?

Anyway. In the tasting room Ann and I try clear, newly made raw spirit, plus Macallan at 12, 18, 25 and 30 years old. I'm just nosing because I have to drive afterwards.

Even the raw spirit doesn't smell too terrible; it reminds me of Pear Drops, the synthetic-tasting sweets I used to like when I was a kid. Otherwise, quite clean and spare. Faced with the choice, you'd definitely knock this stuff back in preference to a few rough vodkas I've had the misfortune to have tried over the years.

The later and older expressions of the whisky itself just get better and better. With the 30-year-old I do take a small sip rather than just sniff. The oldest

Macallan I'd tried until this point had been a 25-year-old.

There is, obviously, lots of sherry-wood influence in the taste, and that influence increases with age, but the subtlety of the whisky is such that the result is a spectrum of different flavours which owe a distant debt to the alchemy between the spirit and the cask, rather than just a single dominant taste of sherry (if you want to test this, buy a cheap blend and mix it with sherry; it really isn't the same at all). There's honey, Christmas cake, heather, a whole fruit bowl of citrus tones, smokiness, syrup, peat (usually fairly elusive, but poking its head out of the thickets of other tastes now and again), vanilla, leather, straw, ginger and even other sorts of wood beside the oak you'd expect in there; cedar is one, and I thought I smelled something like the balsa wood we used for the initial few lessons in first-year woodwork class.

It all sounds like a clanging, clashing orchestra-tuning-up kind of mishmash, but of course not all these tastes are in every expression, and the beauty of Macallan is that every single bottling comes out like a coherent whole, like a symphony, everything working together, all the tastes in harmony, complimenting their neighbours and creating something rich and deep and worth going back to again and again.

You can pay gaggingly large amounts of money for very old Macallan. If you do have the money though, by all means go for the older stuff, because with Macallan, as far as I've been able to tell, you do tend to get what you pay for; this is a whisky that generally just

319

gets better and better as it gets older, and while you will pay through the nose for the privilege, at no point are you going to get ripped off, paying more for less.

The only proviso would be to do with opulence of taste. I love Macallan because it's just so packed with strong flavours, and the fact that the longer it stays in the cask the more wood and sherry elements it's going to pick up means that of course for me older will equate to better. For people who prefer a lighter, less intense dram, or who just don't like the sherry and wood notes, the 10-year-old might be as deep into Macallan Land as they wish to venture, as even the extra two years of the 12-year-old makes a difference, producing a more sweetly potent, heavily flavoured whisky.

The Gran Reserva I tried to impress John from Florida with the night before is eighteen years old, but a deliberately more forceful expression than the usual eighteen as it's matured entirely in first-fill sherry casks (hence the name). This is an immensely powerful, imposing, woodily dominant expression, and while I love it, I can understand it might be just too much for people who prefer a more delicate dram, and would not be appropriate for every occasion or even every time of day.

Personally I think Macallan's good at almost any age — well, maybe not seven, *capisce* — with the widely available 10-year-old serving as a perfectly fine introduction to the oeuvre, while the best compromise between reasonable price and sock-knocking-off taste is probably the standard 18-year-old. This expression is released most years as a specific vintage, the aim being to produce a balance between consistency and year-on-year change. The consistency is achieved by tasting as many as 100 casks, choosing about 50 of those, marrying the whisky from those casks together and leaving it vatted for a month, then performing a sort of mini-bottling and tasting the result (for the 25-year-old, the married whiskies stay vatted for a whole year before being evaluated).

The tasters are brought rather centre stage at Macallan. They've built a new and very tasteful tasting room with more groovily contorted but sexily smooth pale wood and comfy stools with wrought-iron legs. This is where you sit if you do the extended tour. It has a wall-wide window through which you can watch the distillery's tasters do their work; sniffing and slurping, spitting and noting and choosing. This struck me as a bit of an invasion of work-space privacy (it reminded me of the overlooked coopers at Strathspey Cooperage) and I waited until the guys were out of the room before taking a photo through the wide-screen window. I think I'd find being watched a real distraction if I was trying to do something as concentration-demanding as choosing between a hundred-plus different whisky barrels, but maybe that's just me.

On the other hand, it has to be a bit of a compensation that you're getting to work day-in, day-out with unarguably one of the very best whiskies in the world.

One last thought, to let you savour that expensive Macallan with an even clearer conscience. The distillery is part of the Edrington Group, which also includes the Bunnahabhain, Glengoyne, Glenrothes-Glenlivet (so somebody still uses the G-word), Glenturret, Highland Park and Tamdhu single malts and the Cutty Sark and Famous Grouse blends. The Edrington Group is in turn largely owned and run by the Robertson Trust, a charitable body since 1961 which was set up by three sisters called Robertson who had inherited significant parts of the Scotch industry. The Trust gives about five million pounds a year to good causes, mostly in Scotland, so drinking any of these drams is practically a charitable act in itself. Good grief, how virtuous do you want to feel?

Stop Press Handy Anti-Midge Tip.

During our visit to Macallan, Gary and Margaret, our hosts in the Visitor Centre there, recommended Avon Skin-So-Soft as being an unintentionally effective anti-midge treatment. As you'd imagine that making your skin softer would serve only to help the midge introduce its proboscis into your epidermis, it must be something about the smell.

Later in Glenfinnan, we're assured it has to be the Skin-So-Soft Bath Oil.

Later still we're told the spray works just as well.

Just thought you ought to know.

CHAPTER
TWELVE

Porridge and Scottishness, Football and Fireworks

I don't like porridge. There, I said it. The reason I don't like it is not so much because of the taste — the stuff doesn't actually have much of a taste of its own, though what it does have I don't find very attractive — as because of the way it feels in my mouth. There is, for me, something unbearably, slidingly glutinous about porridge that pretty much does turn my stomach. Frankly, any time that I do try it, I can't get over the feeling that I'm basically eating wallpaper paste.

Now, I wish this was not the case; I feel a bit bad that I don't like porridge, because I am Scottish, after all, and I even feel — albeit to a relatively small degree and with the usual liberal corollaries regarding nationalism, bigotry and the randomness of birth and subsequent identity — proud to be Scottish, and porridge is an undeniable part of my heritage. It's arguably an important part of that heritage, because the seed it's made from, oats, has played a vital role in keeping

323

Scottish people fed over the centuries. Without oats —
and barley — we might have had something like the
Irish potato famine to add to our catalogue of Rubbish
Things That Have Happened To Us.

So I keep trying to like porridge. I attempt to eat a
bowl every year or so, especially if I'm in somebody's
house who is known for making great porridge, or if
I'm in a hotel with a reputation for prodigious porridge
or brilliant breakfasts or just good food in general. I
have tried it with the usual things people add to
porridge to make it, well, taste of something other than
porridge, I suppose (and this is the main piece of
evidence I'd offer for this dislike of porridge not being
just me; if the stuff's so bloody marvellous, how come
you have to add all these other things to it?).

To this end, and to counter that familiar feeling that
I'm eating something which would be better used to
make rolls of anaglypta adhere to a wall, I've tried it the
purist's way, with a little salt (this makes it taste like
salty wallpaper paste), with honey (it tastes like sweet
wallpaper paste) and with strawberry jam (guess
what?). Personally, nothing works. I just keep thinking
the salt would taste better on an egg, and the honey
and jam better on a bit of toast. There would seem to
be these two basic approaches to adding stuff to
porridge to make it remotely palatable; the sweet route
and the savoury. The sweet way generally means
preserves and the savoury starts with salt and ends
with, well, Marmite, in the case of one of my
sisters-in-law (if you're grimacing at the thought of
Marmite stirred into porridge, you are not alone).

And/or you can add milk, which doesn't really make the horrible, sloppy, squelchy stuff taste any better but does at least dilute it. Even this is a mixed blessing, of course, because although this means there's less of the oily, mealy mass to consume in each grisly mouthful, the whole dish takes longer to consume, if you're in one of those I'll-finish-the-damned-stuff moods, or just don't want to disappoint your hosts.

What is odd is that I do like oatcakes, which, once you've crunched through them, produce a mouthful of something not unlike porridge.

Then, of course, we have barley as one of our other historically staple foods. Which is fine when it's made into whisky, but, again, I can't stand it when it's in Scotch broth. That glutinous thing again. And another national dish that I feel I ought to like but just can't bring myself to eat.

But then for a long time I rejected a lot of traditional Scottish stuff, like the kilt, bagpipes, haggis and drunken self-pity. I was twenty before I wore a kilt because I associated the things with the whole ghastly chintzy, gaggingly clichéd image of Bonnie fucking Scotland; Eileen Donnan on a shortbread tin with a sprig of heather in the foreground and the sound of Jimmy Shand or Andy Stewart in the background; Scotty dogs and some thick-necked twat in a skirt trying to outwit a telegraph pole. For a long time I wasn't even that keen — whisper it — on whisky.

Well, tastes change. I now own a rather splendid dress kilty outfit in one of my clan's tartans; a simple black and white pattern that looks rakishly elegant with the black and silver Prince Charlie dress gear. Technically this colour scheme is the clan mourning tartan, but what the heck. I still don't like massed bagpipes but I can tolerate and even enjoy a well-played single set, I now quite like haggis — though the best form I ever tasted it in was haggis pakora, an inspired example of Indo-Gael fusion that I did my best to take to ridiculous extremes in *Whit* — and as for drunken self-pity, well, I'm still working on that. I've not really had much excuse since I first got published, however there's still plenty of time. Twenty-five years of desultory support for Greenock Morton Football Club, watching as they slid towards oblivion and the Scottish Third Division have to have had some effect, after all.

Whisky I decided I liked long ago.

It's the last weekend of the season. Morton have one more game — a home game against fellow promotion contenders Peterhead — with which to secure promotion to the Second Division and the Third Division championship. Les, Ray and I think it behoves us to be there.

We're going to stay in Glasgow for the weekend with our friends the Fraters. Bruce is a partner in a surveyors' firm and Yvonne — an old friend of Aileen's — is a PE teacher. Their children are Ross and Amy. Right now Ross, who's nine, wants to be anything that'll earn him lots of money (though I secretly know he's going to be a famous artist). Amy, who is a couple of years younger, is very lively, has bubbly blonde hair and is interested in extremes of pinkness and purpleness. They're a nice, normal, busy family, but they are slightly unusual in that Bruce is a diehard Rangers supporter and Yvonne is an equally committed Celtic fan. (Ross isn't entirely sure who to support as long it isn't bunch of losers like Morton, and Amy, having established that neither Old Firm strip features pink or purple, isn't particularly interested.)

Bruce has very generously offered to drive us down to the match in Greenock and is even going to come in to watch the game. For somebody used to watching Rangers, this is definitely slumming it. Bruce has been to three or four Morton games and I think he comes along partly out of basic palsolidarity, partly out of sympathy for us — we tend to need all the support we can get — and partly, perhaps, the better to appreciate Rangers when he sees them play. It's a telling contrast that can't help but flatter Rangers. Morton and Rangers met a few years ago in a Cup game played at Love Street in Paisley, and Bruce sportingly came with us into the Morton end. Morton did not disgrace themselves — we were quite proud we only lost one-nil — but the difference in the teams was blatant. It wasn't just the speed and the skills, either. It was sleekness. The Morton players, despite being considerably more fit than any of us (Les and Bruce both run and cross train, Ray plays five-a-side and I . . . don't), looked like raw, gawky schoolboys next to the Rangers players; donkeys compared to thoroughbreds. Next to our guys, the Rangers team — big, tanned, glowing, rippling with energy — looked like a different species. I understand that the technical term is "Athletes".

I drive through to Glasgow in the Land Rover via the distilleries at Deanston, Loch Lomond, Inverleven and Auchentoshan. It's actually rather a dull day for a change; clouds in the sky, some greyness, even a few light showers. After all the fabulous weather recently, this is positively refreshing. The roads I take constitute a kind of Sensible Route Bypass (GWRs are often Sensible Route Bypasses given a less pejorative title). The Extremely Sensible Route from North Queensferry to Deanston, near Stirling, is to cross the Forth Road Bridge and take the M9 to just south of Dunblane; the alternative Fairly Sensible Route is to take the main road to Kincardine then head for Alloa and then Stirling. Naturally I ignore these and take a variety of GWRs and WDRs (Wee Daft Roads) taking in the mellifluous delights of Coalsnaughton, Fishcross — ah! Romantic Fishcross! — and Menstrie before trundling through Bridge of Allan and taking the long-time GWR to Doune.

These are old stamping grounds for me; I walked all around this area when I was at Stirling University between '72 and '75, roaming as far as Gartmorn dam east of Alloa in one direction, and as far as Doune Castle in the other. I'd gone to Doune because I heard the Python team were there doing some filming. There was nothing happening and nobody about when I turned up one Sunday, but I did get to see the giant wooden Trojan Rabbit. About a fortnight later the notice appeared on the University notice board which led, a week later, to the not so minor miracle of the successful mobilisation of 150 mainly male students at 6.30 on a Saturday morning.

Suitably dressed in medieval-looking stuff — basically knitted string, sprayed silver to look like chain mail — we were whisked up to Sherrifmuir — scene of a real battle in 1715, during the first Jacobite rebellion — for a long day's filming, part of which consisted of us shouting things like "Get on with it!" and "Betty Maaaarsden!" No idea why.

When we'd finished I got a lift back down to the campus in the Black Maria police van that suddenly turns up at the very end of the film; between the peat and some weird leaching effect of the silver-sprayed, knitted-string socks, my feet were black for a week. All for two pounds, which was the Equity rate at the time. But then I think most of us would have paid ten times that for the privilege.

Deanston is a dramatic-looking distillery in a handsome setting. It's another converted mill, this time an old textile mill designed by Richard Arkwright. It was converted into whisky production in the boom years of the sixties but was closed between 1982 and 1990. The mill overlooks the river Teith, which is a major tributary of the Forth (actually, going by relative amounts of water contributed to the blend, it's more the other way round, so we might, conceivably, have had the Firth of Teith, the Teith Bridge, the Teith Road Bridge and, presumably, the Mouth of the Teith. Narrow escape). The river not only provides the water to make and cool the spirit, it also powers the mill itself, though not through water wheels as it did in

329

Arkwright's day; there are two water turbines producing electricity, with any that the distillery doesn't use itself going into the National Grid.

The daftness of the whisky regions comes into play here; like Glengoyne, Deanston is supposedly a Highland whisky, but it isn't. This area just ain't the Highlands and Deanston tastes like a Lowland whisky; quite light, very clean, the delicacy of the nose matching the paleness of the whisky's colour, and with a very pleasant mix of nut-like spiciness and gentle creaminess about it. Deanston is a highly valued blending whisky, but it's worth seeking out as a single malt; definitely another of those whiskies that could benefit from a decent promotional push.

I take an appropriately meandering route across the floor of the Forth's flood plain, along a slow, tightish road past damp-looking fields heading vaguely towards the Trossachs, then head south past Scotland's only Lake, the Lake of Menteith, crossing the Forth a mile or two later, traversing Flanders Moss.

From the commanding height of the Defender, I check out the Forth — barely more than a stream here — as I drive over the bridge. I committed a lot of these bridges to memory when Les and I were planning our downriver trip. This consisted of us putting two canoes in the waters — the very shallow waters — a mile west of Aberfoyle where the Forth is formed by the confluence of Duchray Water and the outflow from Loch Ard, and then — after we got past the shallows where we were pushing ourselves along with the flats of our hands on the gravel as much as actually paddling

— floating and paddling down river to Stirling over the next three days.

It should have been two days but I needed a day off in the middle because my shoulders and arms were so sore (my Uncle Bob expressed genuine surprise we didn't paddle upstream. Different generation; two of my aunts swam across the Forth just upstream from the Forth Bridge. There had been some publicity — even at slack water, swimming the Forth here is no joke and it didn't happen very often — and when Aunt Jean got to the far side and saw there were lots of people and even a few reporters waiting on the slipway at South Queensferry for her and Aunt Bet, she just turned around and swam back again. Like I say; different generation).

Loch Lomond distillery is a bit of a shocker if you're expecting a wee farm-like gem set amongst the heather with a breezy view over the sparkling loch. It's a factory on an industrial estate. It used to be a calico dye works, so it too is a conversion job. They don't do tours but next door there's the Antartex Village shopping complex; a slightly rough-looking converted factory with garish red external walls and god-awful piped music of extreme Heederum-Hawderum-ness that's patently been dredged from the very lowest, most crud-encrusted sump of the great festering bilge tank that is Scottish Cliché MacMusic from Bonnie Glen Grotesquo.

This drivel even extends to the car park so there really is no escape. I have a walk round, watch some skins being prepared to make leather jackets, stop off at the café for a cup of tea and a scone, walk round some more, find the Whisky Shop — a good selection, and I buy quite a few bottles — and, as I pay, realise that although I've only been in here 30 minutes, I swear this is the second time I've had to suffer "Oh Ye Canny Shove Yer Granny Aff A Bus". I ask the assistant how he stands this music all day. He just smiles and asks, What music?

Loch Lomond — another so-called Highland distillery, though only by the skin of its aluminium cladding — is a bit of a multi-tasker; it's set up so that it can produce quite different expressions according to which of its different stills are used. There's Loch Lomond itself, plus Inchmurrin and Old Rhosdhu and, potentially, several others. There's another distillery not far away on the banks of the Clyde near Erskine called Littlemill (correctly a Lowland) which is owned by the same company. This has just started production again after nearly ten years mothballed, and the same people own Glen Scotia in Campbeltown, so the Loch Lomond Distillery Company could end up with quite a selection.

Loch Lomond Pure Malt (no age statement on the bottle I bought) is surprisingly seaweedy. It's a light, leafy Lowlander like the Deanston, with some sweetness in there too, but it has a definite scent of the sea shore about it. Definitely different. I like it for its eccentricity.

I've also picked up a bottle of Inverleven at the Whisky Shop in Antartex Village, a 16-year-old from '86, and — after stopping to take a few photos of the long red façade of the old Argyll Motor Company factory, also in Alexandria — Inverleven distillery is the next stop.

Bit high rise for a distillery, but all the more dramatic for that, with soaring red-brick walls rising almost from the middle of Dumbarton, wide-stanced but with strong verticals from chimneys, pipes and tall, narrow windows. It has a nicely asymmetric and yet balanced look about it, and the way the set-back of it works, outer components leading in towards higher, narrower units, reminds me of a castle. It's actually in quite a pleasant situation, too, close by one small tree-filled park and across the river Leven from another, at the point where the Leven debouches into the Clyde in the shadow of Dumbarton Rock and its uneven straggle of twin-set fortifications.

The 16-year-old Inverleven is not quite so well built or dramatic as the place it's made, but a very approachable dram all the same; distinctively fruity with some smoke and peat, and dry and smooth at the same time. Chocolate Orange, was what I thought.

Last stop is Auchentoshan, just east of Old Kilpatrick, barely a mortar round's lob from Jim and Joan's place in Dalmuir and spitting distance from what's left of this end of the Antonine Wall. I really must get one of those clip-on GPS units for my PDA. I spend a very frustrating half-hour or so trying to get to the distillery, going down one road that looks like it heads straight there only to find that it doesn't, trying another that also looks promising but then loops round without even going close and then another one again, still without success. What makes it especially annoying is that for most of the time I can see the damn distillery, sitting there in watery sunlight looking quite smug in a trim sort of way. The only plus during all this tortuous maze-running is finding an interesting but deteriorating thirties art-deco style sports pavilion across some playing fields north of the rail line.

I finally work out that the way to get to Auchentoshan is not through any of the housing estates that surround it on three sides, but from the north via the main Glasgow-Dumbarton dual carriageway, just east of the Erskine Bridge approach road complex; there's a single wire-fenced approach road leading off the westerly carriageway straight down to the buildings by the side of the dam that holds the cooling water. Wrong maps, again.

So, Auchentoshan. It's an unusual whisky because it's triple distilled, rather than double. Auchentoshan's the last surviving fully triple-distilled Scotch, representing a style that used to be much more common. Partly this reflects improvements in distilling technology. Distilling is about reduction, about refining. Stills don't make alcohol — the mixture of hot water, yeast and the sugars in the barley accomplish that. A still is just a way of separating that already existing alcohol from all the rest of the stuff that's been left behind after the fermentation process has ended. In the old days a lot of places needed to go through the boiling-cooling process three times; now — with better control over every part of the process and fine-tuning the extent of the middle cut that's taken — twice is generally all that's required.

The result of triple distilling, other influences being equal, is to produce a light, delicate, usually quite floral and perfumy whisky. This probably suits a Lowland style of whisky better than an Islay South Coaster, say, though it would be interesting to experiment (I think there should be a big experimental distilling rig in a Scottish university where they can use all sorts of different types of heating, varying shapes of still, adjustable-length and adjustable-angle Lyne arms and so on ... you might not find much that's actually applicable to real-world distilleries, but it would be *interesting*!). As a finished whisky, Auchentoshan depends more than most on its casking, and the star of the readily available expressions is the Three Wood (no age given), which moves promiscuously from bourbon casks to oloroso barrels before ending up in the embrace of Pedro Ximenez. The result of all this serial experience is a seductive, full-bodied, rather fruity ... well, let's not get too tabloid here, but this is generally agreed to be a fine dram, though when I do taste the Three Wood I find it a bit oily for my taste (my three fellow tasters agree, so it's not just me). It's almost as though one of the barrels which went into the marrying process had held diesel or something. It's another whisky which apparently ages particularly well, with 21-, 22 (22?)- 25- and 31-year-old bottlings amongst others, all of which sound — I confess I haven't tasted them — well worth the finding. Providing they don't taste like the bottle I bought. By all accounts, though, another very different and very pliable, very adaptive whisky.

★ ★ ★

There's a Banks Trap in Broomhill; a small but well-formed retail park which cunningly contains a really big outdoor shop right next to a really big Oddbins branch. The outdoor shop is so big it has displays of assembled tents lying around and full-size canoes hanging from the roof and the Oddbins is so big it has a walk-in beer cooler and a separate and very sizable Fine Wine section, not to mention a giant walk-in cigar humidor. It's almost like somebody's been taking notes of my weaknesses. It only needs a Porsche dealership next door in one direction and a decent Indian restaurant in the other and you'd never prise me out of there. Though a sizable bookshop would probably be required too. And maybe a motorbike showroom. Oh, and a CD/DVD store. And a chandlers. And an electronics and gadgets shop.

Anyway, stuff is bought. The Defender swallows boxes and cases containing different types of Guaranteed Fun. Finally it's time to head for Bruce and Yvonne's.

We're getting a chaps' night out. We take a taxi to the Ben Nevis bar on Sauchiehall Street for a couple of beers, then stroll round to Mother India for a superb meal that's interestingly different from the usual sub-continental run of dishes (much as I love them all). The variety of really tasty fish dishes is especially impressive.

Greenock. Cappielow, hallowed ground of the mighty Greenock Morton Football Club. We get there in far too much time because on the last occasion we tried to get in to a really important match, a decade ago when Morton had a slimmish chance of ascending into the Scottish Premier League (and, oh, how long ago that seems now), we didn't get in. We were there an hour ahead of time but there were just so many people queuing already that the ground was full before we got anywhere near the turnstiles.

This time we're there an hour and half ahead of kick-off time and have no problem. We meet up with Jim and Dave and our friends Ronnie and Nipper. Jim informs us he has stopped smoking. I think this is what convinces me that miracles really do happen and Morton are definitely going up. Actually I'd have thought a comparative miracle to Jim stopping smoking would be Morton winning the European Cup, but sure enough, even during an often tense football game, Jim does not light up.

It's a long wait before the game (it's a *really* long wait, because the ground is heading for maximum capacity again and the kick-off's delayed by quarter of an hour to let as many as possible in) and my feet are sore because this morning we walked from Bruce and Yvonne's just off Crow Road to Byres Road and back, to shop at Fopp and have a look round an antiques fair. This end of Cappielow, overlooking Sinclair Street, still has terracing rather than seats and so I lean on the blue, drainpipe-wide rail and take the weight off my feet that way.

However it's good to have the time to talk to people, the weather stays fine and when the game does eventually start it's all okay, because Morton play well, they score a goal, keep a clean sheet and so go up as champions. It's not a great game except in its consequences, but it's not a poor game either; Morton deserve to win and there are no especially dubious refereeing decisions or particular reasons for Peterhead to feel aggrieved; they was not robbed.

Agreed, there is a slight stramash on the touchline when tempers run a little high towards the conclusion of the 90 minutes and it looks like a few fists are thrown, albeit ineffectually, possibly some of them belonging to coaching staff, but even this is quickly sorted out and doesn't unduly disturb the flow of the game.

Fitba and the Greater Morality.

One of the things I dislike about football is its potential for deeply unfair results (this, as you might imagine, is a well developed and deeply felt theme amongst Morton supporters). Because games are so often decided by a single goal and so much depends not just on the imperfect skills of the competing teams but also on the imperfect skills of the refereeing team, it's all too common to see a result against the run of play. I suppose it all comes down to the clunkily digital, almost binary nature of the scoring system.

The tallying system in a game like rugby, for example, with its multitudinous points, makes unfair results less likely. There are still refereeing mistakes and instances of unfairness, and you still see the occasional iffy result gained more on luck than on skills prevailing on the day, but the mistakes tend not to have quite such a potentially crucial effect on the game, and manifestly contrary results are fewer.

And I do think they should have a fourth referee watching replays on TV, wherever possible. Some disagree, taking a purist line on this, saying that by not using this technology the spirit of the game is preserved; it means that everybody is playing under the same rules, throughout the world and at every level, whether it's a season-end Sunday League match after all the consequential stuff has been decided or the final of the World Cup.

Yes, but. The whole point is that the result of one match matters to a few tens or hundreds of people while the other matters to hundreds of millions of people, maybe billions, and the vast numbers of people sitting at home watching a replay showing a piece of blatant fouling that's gone unpunished, or an innocent action that was falsely awarded a card, can plainly see that an injustice has been committed (you could ban TV companies showing replays, but people would just use their video recorders). If you can use technology to prevent that, when it is so cumulatively important, then you should.

People hate injustice; a very large part of what society is all about — what civilisation is all about — is protecting the innocent, letting people just get on with their lives and their livelihoods, and either deterring people from doing bad things to others, or punishing them if they do. When we see a perfectly good, legal tackle in the penalty box which the tackled player responds to by taking a dive, getting the defender sent off and gaining a penalty, and it's all shown in forensic, repeatable detail in front of us (and especially if this decides the match), the sense of outrage we feel is about a lot more than football.

Compromising the purity of the game's spirit is a small price to pay, and besides, as soon as the concept of the professional foul was introduced, the moment footballers began to be traded for money, the instant that the first club became a quotable commodity on a stock exchange, the essential purity of the game, its rules and spirit were already just a long gurgling noise issuing from somewhere deep down the pan.

We discuss waiting for the Third Division trophy to arrive — apparently there's been a helicopter on standby waiting to take the cup to wherever it was needed — but then the rain starts (not that the Morton players notice — they're already soaked with champagne) and so we leave.

Tired but happy, and in sore need of a celebratory drink.

Another Glenfinnan trip, another couple of distilleries. I'm alone in the M5 this weekend, heading up the A9 to Pitlochry before continuing on to Les and Aileen's with a boot full of what you might call Found Fireworks or Opportunist Pyrotechnics.

I have a weakness for explosions. Over the years this has manifested itself in many different ways, and on a couple of occasions has solidified, as it were, into two groups of letters: BAM and FLEE.

BAM stood for Banks And MacLennan, but it was the obvious schoolboy onomatopoeia that was important (entirely appropriately, as my pal Andy MacLennan and I were both schoolboys when we came up with the name). FLEE stands for Fife-Lochaber Explosive Entertainments (Ltd.) and is a more sober and serious enterprise altogether in as much that it's a properly registered company with Companies House (Company number SC2 13224, if you really want to know).

Now, obviously, if I'd ever been in a war, under fire, had anybody close to me die in an explosion or lived in Northern Ireland during the seventies and eighties, I probably wouldn't find explosions or explosives quite so entertaining. However, I've been lucky enough to live a quiet and sheltered life and, to me, explosives have always basically been of a recreational nature.

I'm tempted to blame Gerry Anderson and *Thunderbirds*. There were a lot of explosions in *Thunderbirds*. I loved the fact that after the initial titles, while you were being informed that the series was filmed in Videcolor and Supermarionation (whatever the hell these were supposed to mean), there was an establishing shot of some huge desert installation; a refinery or a power station or something which the camera lingered on after the lettering faded . . . and then it just blew up! In a series of huge, totally gratuitous, completely plot-independent explosions! I was at an impressionable age at the time when I first saw this and remember thinking, Wow! Brilliant!

Except I'd be lying, because me staring enraptured at the perfectly gratuitous screen-borne exploso-fest was just an example of one already long-confirmed explosion freak acknowledging the spoor of another. Long before my first exposure to *Thunderbirds* I'd discovered I loved drawing explosions, throwing stones into the sea because splashes were basically water-borne explosions and even chucking dried clods of earth across my dad's vegetable garden because when the clods hit they flew apart as though exploding, and the dust looked like smoke. And I always really liked fireworks.

In the sixties they'd practically sell you fireworks while you were still in your pram, and the bangers were more powerful (no, really, they were). Good grief, back then you could buy Jumping Jacks. Jumping Jacks were fireworks designed to explode serially — and unpredictably — and jump around in random directions with each detonation. Can you imagine that? If you work in Health and Safety you're probably about to faint (if you're Chinese or from certain parts of southern Europe, you're probably thinking, Yeah, so?).

So we had fun with fireworks.

On the other hand, of course, I was just one of the many lucky ones and lots of kids blinded themselves — or others — lost fingers and/or were badly burned or scarred for life. I wouldn't even suggest repealing any legislation that restricts the sale of fireworks to minors.

At Gourock High I became friends with Andy MacLennan. We'd meet up and muck about with carbide and water mixtures, then with pressurised petrol containers and finally with a compound of sodium chlorate and sugar, in all cases producing explosions.

The power went up as we went along. The carbide and water stuff usually resulted in fairly gentle detonations like large pops; we rarely had to move out of the MacLennans' back porch, which is where we used to perform these experiments. The pressurised petrol paraphernalia made a noise like a jet engine towards the end and then banged fairly loudly and created a mushroom cloud several metres across and ten metres or more high and was quite spectacular in the context of my mum and dad's carefully tended back garden.

And the sodium chlorate and sugar stuff produced supremely-fatal-if-you-were-too-close, military-standard supersonic-shrapnel-type, serious fuck-off explosions. We had to head into the hills above Inverkip to let those off in peace, though we did try to blow up a donated model yacht in front of a hundred other Greenock High pupils one lunch time, in an old reservoir almost entirely surrounded by overlooking houses. That particular display didn't work (water ingress resulting in fuse extinguishment) but we had others that did, up in the hills near the Daff Reservoir.

We'd invite a bunch of friends and head up into Forestry Commission land in a convoy of cars, and then one of us would keep people entertained with some small explosions — the equivalent of quickly prepared and presented starters — while the other one got on with the preparation of the main course, our feature presentation.

We blew a *lot* of shit up.

Actually when we got to the sodium chlorate and sugar stage, we had problems creating anything *other* than explosions. We kept on trying to make guns, but they always blew up. We tried making rockets. They blew up too. Easy-refill burners for the first generation of bombs; exploded. Rocket-propelled cars; guess what? (Actually the rocket-propelled cars worked fine.)

It has to be said that continually trying to make a gun with a wooden breech block was possibly being a little naïve — I'm sure our Physics, Woodwork and Metalwork teachers would have been appalled.

On the other hand the rogue exploding burner taught us we didn't need burners in the first place. That was Andy's Close Shave; the very suddenly — and indeed very highly — airborne burner, constructed largely from a half-kilo of lead, came inches away from taking MacLennan's head off. I had a couple of near things myself, though apart from giving ourselves ringing ears and bright spots before the eyes now and again neither of us harmed so much as an eyelash.

BAM eventually graduated to electrical detonation of the sodium chlorate and sugar bombs and we tried our hand at making gunpowder (technically possible, but overly complicated) before disbanding BAM for good when we went to our respective universities. This was probably just as well in 1972 as the IRA of the time were doing their damnedest to take all the fun out of explosions.

344

A few years ago, struck by an excess of nostalgia, I bought some sodium chlorate weed killer for the first time in 30 years, but — rather unsportingly, I thought — the manufacturers are obliged to add a flame retardant to the stuff these days, and it just doesn't work as an explosive component any more.

FLEE is a rather more above-board concern. FLEE has headed note paper, a bank account and its own cheque book. We even have corporate pens, key rings and coffee mugs, for goodness' sake. Les is Company President, I'm Managing Director and Chairman, Aileen is Finance Director and Ann is Company Secretary. There's a place on the board waiting for Eilidh as Creative Director once she's legally old enough to fill such a post, at eighteen.

The whole idea was to get our hands on some serious fireworks again after they were banned from sale to the general public and restricted to professionals. We'd fondly imagined that just having a proper company would be enough to be accepted as pros, but it isn't. We still can't buy bigger fireworks than anybody else. Still, the key rings are cool.

It's all because Glenfinnan has its own fireworks display on November the fifth. Glenfinnan is just a wee village and the Community Council can't afford to set aside very much each year for a fireworks display, but it's fun all the same. A good decade or so ago I managed to inveigle my way onto the pyrotechnics team (Pyrotechnician, we've decided, sounds so much more professional than Nutter Running Round Letting

Off Fireworks In The Dark) so I get to help let the fireworks off.

Sitting round the bonfire a few years ago, lamenting the fact we used to be able to buy even bigger fireworks, we came up with the idea of FLEE. It was going to be called BIFF originally, but that had already been taken. Anyway, in retrospect, Companies House might have baulked at Big Impressive Fuck-off Fireworks.

There's even a link between whisky and pyrotechnics, my chum Gary Lloyd has discovered. Back in the sixteenth and seventeenth centuries they used to test the proof of the spirit by mixing it with gunpowder and setting light to it! Seriously. If the soggy mixture blew up it was too strong, if it went out it was too weak and if it burned steadily it was about right. How blinkin cool is that? Very rough and ready, in the sense of being wildly inaccurate, but still. Almost a shame they came up with more precise ways to measure the proof strength. Though I'm sure that if this remained the way they tested the stuff in the distilleries nowadays they still wouldn't let you take flash photos of the process. You know; just in case.

This weekend is not about that, though. This weekend is about me attempting to resurrect the past and produce some blevies for the boys, some vapour explosions like the BAM mushroom clouds of old. It's stuff for this nonsense the M5's boot is full of. Technically I should probably have one of those orange HazChem stickers on the boot. That would look *so* cool. But I bet the bureaucracy's a nightmare.

(As it turns out I never do get to let this lot off because the weather's against us and the midges are out.)

First stop is Blair Athol distillery. In Pitlochry. Blair Atholl is a completely different town six miles away. The distillery which bears (most of) its name isn't even on the right side of Pitlochry to be accidentally associated with it; it's on the south side. This wouldn't even be the Blair Atholl Road in the old days, it would have been the Perth Road or the Dunkeld Road. Exactly why this distillery situated quite firmly in Pitlochry is called Blair Athol (somewhat bizarrely missing out the second "l" that the town takes) seems to be a bit of a mystery. Oh well.

They're in the throes of commissioning a newly refurbished Visitor Centre and shop when I arrive on a rainy Friday in late May. The staff seem jolly despite the degree of mild chaos that attends this and it's here the lady recommends Caol Ila as a good malt with a cigar. The Visitor Centre is in the modern style, with lots of blonde wood and exposed metal. Visitor Centre Vernacular is changing slowly with the times; there are more frosted glass panels around than polished dark wood ones, and sleekly tapering steel posts joined by tensioned wire ropes are replacing turned wood banisters and rails.

The distillery itself presents some visual treats, including a just-this-side-of-kitsch little courtyard dripping with ivy, cozily proportioned buildings and trees turned black with the same fungus that coats the warehouse walls both here and elsewhere.

At Blair Athol, as well as some of the place's own whisky, I buy a few bottles from other Diageo distilleries I've been to and photographed without having done tours of or made purchases at. I suppose proper whisky writers would call up the distillery or head office and arrange a private tour of these not-normally-open-to-the-public places, but generally I'm trying to do this in a punter stylee — albeit a punter with deep pockets — and so I'm denying myself such privileges.

Besides, some of the people in the distilleries might have read my books and, when I make my request for a private tour, be inclined to say, No! Now, if you were that Irvine Welsh or Ian Rankin . . .

Blair Athol is an extremely fruity dram, full of ginger, peach and dried fruits. It's not overly sweet, certainly not cloying and arguably quite dry, but the fruit does kind of leap out at you. I remember trying a Blair Athol some long time ago and being very unimpressed, but whatever was wrong then is all right now. I stagger back to the car with my case of clinking, clanking bottles and head out of town up a wee wet twisty road to Edradour, Scotland's smallest distillery, nestling in the folded hills above Pitlochry.

Edradour is a little gem of a place, a sort of distillery in miniature you want to wrap up and put under the Christmas tree. It looks just like an old farm because that's exactly what it once was. The place is all white with red detailing, the buildings clustered around the rushing Edradour Burn that provides the water for cooling — another stream, the Moulin Burn, provides

348

the water for production. When I arrive, in the middle of another heavy shower, two guys are standing stripped to the waist in the tiny mash tun, shovelling still steaming draff out through a waist-high window and onto the trailer of a tractor parked outside.

The pale copper stills are tiny, at the legal limit for size. Any smaller and the Excise people would deem them compact enough to be both portable and too easy to hide, hence illegal. It's all so compact. It's like finding a distillery that fits into a double garage. There are only three people working in the distillery itself — there are twice as many in the shop and on the tour side of the operation. The tour and tasting are free, too, which seems particularly decent in such a small operation.

Edradour has a thing called a Morton (huzzah!) Refrigerator, the last still in use, certainly in the whisky industry. I'd read about this device and been looking forward to seeing this (which, now I think about it, makes me a bit sad, but there you are). A Morton Cooler-Downer might be a more satisfactory name for what it is. It's a long, low, open red-painted thing with lots of rivets, like a wide, shallow tin bath, full of sets of vanes or baffles stretching across it. Looks like the water goes up over one baffle then down under the next, up over the following one, and so on. Oh well, not as dramatic as I'd been hoping for, but interesting enough. Used on farms to cool milk. So there.

The distillery has outdoor worm tubs, pipes gurgling and pool waters steaming as the latest shower patters the surface. In the Visitor Centre, built in an old malt barn, there's a good, informative little video, displays of old distillery implements and a guide to answer questions (my guide is Elaine. When I mention I'm writing a book, she tells me the new owner, the chap behind the Signatory brand of special bottlings, is on the premises. She asks if I'd like to meet him. My natural shyness, which does surface occasionally, makes me say no).

Back in the shop I buy a bottle of the cask strength 14-year-old in a very attractive bottle that looks a little like a wider-necked Absolut bottle. This is another bottle that doesn't last long once Ann, Dad and I get stuck into it; rich and powerful, smooth and creamy. Macallan-like, in fact, which is very high praise.

There is something intimate about the act of drinking Edradour once you've seen the place. It's an easy distillery to feel close to; small enough, you feel, to embrace. The whisky is big and powerful, but even so you still find yourself thinking about those dinky little stills, the mash tun the size of a kids' paddling pool, the croft-like feel of the whole set-up. Of all the distilleries I've been to so far, it's the one most likely to bring a happy smile to my face when I think about it. Must get another bottle.

CHAPTER
THIRTEEN

Just the Whole Gantry, Then

Here's a handy tip: when a cocktail recipe begins with the words, Take A Pint Glass . . . beware.

My friend Roger invented the Blue Moon in a bar in Sheffield when the owner foolishly invited him to order any cocktail he liked, on the house. You fill the glass half full of ice cubes, then introduce measures of: vodka, gin, white rum, tequila, Cointreau, Pernod and blue curaçao. Add a dash of lime juice and top up with lemonade. My variation is to top up with soda water to produce a less sweet-tasting drink. The result, whether using lemonade or soda water, is an electric blue pint of almost luminous intensity which smells slightly of aniseed and is pretty much guaranteed to sweep your legs from beneath you somewhere around halfway down the glass, especially if the measures are 35 mill rather than 25. Roger says they aren't called Blue Moons because of the colour but because they're so horrendously expensive it's only possible to afford them once in a blue moon.

I've known Roger since '87. He's gone from working in a video store to being a script writer, so displaying consistency and ambition. Over the last few years he seems to have developed a habit of writing the screenplays for various of my books which never then get made into films — *Espedair Street, The Bridge, Dead Air* — though we live in hope, I guess. The scripts are fine — inspired, in fact — but it's just the usual film industry yes-no-ery when it comes to getting films financed. We've been through, I think it's fair to say, a few scrapes together over the years. Roger is one of these people that makes me look eminently sober, sensible and sedate. I've already written his epitaph: *Here lies the body of Roger Gray, the man who led himself astray.* Roger thinks this is a really cool epitaph and has, worryingly, at times seemed almost enthusiastic about securing its imminent deployment on his gravestone.

Something of a tradition has grown up in the last few years or so of Roger staying with us over his birthday and the two of us — sometimes with other accomplices, sometimes not — having Blue Moons in the Café Royal Bar, on West Register Street, Edinburgh. For years we've turned up there in late April to find another new lot of bartenders who invariably look completely blank when we mention Blue Moons and who often have to be persuaded that making something like this is even legal before actually starting to put the blighters together.

We'd always kind of hoped Blue Moons would have become legendary amongst the staff in the intervening twelve months, or at least be remembered from one year to the next, but it has never happened. Until this year. When we turned up in the Café Royal in 2003 — in May, a little delayed — the bar manager we talked to not only remembered us and the Blue Moons, he'd made sure there was a bottle of blue curaçao in the cellar for when we did appear.

So we were happy. But then it's hard not to be when supping a Blue Moon anyway. Our record, of which I assure you we are not proud, is three. Frankly, two is pushing it. Just one will tend to get you outrageously drunk if consumed at any speed — drunk to the point, for example, that having a second one gradually starts to seem like a fairly sensible and indeed only logical course of action. Quite how an idea that — it is solemnly agreed by all concerned beforehand — is Totally Idiotic somehow blurs through Well, Not To Be Dismissed Out Of Hand into Maybe Not Such A Bad Idea After All and then finally emerges fully transformed into Another One? Why, What An Absolutely Brilliant And Indeed Utterly Imperative Concept! is just one of life's more intractable mysteries. The tricky thing is that it can only really be fully appreciated somewhere around two-thirds of the way down a Blue Moon in the first place, by which time all bets on common sense, logical thought, joined-up cogitation and indeed reliably focused bicameral vision are already long since profoundly off.

When you drink a Blue Moon you can actually feel your body becoming drunk; usually from the legs up. When this starts to happen getting off the bar stools in the Café Royal — if we haven't managed to bag a table — takes some forethought and planning, because while your brain is innocently labouring under the delusion that it's just sitting here drinking this kind of harmless-looking blue drink and feeling dreamily, unaccountably happy in a la-la-la sort of way, your legs know differently, and are no longer in reliable, uncorrupted communication with — or under the full control of — your brain. Neither of us have ever fallen over, but it's always a concern.

The Café Royal and I have some history. It was here I had a drink with Mic Cheetham before she became my agent and discovered she was a Laphroaig fan too. I'd been in the fortunate position of being able to take my pick of agents after years of not having anybody to represent me. Until this point, James Hale, my editor, and Mary Pachnos, Macmillan's rights director, both of whom were good friends, had made sure that I got a fair deal from the company, but when they were leaving Macmillan and I was leaving Faversham for Edinburgh, it seemed sensible to have independent professional representation.

I talked to half a dozen agents, all of whom were very pleasant and friendly and obviously extremely well qualified. To a man they each offered tea or coffee — one was going to take me to tea at the Ritz, though the hotel wouldn't serve us because I was wearing black 501s — but Mic — Mary Pachnos's suggestion as a possible agent — was the only one who suggested cracking a bottle of wine. Ah-ha, I remember thinking, this is a woman who knows that the way to a

Scotsman's heart is through his liver. A day later, when I was back in Edinburgh, supposedly thinking about my choice of agent (it was Mic, because we'd got on so well, but I didn't want to hurt anybody's feelings by seeming too precipitate), she flew up to see her son, who was at Edinburgh University, and to convince me that she was the right agent for me. I think the Laphroaigs settled it.

I set a scene in *Complicity* here in the Café Royal. I'd noticed that they had a drinks gantry open from both sides with two identical bottles set back to back, so that it looked like a single set of bottles standing in front of a mirror. How cunning, I thought, and just the thing to confuse a very drunk person, so I had my central character, Cameron Colley, already slightly paranoid, start to think that he'd become invisible or a vampire or something when he thought he was staring at a mirror which wasn't reflecting him.

That whole scene is a bit of a writer's conceit; the friend Cameron's talking to — who's called Al, has a wife he refers to as Andi and makes just this one appearance in the novel — is Alexander Lennox, the never-directly-named central character in *The Bridge*; alive and well and, the implication is, married to Andrea, the woman he loves and thinks he might have lost during the course of the earlier novel. The idea was that *Complicity*, for all its final bleakness, does have a happy ending. It's just that it isn't its own happy ending, and it's not at the end.

Oh, and when the two men head out of the Café Royal and visit a florist's round the corner on St

355

Andrew Street, there really was a florist's shop there at the time; it was called Banks's. (It's wee pieces of nonsense like this that help make writing the sheer and total hoot it is.)

This May, Roger, his fiancée Izabella and I tackle the Blue Moons together after a visit to the Scotch Whisky Centre, close by Edinburgh Castle. We head there on foot.

I have never walked along Princes Street or up North Bridge without looking about me at this gloriously displayed riot of architecture, rock, hill and glimpsed, distant river and thinking, I love this beautiful city.

The Scotch Whisky Centre is housed in a fine old late nineteenth-century building on Castle Hill, the continuation of the Royal Mile, and just a door or two away from the Witchery, a restaurant that I happen to know has Grange on the wine list. There's a tour which includes a couple of short films, a live tour guide, a sort of animatronic model distillery with movable walls and bits that lights up (it's a model of the architecturally dramatic Tormore distillery, on Speyside), and a ride round various tableaux illustrating the history of whisky, taken in slowly moving cars shaped like whisky barrels. I found some of this stuff a bit heavy on the hokum, but then I have a very low hokum tolerance. There's a bit on the tour where the supposed ghost of a master blender gives us a short talk when I felt myself come over all literalist and was not far away from standing up and denouncing the thing as a fake and a blatantly obvious video hologram. I mean, I didn't,

356

obviously, but if I'd seen this after a Blue Moon or two, I might have.

There's a restaurant and bar, corporate hospitality spaces and a well-stocked shop selling loads of whisky and the usual collateral-association stuff of the trade; whisky-flavoured socks and that sort of malarkey.

It's actually a decent introduction to whisky as an industry and a drink. For purists and people who've done a lot of real distillery tours it's basically beside the point, but it's not designed for that sort of person anyway. And it does make some telling points, such as mentioning the historical chance that led to the phylloxera blight crippling the wine and therefore the brandy and cognac industry in France just at the time the whisky makers were properly able to take advantage of the fact and push their product as a fitting substitute for these more established — and indeed historically more respectable — spirits.

Izabella is from Poland and while we're sitting drinking our Blue Moons she writes a postcard in Polish to our friend Gary Lloyd and his wife Christiane, who I'm going to see at the weekend. Roger and I write two postcards. Bought on the Royal Mile, these have been chosen for maximum Bonnie Scotland kitschness, Roger's showing a plate of haggis, neeps and tatties with a glass of whisky, mine a pair of cute Scotty dogs and some sprigs of heather. The point is the two postcards only make sense read together because we've swapped every second word. Under the influence of the Blue Moons this seems like just one of the wittiest things anybody's ever thought of since Mr and Mrs Wilde conceived the boy Oscar. We are also spookily convinced of the rightness of our wheeze because when we write our messages out on the backs of beer mats before committing them to our hideously kitsch postcards (proper writers always do a draft first, after all) they are, coincidentally, exactly the same length.

The three of us have already lunched well at Viva Mexico on Cockburn Street — best margaritas in Edinburgh — but shopping, the tour round the Scotch Whisky Centre, the Blue Moons and intensive high-concept postcard writing leave us fit for a decent dinner too, so we head next door to the Café Royal Oyster Bar for food (and some Chateau Musar — you need something robust and powerful to cut through to your taste buds after carpet bombing them with the multiple warheads of a Blue Moon).

Roger and Izabella fly south and a few days later I head in roughly the same direction, taking the M5 to Chester to see Gary and Christiane. I'm taking them their wedding presents; they got married a few weeks ago in Sorrento, Italy, and while we were in Bruges earlier in the year Ann and I bought them some small things for their house. We could post the presents but I want to talk to Gary about music stuff (this, plus the fact it's a long drive, is one reason Ann doesn't come with me).

I've always loved music and I've always loved making up tunes. When I was about eight I can remember sitting in a bus with my classmates going to see a circus in Kirkcaldy, and making up a tune in my head which became a sort of theme for the day. In my memory, naturally, it was and is a great tune, but it's forgotten and gone forever. For some reason I never did take to music at school, and certainly never learned to read or write music. I had to wait until I got an ancient reel-to-reel tape recorder when I was in my early teens before I could save my tunes by whistling them into the thing.

Later, at university, I bought a guitar but I never tried to get into a band, I just sat and taught myself a few chords and developed my unique, eccentric and highly inefficient fret-fingering style. The main change was that the tunes recorded into — by now — a first-generation cassette recorder were in the form of the sound of awkwardly plucked guitar strings rather than hopelessly inane whistling.

Nowadays I have a small but impressive home studio setup. It's not that comprehensive, and wouldn't count as a studio at all by some definitions. I don't have any audio facility, for example — I can't record any acoustic instruments or vocals, but then, as those few unlucky souls who have heard me attempting to sing will confirm, this is entirely a blessing — but I do have lots of machines with a wide variety of numerous flashing lights, which is, of course, a Good Thing. It's basically music processing, and enormous fun, better than any computer game, and Gary Lloyd is the man who showed me how easy it was to get started. Gary once wrote a long musical piece called *The Bridge*, based on my novel. This took years to write and record — certainly much longer than the book took to write —

359

and is probably even more complex than the novel. It has my voice wittering over a few sections of the CD, but other than that it's brilliant.

Over the last half-decade or so I've been very slowly learning how to use MIDI and my musical gear and during the last year I've created a couple of CDs, one with lots of weird synthesiser noodling on it and one comprising of more conventional piano pieces. I sent both to Gary a while ago and now he's got some thoughts to share.

The CD of piano pieces was sent to a few other friends I thought might be interested, and all their views matter too, but Gary, as a professional composer and electronica expert, can probably offer the most cogent advice.

I take the A701 towards Moffat; a fast, still unspoiled road through some roundly impressive Borders scenery, the wave-round hills stamped with great squares of forest. Like the far North-West, the Borders hold some of the best driving roads in Scotland. They're a bit busier than the roads of Wester Ross and Sutherland, but there are more of them too, and they vary from the What-is-this-"police-car"-of-which-you-talk, Earthman? to the A68. If you ever want to see a good road spoiled, drive the A68. I can remember when this roller-coaster of a route was worth taking just for the sheer fun of it, but now it seems to have at least one GATSO camera per mile and it's just a chore. We have only ourselves to blame, I guess; too many enthusiastic drivers must have driven beyond their skills, or luck, and crashed on the A68, and the cameras are their memorials.

The 701 doesn't have any cameras yet, though it does appear to. Somebody's got a mock one in their garden near Tweedsmuir. This is the first pretend speed camera I've ever seen. It looks quite convincing at a glance, before you realise it's set too low, they never site them in gardens and the square lens aperture is a mirror. What's worrying is that the place where it's sited is on bit of a wiggle in the road, slightly uphill when coming from the north-east, and in the midst of a few houses; you'd have to be driving like a maniac to be going much over 60 here.

Which is the other side of the coin for fast driving in the countryside, of course; country roads aren't just routes for fun driving, they're the roads that people live on, too, and if you don't drive with consideration for those people then they're going to demand GATSOs. It's that whole issue of having your own speed limits, modulating speed according to perceived and likely risk and not just going on whether the group of houses ahead has a 30 sign stuck in front of it.

A hot old day in Chester, sticky and still. It's good to see Gary and Christiane. They met on a train when Gary was on his way to North Queensferry. Gary and I have been working on a soundtrack album of *Espedair Street* for a few years now and both of us had made a few journeys, usually by train, to see the other and work on the songs. Originally conceived as the soundtrack for a mooted film of the book — another of Roger's scripts — this project gradually took on a life of its own, especially after Gary had the brain wave of getting

361

other artists to record a song each, as a kind of tribute album to a band that never existed. We've had a holiday from this for a year or so but now it's back on track and we still intend to see what we can do with this idea.

On this occasion it was Gary's turn to travel to Scotland. The Virgin train was, to no one's great surprise, running late and he asked this attractive girl sitting across from him if he could borrow her phone to call me. (I think Gary compensates for having to use all that electronic music gear each day in his work by resolutely not having a mobile phone, laptop or PDA. Until recently he even went to a nearby café to pick up email.) Christiane lived in Dunfermline, just up the road from us, and before too long Gary was making that long journey from Chester to see her. This had the advantage for Ann and me that we got to see Gary fairly often, but it also meant that Gary spent a lot of time on trains, and quite often in trains that were stuck in stations. So he started train spotter-spotting.

As long as I've known him, Gary's been a great note taker; he always carries a notebook (I don't, which is one reason I often feel I'm not a Proper Writer) so he started a page at the back dedicated to the guys that hang around on station platforms watching trains. Years after Gary told me this, Paul Merton on *Have I Got News For You* came up with the same idea, but he didn't have the time to develop it the way Gary did. Gary had columns to record whether the train spotter he'd spotted had a notebook, tape recorder, still camera, camcorder, one of those fisherman-type gear bags you can sit on, an anorak and, crucially, a thermos flask. There was probably a thesis in there on train-spotting attire, behaviour and associated paraphernalia, but then Christiane upped and left Dunfermline for Chester, and Gary's research time was vastly decreased.

We walk into town along the canal, catching up.

The two of them went to see Goldfrapp in concert the night before, in Manchester. Christiane describes Alison Goldfrapp as being dressed, "like a demonic air stewardess on a special Concorde flight to hell."

It's so hot that in one bar I have a whisky with ice, and decide that on a really hot, humid day a sweetish blend with ice cubes is actually not a bad idea. Only a blend, mind you. I'll take some convincing a malt is to be treated like this.

Hmm. Blends. These are not, of course, strictly speaking, part of the brief for this book, but then I'm in England right now and so such heretical thought might be tolerated. It strikes me that in principle, especially if you restricted yourself to malts, with no grain whisky being used to bulk out the mix, it should be possible to create whiskies that taste (in theory, as I say) as good as the best single malts, yet different — and different in an interesting and worthwhile way — to any given single malt. In the shape of their gold- and blue-label bottles, Johnnie Walker already make a couple of blends that damn well ought to be as good as the best single malts given their prices, and these may well show the way. Merely a thought.

According to my diary we have a very good curry in a restaurant called Al Quaeda, but I'm sure that's just a nick-name.

The next day is hot too. Gary and I talk over the piano pieces, listening through each one in turn. He's got a lot of stuff noted down about them. I'm mostly just glad he doesn't dismiss them out of hand, but I can hear what he's referring to as he picks out specific points and makes general observations. We take a break out at a weird little place called Parkgate, a seaside village with no sea, just a grassy plain with a few barely visible little creeks and pools of water, extending from the grass-front promenade out to the horizon, which is where the sea retreated to over the course of the last hundred years or so. Over rapidly melting ice creams we discuss whether instead of rowing boats you could hire lawn mowers to potter about on the sea of grass (apparently you're not even supposed to walk out there because it's Really Dangerous).

I head northwards later, encouraged; Gary's response to the music has been positive and practical. He's quite analytical, so it just comes naturally to him, I suppose. Unlike a lot of analytical people though, he has extraordinary enthusiasm.

Gary and Roger are both about the same age, a good eleven or so years younger than I am, but even when I was their age I'm not sure I had the same passion for work, for people, for arts and entertainment, interesting and/or weird shit and just life in general that these two have. They are both very clever and good at what they do, but even more than those qualities I think it's that existential enthusiasm that I most admire in both of them. Sometimes I feel like I'm almost parasitical on these two, a jaded older brother osmosing their fresh fascination with everything remotely interesting around them.

And so to Bladnoch, the distillery that sounds like it's in Wales. Actually it's the closest distillery to Wales. And England, obviously. Bladnoch lies way, way down on the south-west corner of Scotland, near the town of Wigtown, which is sort of between Dumfries and Stranraer.

This bit of countryside is just packed with great roads; my route has taken us down some effectively deserted bits of tarmac through rotundly spectacular great hills and deep green valleys; wonderful open, rolling scenery incised with immensely fun roads. Near New Galloway, I stop to take a photo of a piece of sculpture sitting on a rise overlooking the road, a giant egg-shaped thing made of small rough slabs of red sandstone. There's no plaque or notice to say who it's by, but there's something of a tradition of this sort of thing in this neck of the woods; further south there's a whole collection of Henry Moore sculptures sited sitting in poses of calm liquidic ease in middle-of-nowhere fields.

The area I'm in now is the Galloway Forest Park, and the road and the scenery both just get better. This is one of the least known bits of Scotland, and one of the most rewarding. It lacks the grand verticality and sheer scale of the West Highlands, but makes up for

365

that with a more accessible, even friendlier landscape of rumpled hills, fertile valleys (down here they don't feel like glens), high moors, a fine smattering of castles, small, winding lochs, lush fields of positively Irish greenness, huge forests and neat, idiosyncratic towns with names like St John's Town of Dalry, Newton Stewart, Castle Douglas and Gatehouse of Fleet. And all this is before you even get to the coast, which feels sometimes like the least Scottish bit of Scotland (with the possible exception of St Andrews on Graduation Day). The Solway coast can feel almost like part of Dorset. Or South Wales. Hence Bladnoch having that Welsh connection, you feel (I mean, wrongly, obviously).

Bladnoch distillery disappeared off the extant distillery map some years ago; United Distillers — as they then were — owned it from 1983 to 1993, when they closed it down and removed all the stocks of whisky, the pipe work and other whisky-making bits and pieces (save for the big, expensive-to-break-up things like the mash tun, washbacks and stills) and sold the buildings as very much not a going concern, with the condition included in the deeds to the place that it could not be used as a distillery in the future. And that certainly seemed to be that for Bladnoch.

Then an Irishman called Raymond Armstrong decided he wanted to buy a holiday cottage on the Solway coast. He bought Bladnoch. Now, there is a cottage sort of attached to Bladnoch, but basically this is a whole sprawling complex of light-industrial buildings with what certainly looks like several acres of warehousing space adjoining; how the hell you'd cop for this lot while looking for a wee holiday home by the coast quite defeats me. Whatever; Mr Armstrong signed the papers, then thought, actually, it would be interesting to try his hand at distilling. Either he's a real sweet talker or United Distillers were much nicer than Ravening Capitalist Mega Corps are supposed to be, because they agreed to alter the terms of the no-distilling clause to let Bladnoch make up to 100,000 litres of spirit a year (it could make over ten times that at full production), and so Mr A, after installing the necessary pipes and ancillary bits and pieces and attending to the legal paperwork, had his working distillery.

Sitting just outside Wigtown in the midst of fields beside the lower tidal reaches of the river Bladnoch, across from a pleasant little pub with colourfully impressive hanging baskets, the distillery is attractive and welcoming. When I arrived they had a pair of six-week old kittens called Sherry and Bourbon wandering around the courtyard and Visitor Centre in that dazed, not entirely coordinated, what-am-I-doing-here-again? manner that kittens tend to exhibit at that age.

Bladnoch is basically a one-person-operated distillery; with its necessarily sedate production schedule, each stage of the process is carried out in discrete steps and only needs one person to oversee everything. Many more people are required to staff the Centre and manage the place than it needs to actually make the whisky. Perhaps because of this there is a distinctly relaxed air about Bladnoch, a sort of gentle feel to the place. Also, the tour's a very reasonable one pound each, so it's not as though they're running it more to rake in dosh from the Visitor Centre while forgetting about the whisky itself. It feels like part of the community, too; the old bottling hall has been turned into a fairly sizable function space — something like a modern interpretation of a medieval banqueting hall — with a stage, bar and lots of space for dancing and general hilarity. Popular with the locals for weddings and birthday parties, apparently, and even on a sunny afternoon, deserted apart from our small tour group, it feels like is does indeed have an atmosphere conducive to serious fun.

Very lightly peated indeed (3 p.p.m.), Bladnoch is a light, flowery, crisp dram, very appropriately Lowland in character. I've already got a Rare Malts Edition 23-year-old at 53.6 abv and it's quite a forceful, dynamic dram for something so intrinsically light in character; a rapier to the cutlasses and broadswords of some of the heavier, more northerly whiskies. It'll be 2010 before the first of the new-ownership bottlings become available from Bladnoch, and it will be interesting to see to what extent the character of the whisky changes then. It's an easy place to like and the people seem enthusiastic. You find yourself wishing them all the best for the future, and looking forward to watching the development of the distillery and the whisky.

I stop in Wigtown on the way back. It's Scotland's Book Town. They're hoping to turn it into a northern

Hay-on-Wye and while it's not really there yet in terms of the sheer numbers of book shops, it too is developing hopefully and seems encouragingly busy. Even has a bookshop that specialises in SF and related stuff, which is no bad thing. I struggle to restrict myself to two shops and as many books as I can carry. I head back via the coast and the A75. The 701 from Moffat is equally inspiring in the opposite direction.

The fake speed camera at Tweedsmuir is still there.

By now it's June and I've started writing the book. We've played host to Ann's sister Susan and her husband Phil as well as to Ann's parents, Denis and Christa, so Ann doesn't feel too left out or lonely as I sit in the study clattering away at the keyboard. We've been abroad with Denis and Christa in Cyprus back in March, of course (cue that unexpected snow in Pissouri) and we went to Berlin — one of my favourite cities since I hitch-hiked there from Hamburg in 1975 — with Sue and Phil back in November. Cue perfectly expectable temperatures of umpteen below. On the way to Berlin, changing flights at Birmingham Airport, I picked up a copy of *Whisky* magazine. By November I'd already signed up to write this book, and besides, the magazine had an article about whisky bars in Berlin. We don't actually visit any of these bars, though we do stroll round the Charlottenburg Palace and visit another great palace, in this case of retailism, KaDeWe. KaDeWe is a monumental department store whose two top storeys are devoted to food and drink. These two floors make Harrods Food Hall look like a corner shop.

Seriously; if you ever go to Berlin, don't miss KaDeWe; if you have any interest in food and drink *at all* those two top storeys are just another vision of heaven.

Later I take out a subscription for *Whisky*, strictly in the interests of diligent research.

I've settled into a routine of writing, doing all the usual domestic stuff, and — to try and keep even slightly fit while being basically sedentary through most of the day — augmenting my usual short walks round the village with longer walks in the forests and hills within a half-hour's drive.

There are still distilleries to be investigated, however, and malts to be drunk. The next couple of unwitting guests to be press-ganged into some gratuitous distillery-researching are the Obasis.

Michelle Hodgson used to do my publicity. She's working for the *Guardian* and *Independent* these days and — as an aspiring writer — writing novels in her spare time, but for a good decade or so she was the person who had the task of arranging my promotional tours round the country and then accompanying me round the bookshops for a fortnight at a time. Michelle did this for lots of other writers too, of course, but my book-a-year schedule meant that she probably had to endure more time with me over those ten years than any other scribbler. Despite this, she became good friends with Ann and me — to the extent that our spare room was renamed the Hodgson Suite — and we've kept in touch since she left Little, Brown.

Michelle is another of these approximately-eleven-years-younger pals, about the same age as Gary and

Roger. The girl takes her novel research seriously. She lived on Guadeloupe in the Caribbean for almost half a year to research a novel set there, and moved out for three months to Benin, next door to Nigeria, a couple of years ago, to work on another book. In both places the national language is French, which Michelle is fluent in, and part of the idea was to go somewhere hot and exotic, certainly (research should be fun, as I've always thought and am trying to prove), but more importantly somewhere hot and exotic off the more usually trodden tracks for English speakers. Ann and I duly went out to Guadeloupe for a week when she was there — just to make sure she was okay, obviously — but missed out on Benin.

Maybe just as well. While Michelle was there she contracted malaria. She got through it, and it was one of the not-quite-so-serious, non-recurring types, but it sounded unpleasant enough from the symptoms she described. One of the main reasons she got through the illness was a young Nigerian man called Tom Obasi, who looked after her while the disease was at its worse. They were married a few months later.

Why Roger and I have mixed feelings about Brad.

Bradley Adams is a great tall chunky man of quietly riotous good humour and a passion for films and for making films that can even get through my near-invincible filmic disillusion. He was the producer of *The Crow Road*, and, if the money is ever got together, will produce the films of my books that Roger has been working on the scripts of. He has an enormous reservoir of Really Funny Film Stories (many of them libellous), is great company and, in a modest, unassuming way, is profoundly impressive.

Roger, Brad and I were sitting in the secret underground HQ of Brad's production company in Soho (well, I usually get lost when I'm trying to find it and it is in the basement). We were in what I think is supposed to be the script development room but which always feels to me like the staff room or the common room or the officers' mess or something, sitting round the table drinking wine and chatting. Roger and I were about to leave to meet Michelle for the first time since she'd got back from Africa, before rendezvousing with Brad again later so I could do research for my novel *Dead Air* (this consisted of going to a huge early Christmas party being thrown by Working Title Films at the RAC Club on Piccadilly, then going on to the Groucho Club and the Soho House and then the Century Club where I had a great time but then completely forgot all about until we had the book's launch party there, coincidentally, most of a year later. After that we went back to Claridge's and sat talking nonsense, mostly, all night).

So, just before Roger and I were about to leave the secret bunker to go and meet Michelle, I mentioned to Brad that Michelle had gone to Africa and got the two big "M"s: Malaria and Married. This was an observation of such minor wit even I wasn't remotely proud of it, but people kind of expect this sort of thing when you're a writer and it's hard to get out of character sometimes. Brad just nodded once and said, "Ah yes; first bitten, then smitten."

Roger and I looked at each other, faces falling.

We were supposed to be the writers; we do the quips, the funny dialogue, the one-liners. Not producers. And we rarely expect to generate all the above stuff in real time; it can often take hours of work (or what certainly *feels* like hours of work) to create what looks and sounds like a single snappy off-the-cuff remark.

Naturally we pointed out this basic film industry professional demarcation issue to Brad at the time, but I doubt the scamp took any notice.

In any event, maybe now you can see why we both love the guy and — when he says something like that — really *really* hate him.

So, Michelle and Tom come to stay in what is now the Obasi Suite. We go to the Omar Khayyam, come home and play lots of pool. This mostly means Tom and me being competitive and me being lucky. Tom is a breezily cheerful guy with a neat turn of phrase. He looks fit as an ebony fiddle (well, maybe a viola) but declares that he has to be careful not to eat too much because as he tells us, "I am vulnerable to expansion". Nobody who sees Michelle and Tom together could doubt they married for love, but he's had predictable problems getting a residency visa for the UK. It's been sorted out now and he's set up his own company to install security camera systems, though what he wants to do is start up an import-export business shipping goods to and from Nigeria.

The next day we load up the M5 and head for Mull, to visit the Tobermory distillery. Music comprises three CDs of soul classics, *Buzzin'*, the second Bumblebees album, *Specialist in all Styles* by Orchestra Baobab and *Loss*, by Mull Historical Society.

We take the Glen Devon route to Crieff, then head on down the A85 for Oban. The stretch between Tyndrum and Dalmally is the best bit, with intestinally sinuous curves and fabulously long, open straights, then after Lochawe village there are more fast lengths along the side of Loch Awe through the Pass of Brander.

There's a power station built into the mountain of Ben Cruachan and one day I really intend to visit it. The power station uses off-peak electricity generated by other power stations during the night to pump water out of Loch Awe up to the Cruachan reservoir 1500 feet up the mountain. It takes so long to shut down your average power station efficiently that it's cheaper to keep them running overnight and use the power for schemes like this. During the day, when there are peaks in demand, the water's released from the reservoir and flows back down to Loch Awe through some humungous pipes and a huge turbine hall hollowed out of the middle of the mountain. The turbines drive generators and the electricity they make goes into the National Grid.

There's a Visitor Centre here so it's not as though you need to ask somebody nicely before you can see all this, which basically sounds like exactly the sort of Big Engineering Stuff that I'd really get off on, but the trouble is that when we pass here we're usually either, as today, on the way to catch a ferry, or on our way back after a holiday and just wanting to get home. Plus it is a great bit of road, so we tend to have already gone whistling past by the time we think it might be an idea to stop and have a look. Still, one day.

At Connel, tyres swishing through the remains of a light shower, we look for the Falls of Lora, but the tide's wrong. The falls are tidal rapids caused by a broad lip of underwater rock at the narrows where Loch Etive joins the sea; twice a day, unless it's a neap tide, the whole width of the narrows fills with wild, surging surf. It's kind of nature's equivalent of the Ben Cruachan pump-it-up/let-it-flow-down setup. Actually it's mildly surprising it hasn't been dammed with a tidal barrage.

The falls lie almost underneath the bridge at Connel. This is an old, narrow girder bridge which used to carry both road vehicles and trains, when the line still ran to Ballachulish; traffic lights stopped the cars when a train was approaching (I remember seeing this happen, back in the early sixties when we were on holiday and Mum and Dad's car was stopped at the Connel side. The steam engine roared past only feet away from us. I recall being immensely impressed). Even without the trains the bridge is still too narrow for two-way traffic, so the lights at both ends remain.

The ferry is inbound a mile or two out of port as we arrive in Oban. I've always liked Oban; it can get so busy in the height of the season that the whole town is basically full, with nowhere to park and nowhere to

375

stay, but I suppose that's down to geography. The place grew up around its harbour, and the same intricate foldings of the landscape that made the anchorage sheltered by hiding it from the open waters mean that the land nearby is highly convoluted, all steep hills, cliffs and outcrops of rock with relatively little flat ground available. At such times, if you don't need to go through it but it lies en route, it's arguably quicker and certainly much more pleasant to take to the network of wee roads east of the town which I tend to think of as the Oban bypass, but for all its its dizzy bustle the place has real charm and the ferries, fishing boats, yachts and trains give it a buzz that by Highland standards makes the place positively colourful.

As the ship quits the harbour, we pass the ivy-smothered ruins of Dunollie Castle. I climbed this once, on a day trip by train from Edinburgh, and did a circuit of the walls' broad summit. That was after the first instance of What Happened To My Car, back in 1987, when I was travelling by train quite a lot because I'd picked up a twenty-month ban for drunk driving. Broke Jim's ankle, wrote off a very large Volvo and demolished a not insignificant part of a Kentish farm. Long story.

I do not have chicken curry and chips on the ferry.

We pass Duart Castle shortly before docking at Craignure. This is another much filmed location; the most recent film I remember seeing it used in was *Entrapment*, but it's been in a few others. We're staying at Druimard Country House Hotel, in Dervaig, right beside the small but perfectly formed Little Theatre of

Mull, about twenty minutes away from Tobermory, the island's capital.

The food at Druimard is excellent, though only Michelle and I turn up for breakfast. Tom, like Ann, seems to number Sleep and Having a Long Lie amongst his hobbies. I am tempted by the kipper, but we'll be in the M5 for a good few hours today, and in-car belching etiquette dictates that scrambled eggs are probably a safer bet. When we eventually round up our respective spouses we head over the wee twisty road for Tobermory, like Oban another clinging-to-the-land-by-its-fingernails kind of town, but very colourful.

Tobermory has probably been on more postcards and magazine and book covers than any other Scottish town of its size just because it's so picturesque (and these days it's almost better known as the BBC's Balamory); every harbour-front building save the church seems to be some freshly painted and very bright primary colour — usually with contrast detailing round the edges and apertures — and the whole wildly motley crescent is backed by wooded cliffs and reflected in the clear waters of the harbour. One of those places you practically have to have a degree in camera klutzhood to take a bad photo of.

At the distillery, we register an interest in taking a tour — they need a few more than just us to make a quorate tour group. However after a look round some interesting craft shops and a chandlers on the spectrum of seafront, we get together with some more people to do the look-round.

Tobermory distillery instantly gets the prize for Hottest Still Room So Far. It's not even that hot outdoors but the still room is small and relatively cramped, and with the stills operating as they are now, you can feel the heat increase with pretty much every step you take up from the room's floor to the walkway set around the stills' centres. I remember walking uphill in the largest of the big quilted-looking biomes at the Eden Project in Cornwall the summer before, and experiencing the same feeling there, each pace underneath the giant bubble-wrap semispheres seeming to make the air hotter and more humid. It doesn't feel too claustrophobic in the still house because there's a big new window looking out onto the road outside, but the heat is such that you can see people start to wilt almost as soon as we walk in.

The distillery sits in a relatively cramped site jammed against the bottom of a cliff, across the main road from its old warehouses, which have been turned into rather attractive council flats. The main road down into the bay-front centre of town runs past them, but the traffic noise must be partially masked by the susurrus of sound coming from the distillery's water supply, the Tobermory River, which tumbles down the steep stepped channel between the flats and the road. These days the spirit is taken to be matured in that big old converted mill by the Teith at Deanston, near Doune. Usually reliable sources indicate that this has, as you might expect, changed the character of the whisky so that it's less island-like in flavour, missing some of the seaweedy notes it used to display and tasting a little more like a Lowland malt.

The water is so naturally heavily peated there's no need to add peat to the malt for a hint of the flavour to come through in the finished dram, though phenolised malt is used for the Ledaig expression. Ledaig means "safe haven" in Gaelic and was the old name for Tobermory, which — just as Oban is protected from on-shore winds by the island of Kerrera — is sheltered by Calve Island. The washbacks, housed in a Velux-windowed building set hard against a precipitous tree-lined slope, are made of Douglas fir, replacing the more usual Oregon pine.

The stills each have an odd-looking Lyne arm which looks like a drawn-out S lying on its side. Incredibly, Tobermory risks setting the entire atmosphere of Earth on fire and sending the planet spinning into the Sun by letting people take flash photos in the still house. Obviously these people don't know the primal forces they're meddling with. However it's not my job to set the poor fools straight so I keep shtum and click and flash away with me Minolta.

The 15-year-old Ledaig I buy at the distillery is a nicely rounded dram of some peatiness and smoke, halfway between a typical Island Whisky and a Lowlander; a peninsular whisky, perhaps. There's a kind of high, keen edge to it that then fills out into a kind of spicy chocolate flavour. Tobermory itself, usually bottled at ten years old, is a lighter whisky which still seems to have that touch of peat and sea about it, and focuses the spiciness of Ledaig down to a sort of nutty pepperiness.

I don't grudge the people in the flats opposite the distillery their homes, but you do wonder what the expressions of the last couple of decades would have tasted like had they been matured within sniffing distance of the sea.

The last thing we do before leaving for the ferry is buy some Mull Cheddar, one of the best, tangiest, most fiercely flavoured cheeses you can buy.

A couple of weeks later on a hot, bright sunny day Ann and I take the wee car through Glen Devon to Crieff and Gilmerton and back round to the Famous Grouse Experience at Glenturret. We go via the small, very peaceful little chapel at Tullibardine, an old family chapel no longer in use but sitting very prettily in a stand of beautifully shaped Scots pines, and wonderfully cool inside on such a hot day.

The route has also taken us past Gleneagles, the stupendously grand but surprisingly welcoming überhotel where, in the big art deco bar to the right as you enter through the main doors, there is a very thick brown book detailing lots of whiskies. Lots of old, rare whiskies. Lots of old, rare, very expensive whiskies. Lots of old, rare whiskies which are so expensive the prices make you blink and look again, because you could buy an entire case of quite decent whisky for the price being asked here for a glass. It is a decent glass, in the sense that the standard measure is a small double — 50ml — but even so.

I have never gone entirely mad with this big brown book, but even keeping to the humbler examples there are interesting and out-of-the-way whiskies to be sampled if you choose carefully, and it's really rather comforting to know that you're in the presence — at the other end of the scale — of Extreme Whisky Pricing. I only hope that the people who do shell out hundreds of pounds for a dram aren't doing it just to impress partners or people they're trying to do a deal with. And that they don't add bleedin' Cola.

We stayed at Gleneagles over a long weekend with the McFarlanes, three years ago. Gleneagles has wonderful staff, brilliant food and drink, and has all sorts of sports and activities to take part in if you feel so inclined, or you can just be outrageously pampered. I believe golf is played there on occasion, too.

We went in opposite directions at the end of the weekend, the McFarlanes north to Glenfinnan, us south to North Queensferry. Ann and I were in the Defender at the time, which we'd bought a week or so earlier. It was still unchipped, with its original lowly horsepower quotient, and as we headed out of the car park towards the Glen Devon road, we were behind a brand new silver 911 Turbo. I naturally expected this beast to disappear into the distance in a red-shifted blur within about half a second of exiting the hotel grounds, but it didn't. Instead it dawdled, rarely doing much more than 50. We stuck behind it in the Land Rover, driving fairly sedately, easily keeping pace. I swear if I'd really wanted to there were a couple of places I could have overtaken the guy. I didn't — it would have seemed almost sacrilegious, and would basically have been showing off, even borderline aggressive — but I could have. I have no idea why the car was being driven so slowly, but it just goes to show; it ain't what you drive, it's how.

Glenturret is one of the smallest distilleries in Scotland (just one pair of stills), and one of the oldest (founded 1775), however it's also one of the most up-to-date and visitor-friendly. It lies leafily beside the river Turret, only a mile or two from Crieff, and is set up to receive lots of visitors in a Centre displaying all the shiny newness of that Visitors Centre Vernacular, Reformed: blonde wood, lots of wee halogen spotlights, serious glass and cable-linked stanchions. Oddly, the stills themselves are one of the less visually appealing parts of the whole experience; they're inelegant, almost square-looking things, but I suppose of all the qualities of a still its looks are the least important. There's good Scottish food in a proper restaurant, various audio-visual bits and bobs, a well stocked shop and two statues; one of a giant grouse, at the entrance to the car park (for this is the Famous Grouse Experience, both it and Glenturret being owned by the Edrington Group), and another, much smaller one of Towser, the old distillery cat credited in *The Guinness Book of Records* with offing just under 29,000 mice. Actually with offing 28,899 mice, which is a very suspiciously precise number.

Roughly on a par with that warheads-ready-in-45-minutes piece of shite, come to think of it.

Well worth seeing, Glenturret, and well worth drinking, too. I go for the standard 12-year-old, which is all fruit and nut, like an extremely alcoholic chocolate bar. There's dryness too, especially in the finish, with lolloping hints of grass and flowers. So; a chocolate bar sampled in a sunny meadow. Like an ad-exec's dream from the seventies, really.

It's a whisky that would probably particularly benefit from a vertical tasting, where the same drink is sampled at various ages. Reading what people have written about some of its older expressions it sounds like Glenturret changes more than most as it matures, and keeps on developing and getting better. Would that we could all perform the same trick.

CHAPTER
FOURTEEN

The Ends of the Country

Welcome to the Free World.

In the July 17th 2003 edition of the *Guardian*, in an article headlined "We are now a client state", David Leigh and Richard Norton-Taylor set out the case for Tony Blair having finally surrendered to the United States of America most of the few remaining shreds of British sovereignty.

They point out that Britain cannot target, maintain or fire its Tomahawk cruise missiles without US authority, that this same restriction has applied to the Trident missile system for the last decade and a half (so that Britain's "independent" nuclear deterrent never has been; basically the British taxpayer has been paying for at least one sturdy spoke of the US's nuclear umbrella all these years), that Britain has already entirely and formally given up sovereignty in various British mainland bases and several overseas ones, like the Indian Ocean bomber base of Diego Garcia, where the native people were thrown out 30 years ago and left on the docks in east Africa, that we spend a fortune gathering intelligence at GCHQ, share all of it with the US intelligence services — those paragons of vigilance who did such a brilliant job preventing the atrocities on September 11th — but they are under no obligation to share all they know with our lot, that (and this is ongoing through recent and envisaged purchasing and equipment standardisation decisions), Britain is tied into the US war-fighting machine to such an extent that it will no longer be capable of fighting a war without the US's approval and connivance, while being, by extension, entirely expected to muck in with any American military adventure where such participation will help make this year's invasion look less like the exercise in naked imperialism that it in fact is.

They also make the point that your individual Brit cannot any longer rely even on the occasionally dubious protection of the legal system which we pay for through our taxes and at least nominally control through the democratic system of the country we live in. British nationals held in the fantasy counter-reality that is Camp Delta, Guantanamo Bay on Cuba — prop. George Sauron Bush, Esq. — have effectively been abandoned by the Crown and government that is supposed to protect them (well, they haven't got even the basic good sense to be white, they are self-confessed Muslims, Dubya says they're all Bad People anyway so *of course* they don't really count).

Finally, it now turns out that back in March, while we were distracted by all that spiffing fighting, British Home Secretary David Blunkett signed a treaty with the US which means that any British national, living in the UK or its dependencies, can be extradited to the US to stand trial for whatever crime an American court deems they might have committed, with no need for any prima facie case to be established in front of a British court before the alleged miscreant is hauled off. In other words, they just have to ask, and you'll be handed over. The Americans, being the big Uncle Sam daddy rather than the quivering Britannia bitch in this abusively unequal relationship, and very sensibly having a written constitution which forbids such horrors, are of course under no such obligation to reciprocate, and indeed are legally unable to.

So the British legal system and the individual rights of any given Brit are now entirely subservient to the whims of any one of gawd-knows how many public servants and judges sitting in the United States, home of Dubya the Usurper and his grotesque squad of Cold War throwbacks. The Home Office press release covering the meeting during which this historic and unprecedented surrender of sovereignty took place failed to mention it had happened at all. As Leigh and Norton-Taylor suggest, maybe it was through shame.

Equally quiet at the time, once this treaty's terms have finally slithered out into the light of day, are all the right-wing British newspapers which can be relied upon to foam at the mouth whenever they detect the slightest hint that Britain might be surrendering something as important as control over the shape of a fruit to Brussels. Suggest that there might be a standard Europe-wide definition of what you can call "ice cream" or "chocolate" and these charmers are spitting blood about faceless Eurocrats completing the job that Napoleon and Hitler failed to accomplish and dropping dark hints about leaving the EU altogether; abandon us all to the mercies of a protofascist rogue state 3000 miles away over which we have no democratic or legal control whatsoever, and there's not a damn peep.

Last time I checked I did have an MEP to whom I could complain about any abuses within the European system, and who I could, along with my fellow voters, remove from office; I have yet to be informed of the identity of my Congressional representative.

On the 18th of July, 2003, Tony Blair makes a speech before the US Congress (meanwhile a scientist called David Kelly is taking his last walk along a path in Oxfordshire). Blair as good as admits that he and Bush were lying about Iraqi weapons of mass destruction but says that history will forgive them. As one has to suppose it will, when it forgives Quisling, Pétain and Milosevic (I'd include Mussolini, but under Berlusconi the Italians seem halfway to forgiving that particular scumbag already). Then Blair tells America — and, more to the point, the illegitimate, far-right fundamentalist administration of Bush the Younger — that it has a mission to combat evil wherever it thinks it sees it, and bring its form of peace to all the world. "Destiny put you in this place in history, in this moment in time," he tells them. "The task is yours to do . . . Our job is to be there with you."

To which the only reasonable, calmly considered reply any sane Brit can offer is, I think, "Oh no it fucking isn't, you self-righteous warmongering git."

To Aberfeldy with my dad and Uncle Bob. We whisk northwards in my dad's automatic 528i. This is our old car and similar-in-some-ways to the M5 so I feel that I don't do too badly making just the one grab for the selector in a vain attempt to change down. The guys don't make any sarcastic remarks.

My dad is 85 and Uncle Bob is his young brother — a sprightly 70 and a bit. He lives down the hill in our village and is still a bit dazed looking sometimes after losing his wife, the wonderful, vivacious Isabel, last year. Aunt Isabel — Glammy Aunt Isabel as she was accurately christened by one of Ann's nieces — always looked about fifteen years younger than she was, and was just full of life and love. She died very suddenly last summer, with no warning at all, leaving Bob and her children, Vicky, Donna and Bobby, bereft. You always wish a quick, unlingering end for those you love, but you forget that an unexpectedly sudden death leaves people unprepared, just stunned.

My dad is the man I've admired most in my life. I suppose objectively Nelson Mandela is more admirable, but of all the people I've ever met, could ever claim properly to have known, my father is the one I've looked up to the most. Like I said earlier, both my parents made me feel loved and special, and I feel that I owe them both enormously.

Uncle Bob is arguably the really artistic one in our family; he's been an accomplished watercolour painter for 30 years or so and he's had dozens of stories and poems published over the last few years in a variety of magazines (it occurred to me a couple of years back that actually my mum's a fellow professional too, now, as she had a poem published, for dosh, in a magazine). Bob used to be a rigger on the Forth Road Bridge, and it's thanks to him I got to the top of the bridge, twice. The view from up there, 512 feet up — the Forth Bridge is a mere 365 five feet — is simply breathtaking. The first time I went up there was on a beautiful clear day in the early seventies, when I came through to the Ferry on a day trip from Stirling; I thought I'd taken a whole spool of photos, but my camera didn't. The second time, with Les, was on another calm, bright day not long before Bob retired. I took two cameras this time, just to be certain. Loads of photos.

We head straight up the M90/A9 with just the one wee detour at Logierait to take in an old disused railway bridge Ann and I discovered last year that's been turned into a privately owned but open to the public route across the Tay. The 528 clatters over the bridge's slatted wooden deck and briefly grounds its sump on a seriously vicious hard-rubber speed-bump, even at walking pace (there's another one like it at the far end of the bridge; the trick — apart from taking it dead slow, obviously — is to brake as you go over and then release as the front wheels start to drop, letting the rebound on the springs provide the necessary clearance).

389

The Aberfeldy distillery and Dewar's World of Whisky lie a few miles further on, on the outskirts of the town of Aberfeldy.

Now this is Extreme Whisky Glitz. The distillery itself is very neat, clipped and well presented, with imposing grey buildings topped with the traditional pagoda, precise lawns, lots of flowers, sharp paths and a steel and blond-wood bridge into the Visitor Centre, housed in the distillery's old maltings. A nature trail meanders off into the woods and in theory we might have been tempted to go for a stroll, however it's a day of on — off drizzle — a Soft Day as they'd term it in Ireland — and so we miss out on the nature stuff. There's an old and well-preserved saddle-tank shunting engine in the grounds which used to haul the barrels from the distillery to the branch line that went via the old bridge we crossed earlier.

Inside is where the real plushness is. There's a well-stocked shop — the Brand Store, no less — and for a fiver you get given a big flat stick-like thing like two very early mobile phones joined together end-on. This is a sort of personalised, opt-in tour guide, and available in different languages. Scattered round the place there are head-with-headphones symbols with numbers underneath; you key the number into the phone-like Audio Guide and listen to the solid-state recorded patter.

There are really two tours here; this one with the hand-stick thing of Dewar's World of Whisky, then a more conventional distillery tour with a human guide. The W of W tour really starts with a good, not too embarrassing video which is shown in an auditorium that looks a lot like the sort of private film theatre I imagine Third World dictators have in their palaces; lots of red draping with fake white columns round the inset walls, with the three-part semi-wraparound screen — quite effectively used in the presentation — framed in scrolled gilt. This is very much just one side of tasteless but I can't entirely decide which. Actually I can, but it doesn't matter because once you leave the Auditorium and are batched into the rest of the display space, the glitz turns out to be entirely appropriate to the life of Tommy Dewar, the man and retail genius who really set the whole kit and indeed caboodle going in the first place, a century and a half ago.

There's a darkly opulent study recreated in here, a blending room, lots of hands-on computer stuff — create your own blend, play a whisky trivia game, zap an Excise man in Speyside Invaders (okay I made that last one up), that sort of thing — and drawer after drawer full of Dewar family and brand memorabilia. You get the distinct feeling that the Dewars were not great ones for throwing things away. I fully expected to find a drawer full of Tommy Dewar's old bus tickets. Perhaps I missed it.

The bulk of this genuinely fascinating display, however, is comprised of the Dewar's brand advertising materials. Dewar's have always been right at the cutting edge of international advertising. They made the first whisky film advert in 1898 — a film Tommy had projected onto a skyscraper in New York — they were one of the first to advertise on a balloon and they were

391

the first to make a TV documentary on the production of Scotch. Clips of films ancient and recent, multitudinous posters of varying degrees of gaudiness and subtlety and dozens of promotional products make up a spellbinding Museum of Canny Advertising.

The tasting bit at the end of the tour is also a further nosing/blending teaching area, with a bar where you can sample the blend at different ages and the Aberfeldy itself, plus tables to sit at with little smell sample bottles and a Nosing and Tasting Notes form to fill out. There's a café here too.

After this multimedia extravaganza, the distillery tour might seem almost a disappointment, however the guides do their best to live up to the brand vision. Well, our guy wore a kilt, which is a start. Actually he was really interesting. His dad had worked here in the distillery — he was present in a couple of the blown-up old black and white photos displayed on the tour — and he used to skelp about the place when he was a bairn and was given a whisky toddy every night from the age of about one. One month, that is. Claimed as a result never to have had a cold in his life, but developed a concomitant dislike of whisky, blended or malt (which is interesting but definitely not my idea of a good trade-off).

Aberfeldy is at the heart of the Dewar's blend and these days the distillery runs 24 hours a day for five days a week, employing eleven staff including the secretary and manager. There's a big enclosed mash tun with a neat water-skooshing system to keep the window clear, two steel washbacks outside and eight inside, made from Siberian larch rather than the usual Oregon pine. The four big stills have nearly flat Lyne arms and the whole pace is as neat as the grounds outside, all cream and burgundy paint and looking positively polished and gloriously gleaming. This is real engine-room, full-steam-ahead industrial malt-making. About 90 per cent of the output goes for blending and the resulting malt expressions — I choose the standard 12-year-old — are not in a sense the point of the place, which is very much to make the principal component of the Dewar's blend. It's a perfectly palatable dram all the same, bursting with flavours, quite sweet and with hints of flowers and herbs. Big and boisterous and in a way almost asking to be blended, but nothing to be ashamed of. The whisky equivalent of somebody you wouldn't kick out of bed.

Dad, Uncle Bob and I lunch in the Black Watch Hotel in the centre of Aberfeldy. This is fairly appropriate as the Black Watch was my paternal grandfather's regiment. Dad and Bob's father spent three years in the trenches of the Somme and I still have a ring he carved out of a shell fragment. It's worn away a bit now but you can just about make out the figures and letters that spell out *1914 Somme 1917*. He made it back alive and my dad was born in 1918.

One day when he was still in short trousers my dad and his dad were on the far side of the Forth, at Barnbougle estate, across from the family home near Granddad's work place in the quarry near Inverkeithing. They were on the broad beach there, having rowed over from Fife, looking for coal and coke washed up from the Granton gas works down the coast, when a man carrying a shotgun approached from the trees and they got to talking. This proved to be the laird and local land owner, the guy whose estate my granddad and dad were on.

Whether he was coming to move them on or not we don't know because he and granddad got to talking and discovered that, like most of that male generation, they'd both been in the trenches. The laird, of course, had been an officer, but the experience had arguably left them with more to unite them than to separate them, which was maybe one of the few good things to have come out of the whole catastrophic War To End All Wars.

My dad remembers Granddad gesturing towards him and saying something like, Well, at least the boy here won't have to go through the same thing I did.

This was the late twenties. The laird shook his head sadly and told my granddad that he was very afraid he was wrong, and there would be another war, just as big and just as bad, if not bigger and worse, before too long. And quite possibly just in time for my dad reaching call-up age.

Granddad grabbed the barrels of the laird's shotgun before he could do anything to stop him and levelled the gun at my dad's face. My dad stood stock still, staring terrified into the double barrels. The laird stood frozen goggle-eyed as well, though still holding on to the rest of the gun. "If I thought you were right," Granddad told the laird, "and this wee lad would have to go through anything like what I had to go through,

I'd blow his head off here and now, and know I was doing him a favour."

Then he handed the man back his gun and marched off back to his boat, followed an instant later by my still quivering father.

The laird was right about the coming war, of course. Dad served in the Royal Navy during the war, based at Scapa Flow in Orkney for a large part of it. Granddad died just outside the quarry one day when he was 65, playing football during his lunch break.

In the news, Uday and Qusay, Saddam's sons, displayed dead. Saddam's grandson died in the same attack but they don't show his body. It occurs to me that if Saddam is creeping round the desert in a pick-up with one big barrel of anthrax left over from his patently long-deceased WDM program, now is the time he'd use it. Nothing of the sort happens. On the other hand, the continuing attacks on American soldiers in Iraq are supposed to stop now. They don't, and another few die.

The quest continues; I'm off to Inveraray, Campbeltown and — hopefully — Arran. Then if the timings work out I'll join some pals in Greenock for a card school. M5 again, alone, so the CD player is loaded with completely self-indulgent premium Iain-pleasing stuff; both Led Zeppelin *Remasters, OK Computer* by Radiohead, *Strange Brew, The Very Best Of Cream, As If To Nothing* by Craig Armstrong, and a collection that came with the June '96 edition of *Q* magazine called *Mmmmm* . . . (these sample CDs are usually extremely hit-and-miss but this one always struck me as hanging together brilliantly, with not a weak track on it).

I set off along the M8 at what seems like a really early hour to me, however the roads are already pretty busy. When I get to the turn-off for the Erskine Bridge near Bishopton it's 0755 and I've got 25 minutes to get to Gourock for the ferry to Dunoon. I reckon I'm not going to make it so swing north across the bridge, up the side of Loch Lomond as far as Tarbet — this is where Rog's mum lives but it's a bit early to drop in for a cup of tea — then onto the basically brilliant A83, roaring up the Rest and Be Thankful. This is a pass that marked the summit of a once-steep road which must have been murderous for horses hauling people and goods and which was pretty demanding of old cars too. Then we go zapping along through Glen Kinglas. I pass the Cowal peninsula road junction at 0835, five minutes before the ferry I was aiming for would dock at Dunoon, so coming this way has definitely been the smart move.

Out of Lochgilphead I pick up a tail; what has to be a local in a modest-looking Rover driven easily well enough to keep up with the M5 on this twisty stretch of road.

Now, I absolutely don't believe in road racing but we are going fairly briskly — I don't want to hold the guy up, after all. There's one straight stretch where I could go a lot faster but don't, to give my new chum a chance to overtake, but he chooses not to, so I guess we're okay.

It's a bit drizzly and the road is wet from earlier showers; the M5's traction warning light flickers once or twice on the display, indicating that it's sensed a momentary loss of grip. The BMW does finally get away from the old Rover for a bit but we're back together by the time we enter Tarbert, where my shadow pulls in. I always wish there was some hat-doffing gesture to perform at such points; I have no real doubt that if this guy had been driving the M5 and I'd been driving the old Rover — even knowing the road — he'd have lost me in the first couple of miles.

The A83 south of Tarbert, certainly past the Islay ferry port at Kennacraig, is something of a corker; not ultimately fast — too many wee settlements and too lumpy a surface for that — but nicely open and pleasantly undulating. It reminds me a lot of a similar west-facing stretch of seaboard road on the A77 heading from Girvan to Stranraer. It's a clear day in between the rain showers, and in the distance I can see Ireland, cliffed across the horizon.

Springbank distillery's entrance lies on the main road into Campbeltown.

There are now only two or three fully working distilleries in Campbeltown. Once there were dozens.

Blame that whole boom-and-bust thing.

What happened was that back in the latter part of the nineteenth century Campbeltown grew to become, in effect, the whisky capital of Scotland, never quite

397

eclipsing Speyside in terms of its productive capacity but almost equalling it in the number of distilleries in the region and certainly providing a more focussed concentration of whisky-making than anywhere in Speyside or the rest of Scotland could boast. The place fairly reeked of whisky, stank of distilling; soon the local grain supplies proved insufficient and loads were brought in not just from the rest of Scotland but from Denmark and even Russia. The dried draff was exported as far as Germany, allegedly to feed the Prussian army's horses.

The local whisky barons built mansions on the profits. Campbeltown became a boom town, the unchallenged Whisky Metropolis of the west coast. By 1891 this essentially wee daft town in the middle of a watery nowhere with a population of less than 2000 souls had the highest per capita income of anywhere in Britain, and all because of whisky.

It couldn't and didn't last.

A degree of complacency set in, and standards fell. In an industry where you don't reap what you sow for at least three years and probably a lot longer, this is both an ever-present temptation and an act of complete and almost inevitably utter and terminal stupidity. Even more to the point, speculators started to buy up supplies of product, investing in entire warehouses of still-maturing spirit, so encouraging the production of more of the same. What looked at the time like a virtuous spiral set in, investment encouraging production, until the boom's bust point was reached, there was a tiny blip that turned into a big one, the premium was suddenly on quality not quantity, and the whole shaky speculative, down-marketed edifice fell apart. The First World War didn't help matters, however it was the combination of punitive tax hikes by Liberal Chancellor Lloyd George, along with post-war mass unemployment in Glasgow and the local coal beds running out which completed the destruction.

In the twenties, when the US was undergoing its honourably intentioned but basically insane experiment with Prohibition, Campbeltown started to blossom again, but it was still predominantly bottom-of-the-range stuff, and after a reprise of the boom-and-slump trajectory it had experienced two decades before, the place sank back into the productive stagnation that lasts till this day.

The one great shining light in all this sorry tale of commercial darkness is Springbank. Springbank distillery does all the things that almost nobody else does; it malts its own barley — grown locally — it flavours and dries the barley over smouldering local peat, it directly coal-fires its stills, it does not chill filter or use caramel colouring plus it two-and-a-half or even triple distils its spirit.

The result is a whisky of enormous provenance and genuinely magnificent taste, an unparalleled, uncompromising contender for a place in the Top Ten Scottish malts. And, going on past experience, a whisky with a real chance of displacing even the great Havana Reserve as my Best Dram So Far. It has strong hints of Island — even Islay — whisky in character, with a deep, convoluted, yet zesty and somehow youthful character.

399

A real surf-and-turf whisky, with notes of the sea-salt airs and the root-tangled earth about it. The 15-year-old I buy in Cadenhead's shop in Campbeltown itself — Cadenhead's being an outlet owned by Springbank since 1969 — is a surprisingly peaty monster, all competing tastes of salt and soil, riddled with sweetness and a whole spectrum of oily, quayside-tarry notes.

A singular, beguiling, uncompromising whisky from a place that was once a whole region and is now reduced, concentrated down to Springbank itself, plus Longrow and the quite separate Glen Scotia, which I'm sorry to report is the the only other whisky I've tasted so far apart from Auchentoshan which has proved a real let-down. Les and I sampled a 1990 bottle from Signatory at the same time back in May and immediately looked at each other, somewhat aghast, unwilling to believe that what we were tasting was supposed to be a good single malt. Oily — in a bad way — and kind of off, frankly. Signatory is usually an extremely reliable source of rare and interesting whiskies, so I like to think we just got a bad bottle.

Anyway, it's too hard trying to decide exactly where Springbank sits in the hierarchy right now; best wait until I've got them all in front of me and try to decide then.

Longrow, once a bottling from an old set of casks owned by Springbank — who own the name Longrow and have done their creditable best since to produce a quite different whisky from the apparatus that usually produces Springbank — is an even heavier, peatier —

in fact quite intensely peatier — and altogether more forceful dram with a bouquet like a deep breath in a pine forest. My Cadenhead's' bottle is a fairly standard 10-year-old and I like it a lot, but as I've said I kind of like fighting with my flavours, and those of a more delicate disposition might find it too bruisingly combative to enjoy.

I walk round Campbeltown for a bit between showers, soaking up its pleasant sea airs and admiring the Victorian exuberance of architecture obviously built, or at least commissioned, at the height of the town's commercial success.

Then, after a bit of unashamed road-bagging round the glans of the peninsula, it's off northwards to Claonaig on the shaft's east, Clyde-facing coast, to pick up the ferry for Lochranza on Arran, and a visit to what is, at least for now, Scotland's youngest distillery.

The Arran distillery, opened in 1995, looks quite spankingly new. It's set on the outskirts of the village a kilometre or so from the ruins of Lochranza Castle, with the hills rising steeply on three sides. There are two main distillery buildings, plus a smallish warehouse hidden away behind them. The main two buildings have purely decorative pagodas which I think you'd have to be a real knickers-in-a-twist purist to complain about; basically pagodas are stylised signs that shout Distillery! the way that a red and white striped pole used to shout Barber Shop!

One building houses the offices, the Visitor Centre with the usual blonde-wood-and-stanchions décor, a shop, an enclosure of what looks like real growing barley and a impressively large indoor waterfall feature faked to look like a bit of hillside. Upstairs there's a café/restaurant serving interesting, above average fare (I have a very late but delicious lunch consisting of a venison sausage and black pudding baguette, but they do food for normal people too). The only negatives in the café/restaurant seem to be the seat backs, which bend alarmingly when you put any weight on them and feel like they're about to send you tumbling backwards. The other building contains all the whisky-making equipment.

They're having their quiet season at the moment so photos are allowed in the production building, which in appearance is quite refreshingly different from most distilleries. For one thing it's effectively open-plan, with the mash tun, washbacks, stills, condensers and ancillary bits and pieces all in the one big square space. You head up steps from ground level onto a metal mesh floor covered with mats where people are likely to walk during the tour. There are lots of windows and so there's lots of light and there are tubs of pot-plants scattered about the floor, which is an unusual sight at the business end of a distillery (must get hot in here for the plants when it's sunny and the stills are running; on the other hand maybe the greenery benefits from the CO_2 given off by the washbacks. Whatever, they look real and in good nick).

There are attractive banisters in the shape of barley stalks round a well that holds the intermediate- and low-wines receivers. The wash still has a much thinner neck than the spirit still, and the Lyne arms are both almost flat. Our guide tells us that the sharpness of the angle of the Lyne arm's elbow does a lot to determine the fierceness of the spirit, a sharp bend producing a sharp spirit, which is a detail I hadn't encountered before. One interesting point is that there has patently been no evolution whatsoever in spirit safe design over the years, because the one here looks like it could have come out of a distillery established in 1795, not 1995.

Arran has taken the off-site handling of barley a stage further than most, buying its raw material not just already malted but already milled and gristed too. There's no peat in the malt itself, the local water — which was the principal reason for siting the distillery here rather than anywhere else — being judged peaty enough by itself. Most of the production has to be matured on the mainland because the distillery could only get planning permission for that one relatively small warehouse behind the main buildings.

I buy a bottle of the non-chill-filtered whisky at 46 abv. As in the Cadenhead's shop in Campbeltown, you can pour your own bottle of whisky here from a cask set up in the shop; they'll cork it and label it for you while you wait, which is a neat retailing idea (Tommy Dewar would have been proud). There's no age stated on my bottle but obviously it can't be more than eight years old given that the place started up in 1995 and I'm buying the bottle in 2003. It's a fresh, appley dram, sharply sweet with hints of peat and wood. Positively refreshing, and it'll be fascinating to see how older expressions turn out.

The good ship *Caledonian Isles* lands me in Ardrossan (CalMac ship, restaurant, usual menu, late light baguette-lunch no longer filling tum, no evening meal arranged; you guess the rest) and I head home. I've made such good time I'd have to kick my heels for too long in Inverclyde before the card school starts, plus I've caught myself yawning rather a lot already after my early start this morning and I'm not sure I'd be safe to drive back later on tonight. Anyway I need to be up at a respectable hour tomorrow because we're off to Orkney.

I've listened to my six CDs once by now and so channel-hop on the radio on the way back instead, catching some government apparatchik wittering on about how they must be winning the war against drugs because they're intercepting so many more shipments these days. Oh good fucking grief.

Illegality: a thought experiment.

Okay, here's the scenario:

A kid, say ten years old or so, finds a tenner on the pavement. Or maybe they nick it out of their mum's purse. Whatever. They go to an off-licence. They reach up, slap the note on the counter and in a high, childish voice say, "Bottle of vodka, please, mister."

What? Nine out of ten? Nineteen out of twenty? Ninety-nine out of a hundred? (Adjust according to level of cynicism or outright experience.) Regardless of the exact proportion, the vast majority of people behind the counter at an off-licence are going to tell the kid to get out; they can't serve them. And most would say the same thing if the kid asks for a packet of fags.

So the kid goes back onto the street, finds a dealer and says, "Can I have a tenner's worth of heroin, please?"

Again, we're probably talking nine out of ten, nineteen out of twenty or ninety-nine out of a hundred. Except this time the numbers are reversed, and it's only one dealer in ten, one dealer in twenty or one dealer in a hundred who would turn the child away and not sell them what they've asked for.

So what is the best way of protecting our children, controlling mind-altering substances and ameliorating the damage to society caused by these things, given that the demand is unarguably there?

Don't forget that in the off-licence the drink will be of a guaranteed quality and effectively unadulterated because if it ever isn't there will be commercial hell to pay. Don't forget that the dope can be as contaminated, cut and crap as the dealer thinks they can get away with, because nobody's going to complain to their local M.P. or Food Standards lab. Don't forget that tobacco sends 110,000 people to an early grave in Britain alone and alcohol over 40,000.

Seriously; which way protects the best: legal control or simple illegality? Can you honestly see any excuse for sticking with the absurd system we have at the moment? I mean apart from sheer conservative-with-a-small-c idiocy?

Right, rant over.

★ ★ ★

Big silver bird in sky! Well, medium-size silver bird, anyway; a BA/Logan Air twin-prop Saab 340 from Edinburgh to Kirkwall via a brief touchdown at Wick. As we're on the approach into Wick I see the Old Pulteney distillery but otherwise it's been a frustrating flight because there's been so much cloud. Flying — preferably not too high — over country you know is one of life's great pleasures. Must learn to fly. Maybe next year.

I suppose I'm getting a bit demob-happy at this point; the quest is almost over (just the paperwork to do, but then I generally enjoy that too, so what the hey), plus there's a feeling that I'm saving some of the best for last; I know Highland Park pretty well already and there's a lot to look forward to here. I'm also feeling slightly smug because I got through security at Edinburgh with my Swiss Army Card. This is a sort of Swiss Army knife in a credit-card-sized bit of plastic; it has a little knife with a three-centimetre blade and a dainty pair of miniature scissors.

Frankly you'd struggle to hijack a tandem with a piece of kit like this, but thanks to the hysterical and absurd reaction to the September 11th attacks you're not supposed to carry such things on to a plane any more (I did try pointing out in *Dead Air* that if you can't take a blade or even a tool onto a plane, why are we glasses wearers allowed to take our specs on board? Give me a second to pop the lens out the frame and snap it in half and I'd almost instantly have two of the sharpest blades you can find. Sense? Logic? Don't think so). Anyway, I forgot to remove the card from my wallet

406

this morning and I only realised I'd got through the security check with it afterwards. It'd be tempting fate to try the same trick deliberately on the way back, so I'll put the card in my bag and my bag in the hold.

From Wick it's a less-than-fifteen-minute hop to Kirkwall, but at least the clouds have mostly cleared. We fly over the north-east tip of Scotland, over Duncansby Head and John O'Groats and within sight of the real most northerly point of mainland Scotland at Dunnet Head. Then it's out over the white stroked waters of the perpetually restless Pentland Firth and the island of Stroma — lying in the sea like a giant green jigsaw piece — and banking past the fabulously dramatic thousand-foot cliffs of Hoy and the island's Old Man, a wave-washed pinnacle of layered red rock knuckled out from the cliffs like a colossal cubist tree trunk.

To the west, as the plane banks for Kirkwall airport, stretches Scapa Flow, the base for the Home Fleet during the First and Second World Wars. It's where the German High Seas fleet was scuttled after the end of the Great War, and where my dad was based during WWII, when the service men and women far outnumbered the local inhabitants. Way in the distance, built where the rusting hulks of the earlier block ships used to lie, the Churchill Barriers make delicate pale lines across the grey-blue sea, slim causeways between the isles.

Taxi from Kirkwall airport to the Kirkwall Hotel and room overlooking the harbour. Take away the harbour and it would just be a nice view looking out to the

407

shores and hills across the sound, but with the harbour involved it's one of the most fascinating views you could ask for. There are ferries coming from and going to the other Orcadian islands throughout the long hours of daylight, fishing boats setting off high and returning low in the water, catches being landed, and people pottering about on power boats and yachts — many of them from Norway — all the time. On the horizon to the north, one of the big wind generators on Burgar Hill revolves serenely, like a white giant doing cartwheels. The only thing missing is one of the big cruise ships that regularly call in during the summer.

Orkney: a Handy Hint on blending in.

If you ever go to Orkney — and you should — never call Scotland "the mainland". Orkney has its own Mainland; that's the correct name for the big island that Kirkwall and the other sizable town, Stromness, are on. Scotland is called Scotland. The Orcadians don't really think of themselves as all that Scottish at all; they're Orcadians.

Look, these people have two distilleries, some of the best whisky made in . . . the British Isles and a make of beer called Skullsplitter; it's as well to keep on the right side of them.

Ann snoozes. I take a taxi to Scapa distillery for a quick photo, then onwards the mile or so to Highland Park. Scapa is closed, shut up, deserted, and profoundly unphotogenic. Highland Park is smart without being too fussy, and looks happily busy. My taxi driver used to be a barman in the seventies here and remembers when the two Orcadian distilleries were level pegging on production and pretty much reputation too. Back then, he tells me, there was real rivalry between the Scapa and the Highland Park workers; if a Scapa man came into the bar and asked for a whisky you couldn't serve him with Grouse because there was Highland Park in Grouse; he'd have to have a different blend, like Cutty Sark. And vice versa. We talk about how they're going to be starting a distillery on Shetland later this year or early next year, which will mean that Highland Park will have to remove the statement, "The Northernmost Scotch Whisky Distillery in the World" from its packaging. "Aye," the driver says, "the Shelties have been jealous of us having two distilleries and them having none for years."

Since the seventies, Scapa and Highland Park have gone in opposite directions; Scapa obscure, almost completely unpromoted and barely known, bumping along the bottom, mostly quiet with only occasional short bursts of activity, and Highland Park going from strength to strength, celebrating its bi-centenary five years ago with a flourish and a big party that brought whisky connoisseurs and writers from all over the world, releasing various medal-winning expressions of huge repute and just generally establishing a deserved reputation as one of the very best malts made anywhere.

This is a good tour to do; while the open-plan, one-box-solution Arran tour lets you see really clearly how all the different bits of the process fit together, the Highland Park tour winds through the different stages building by building, but has more stages to see in the first place. There's the real-thing malting floors for a start, with the barley laid out in great flat drifts, like absurdly thick piled golden carpets covering the floor. You're encouraged to lift a few grains and sniff them, but asked not to eat them. Given that the distillery workers are wandering about in their work boots through the barley, sticking thermometers into it while you're doing this, it's an easy request to comply with.

The old malt shovels and hand-dragged wooden rakes still lie about the place, although most of the turning of the malt — to stop it matting or overheating — is done by a rather Heath Robinson machine with leather-wrapped paddles that looks like a cross between a rotavator, a big old-fashioned lawn mower and one of the less successful but defiantly eccentric contestants from *Robot Wars*.

Next there's the kilns, proper age-of-steam-looking waist-level fires in big brick and iron ranges that look like they've come straight out of a twenties film set in a tramp steamer. You half expect a couple of swarthy Lascars to appear at any moment, stripped to the waist with grimy bandannas tied round their sweaty heads, to shovel more coke into the furnace. The kilns burn peat for the first sixteen or so hours of the malt-drying process, then switch to coke for the last twenty hours, until the barley only holds about five per cent moisture. The humid gases released from the drying chambers

410

exit the distillery through the two very-much-not-decorative pagodas which rise above the complex of buildings set on a low hill just outside Kirkwall.

You can tell they make a lot of whisky here. The mash tun is huge, they have a dozen washbacks — two steel ones outside and ten inside made from Douglas fir — and the stills are big too, with flattish Lyne arms and outside condensers. When I'm looking round in late July they've just started production again after a six-week silent season for maintenance and general refitting. During this time the workers spent four weeks at Scapa distillery, producing a batch of malt there. The distilleries are owned by quite separate companies — HP by the Edrington Group and Scapa by Allied Distillers — but they've got an agreement to do this and obviously everybody feels they benefit. So at least there will be some 2003 Scapa.

Highland Park bottles at 12, 15, 18, 25, 35 and 40 years, plus the occasional special (I choose an 18-year-old at 43 per cent abv). The 12-year-old is already a phenomenal, fulsome dram, and the stuff just generally gets better and better as it gets older. Sweet, smoky, smooth and opulent, filled to bursting with spicy fruits and a long, hazily luxuriant and powerful finish, this is magnificent whisky.

There is a kind of wide-spectrum plushness about the 18-year-old that is as impressive for the way it's balanced as it is for the sheer amount of flavour packed into it. In the same way that it's much easier to do cool-looking minimalist interior design compared to cool-looking intricate, complex interior design, it takes more skill to create a flavour-jammed whisky that feels rounded and harmonious than it does a relatively bare, stripped-down expression. The 18-year-old turns this trick with seeming ease; a bravura piece of polished burr walnut beauty amongst plain sanded pines. I've sampled the 25-year-old version and it's better still. Tasted in Orkney, looking out into the clear northerly light, these jostle for that Best Dram So Far title.

Highland Park may not be the Most Northerly Scotch for much longer but it'll still be one of the very best.

Work done, we dine at the hotel with Jenny — Ann's eldest sister — and her husband James. James is a Dewar, and distantly related to the whisky family (and even more distantly to me, I suppose, as the Dewars were part of the Menzies clan). Jenny and James moved to Orkney over a decade ago and seem happily settled here. While they were thinking about moving here the four of us spent a few weeks on the islands, staying in a house in Finstown shaped like an up-turned boat — complete with seals cavorting in the sea on the other side of the garden wall — and later touring most of the other islands, staying in hotels and B&Bs. We've stayed with Jenny and James in their house just outside Stromness many times over the subsequent years, often around the time of the Orkney Folk Festival, but on this occasion it seemed sensible to keep to Kirkwall, especially as we're only here for the one night.

It's a good, fun evening but we call it a day fairly early as we've all got stuff to do in the morning. Sadly,

Ann and I will miss the end of Shopping Week in Stromness tomorrow night (does anywhere else have a Shopping Week? Or only Stromness? Never mind). The point is they always have good fireworks on the last night of Shopping Week, even though it does have to be said that fireworks in Orkney in the middle of the summer will basically have to be set against a still-light sky, almost no matter how late in the evening you wait before setting them off (on Midsummer's Day at Jenny and James's house about ten years ago I did that thing where you read a newspaper outside with only the glow of the midnight sky for illumination).

The next day, before we leave, we meet up with Andrew Greig and Lesley Glaister; they have a house in Stromness too. Andrew and I met through Ken, when Andrew had a place in South Queensferry. We used to get together in the Ferry Tap and drink pints of Dark Island beer, brewed — appropriately enough — in Orkney. Andrew and Lesley married last year and have just returned from Borneo where Andrew's been researching his latest novel. Lesley's still recovering from having come back with a nasty-sounding bug, but she's working on the production of a play and at the planning stage of a new novel too. Scribblers three and one civilian, we spend a happy couple of hours exploring an old farm track or two in their car and walking along a beach near the airport in what feels like Mediterranean weather. Ann and Andrew both go paddling.

413

Being Orkney, littered with the detritus of wars as well as 8000 years of occupation from the neolithic onwards, the quiet bay cupped by the beach holds not just the slim white shape of an anchored yacht but the picturesquely corroding remains of what looks like an old destroyer, mouldering away to rust and nothing under the high ubiquitous searchlight of the sun.

CHAPTER
FIFTEEN

Tunnel Biking

Glenkinchie by bike. This is trusty-steed, knight-on-a-quest stuff (it's hard not to feel a bit heroic when you're on a bike. On the other hand Glenkinchie is the distillery nearest to our house, so I'm not being *that* heroic). I'm riding a Honda VFR 800; by general agreement, one of the best bikes on the road today. If that nice Mr Gore had been allowed to assume presidency after winning the election, at this point I'd almost certainly be extolling the virtues of what I still think is the the world's best-looking motor cycle, the Harley-Davidson V-Rod, however after the Bush putsch I started my own trade embargo.

The Honda is red in colour, which is generally a good thing in a motorbike and certainly makes this one look pretty damn splendid. The old VFR 750 I owned before this model was nothing special in the looks department, plus mine was a sort of dull green, which did it no favours, however the new one looks great. It has two double exhausts exiting right up under the seat so it almost looks like a Ducati if you sort of squint at it in subdued lighting conditions.

Ducatis are fabulous-looking and fabulous-sounding machines, but they can be uncomfortable to ride, especially if you're over six feet tall, and the consensus amongst bike magazine journalists seems to be that they're still not as well screwed together as Hondas. The 800 also has brilliant-in-every-sense headlights, which is an area where a lot of otherwise very good, very fast bikes fall down (falling down being something that very good, very fast bikes are in general quite good at anyway).

I'm sort of a born-again biker, though my early biking days were limited in nature. I had the use of a Suzuki 185 GT for about six months back in 1976, looking after it while its owner was abroad, and that was pretty much that.

Then a few years ago I thought it would be fun, and a challenge, to learn to ride a bike properly, so did a course locally, sat and passed my test and, as tends to happen, *really* started to learn how to ride a bike afterwards (all the test can really do is make sure you're not too big a menace to others or yourself before you're allowed out unsupervised to start the actual learning). I'll never be as entirely comfortable on a bike as I feel in a car — it'll never feel as second nature just because I've been learning how to drive cars ever since I was seventeen, whereas I've only been learning about bike riding since my early forties. But oh-my-goodness it's fun. Scary fun, sometimes, but fun.

I'd better emphasise that I can only ever describe the merest foothills of what it is to be a biker, leaving the higher slopes to others; I've never done a wheelie or got my knee down and don't really anticipate ever doing either, at least not deliberately. (A wheelie is when, through the application of just the right degree of Too Much Throttle you get the front wheel of the bike to lift off the ground. Getting your knee down is when you lean over so far while taking a corner that the outside of your knee — or hopefully the slider pad that you're wearing on top of your leathers — makes contact with the road surface.) A lot of bikers wouldn't consider me a proper biker at all because I haven't done both of these, or fallen off yet, and I wouldn't quibble with them. As I've got older I've decided that life is largely about having fun without frightening yourself — or others — too much, and the level at which I've set my bike fun just precludes such doubtless adrenalising shenanigans.

This comes back to the whole thing about not liking being frightened, and fairground rides. The few times I've been on an extreme ride, I've spent the time worrying whether it's all been put together properly, and thinking back to my days as a non-destructive testing technician, imagining hairline cracks propagating around bolt holes and slag inclusions in the welds linking up under stress, while wondering if all this G-force is really that good for the human body. On the other hand, it has to be said extreme rides are probably so ridiculously safer than Drunken Urban Climbing, or one plastered idiot throwing himself off a high wall into the arms of another — even just the once — that the difference is barely worth measuring.

★ ★ ★

417

I'm a solitary biker; I love the feeling of freedom the experience gives, even if you do have to surround yourself with a whole prophylactic suite of helmet, armoured leathers and Serious Boots. Of course, you don't *have* to; only the helmet is compulsory in this country. But the thought of biking in a helmet, shorts, trainers and T-shirt (as you do sometimes see people doing), so that, if something you couldn't avoid does happen, you end up sliding along the road at 50 miles an hour or whatever, scrubbing off speed by the gradual abrasion of your wrist, ankle, knee, pelvic and spinal bones — the flesh having sloughed easily, if painfully, off in the first half-second or so — while your helmet keeps your brain undamaged, entirely conscious and in full-on pain-appreciation mode is enough to make me look upon my insect-spattered leathers with something almost bordering on affection.

Part of the reward of riding a bike is that it makes you absolutely a better driver. The most obvious effect is that you become more sensitive to the road surface. Obviously when you're in a car you have to watch out for things on the road like ice and just lots of rain and standing water (watching out, and then ignoring the signs and taking unexpected upside-down excursions off Highland roads, in my case), but when you're on a bike you suddenly became hypersensitive to the presence of stuff like a little gravel on the road's centre line, a curved smear of mud extending from the entrance to a field, the rainbow hint of colour that indicates a diesel spill, metal manhole covers slicked with rain or a patch of damp autumnal leaves lying in a shady corner.

The point is that a car just sits there. You don't get out of a car and have it fall over. (I'm told this even applies to three-wheelers.) Cars are, essentially, stable. Get off a bike and forget to put its side-stand down and the bugger will fall over with a loud and probably surprisingly expensive clunk. The same applies when you're underway. The gyroscopic effect of the wheels means that once you're going at even extremely modest speeds you're kind of dynamically balanced, but it's still all about equilibrium, about poise.

Compared to driving a car, riding a bike feels like halfway to flying. There's suddenly a third dimension involved. Cars basically stay flat. They'll dive under braking, squat under acceleration and roll in a corner (being in a Citroën 2CV taking an average corner at, oh, twenty miles an hour is an extreme ride all by itself if you're not prepared for it), but the movements are relatively mild. On a bike, with a little experience and confidence, you find yourself leaning all over the place; you, the bike, and the whole tipped world suddenly take on angles you'll never see in a car unless you are, technically, crashing.

All of which is entirely fine, dandy and fun as long as there's lots of nice sticky grip between your one powered wheel and the road surface, but which brings on instantaneous gut-freezing fear the nanosecond you feel that grip start to go and the wheel — and the rear of the bike, and with it *your* rear — start to slip. I've had a few moments on the three bikes I've owned, a couple of micro-skids which I've managed, probably more through good luck than inherent skill, to control, but it's arguably those instants of fear, and the associated gut-level, bone-level appreciation of the dynamics of the balancing forces of grip, power and the relationship between the bike and the road that help make you a better, safer rider in future and to some extent a better road user in general.

Heading across the Forth Road Bridge, I take the main road into Edinburgh rather than the signposted route to the city bypass. This avoids the ludicrous A8000, a stretch of ordinary two-way road between the motorway and the bridge that should have been upgraded at least to dual-carriageway standard 40 years ago when the bridge was built. A bit of jiggery-pokery on some quiet wee roads and I end up on the bypass later anyway. You have more choices on a bike, because even if you do end up in a traffic jam, you can thread your way through towards the front by taking the narrow channel between two lanes of cars, or just overtake a single lane. Routes that you might avoid in a car because you know there's going to be stationary traffic ahead you'll happily tackle in a bike because the jam will only slow you down a bit.

It's a hot old day, and so there are a few Random Indicator Events. These are when people leave their indicator lights flashing long after the manoeuvre they were warning people of has been completed, so that you find cars and vans sitting in any given lane with either set of indicators blinking merrily away. You see a lot more of this sort of thing in hot weather because that's when people are more liable to have their windows open and so can't hear the indicator clicking above the noise of the wind, engine and tyre roar. And of course hot weather is usually bright weather, so noticing the tell-tale on the dash is harder in the glare, too.

Approaching a vehicle sitting in the nearside lane which is indicating it's about to pull out in front of you when there seems no need for it to do so is slightly worrying when you're in a car — *is* this bozo going to suddenly put themself in my way, or is this just a seasonal Random Indicator Event? — but when you're on a bike it's much more anxiety-promoting. You're not worrying about your bodywork, you're worrying about your body. Then you have to decide whether to flash your lights at them, or honk the horn as you pass and use your own indicators to suggest they might like to check the state of their stalks.

A roundabout on a bypass. Big queues ahead. Who does the road planning around here? I head gingerly down the gap between the two lines of traffic. This will never feel entirely natural to me. In fact it feels a bit like cheating, but on the other hand when I'm in my car and a biker threads their way down the central channel, I don't mind; it doesn't lengthen the amount of time I'll have to spend in the jam, after all, so why should I resent it? However I do feel vaguely embarrassed to be doing this. Just all those years of being a car driver, I suppose. The only thing more embarrassing than heading down the central channel is not doing it, queuing up behind the stationary traffic, and then

421

having a fellow biker pass you and disappear towards the front of the jam while you sit there like a prune.

Through Dalkeith; the place specialises in traffic jams and today there are roadworks as well. Sitting in the bright sunlight in my black leathers, I start to get quite hot. Then finally it's open-road stuff again, taking some wee daft roads to Glenkinchie. The route includes a ford, which is something you don't see every day, certainly in Scotland. In fact I can only think of one other ford in Scotland on a public road, on a wee road near the Carron valley reservoir. This ford has a steep exit over badly pitted tarmac, and when the VFR splashes through the water I feel the back wheel slip momentarily as I get up a bit of speed to carry us over the cratered surface, but we get out without any further nonsense. I always seem to end up doing stuff like this on inappropriate bikes.

The first bike I had after I passed my test was a CB 500, which — I read in the bike mags — was an all-rounder. Somewhat idiotically, I took this to mean you could use it like a trail bike and kept taking it up farm tracks and down muddy paths, over rocks and through streams and stuff, and so fell off a lot, tumbling over the handlebars on at least one occasion, though at such low speeds all that ever got hurt were the bike's extremities. Inappropriate bike, see? Should have done all that sort of stuff on a trailie.

On the other hand, the old 500 proved perfectly fine for going through disused railway tunnels. There's an old railway line which passes by Glenfarg on the way to Perth; you used to be able to get up onto the route of

422

the line from a minor road nearby, drive along the track bed — the rails were obviously lifted long ago — then drive into this tunnel. It was a good long tunnel, too, and curved, so that when you were in the middle you couldn't see any daylight from either end. The bike's headlight showed up very little because everything it pointed at was dark earth or soot stained bricks and rock. There was a bridge across the main road at the far end of the tunnel, and I could probably have followed the route of the old track to a way back onto the road, but I turned and went back the way I'd come because it had been such brilliant, eerie fun. The access point is fenced off now, so that's that. Besides, I wouldn't even try that sort of thing on the VFR; too much of a road bike.

And so to Glenkinchie, a neat little distillery in a sleepy but well-turned-out-looking wee village. Pencaitland is south and east of Edinburgh, set in gently rolling wooded countryside, one more nexus in a web of GWRs. The distillery has a daintily clipped-looking bowling green which you pass on your way to the Visitor Centre, and there's a general air of civilised peace and quiet about the place. There's a good exhibition in the Visitor Centre, including a huge and intricate model distillery which was housed in the Science Museum in London for a couple of decades. Two big stills dominate the business end and one of the warehouses is a four-storey affair, stepped back into the surrounding valley's steep side so that the ground and top levels both have entrances at ground level.

Another well-promoted whisky, as the Lowland representative of the UDV/Diageo Classic Malts collection, Glenkinchie is full of heathery, flowery scents, with a long finish. In its own quiet way there's quite a lot going on in here, and to be honest it's beyond my uneducated palate to sort it all out, but there's a definite impression of complexity. The obvious solution is to have more and work out what it is that's going on, but that never quite seems to resolve things. Still fun trying though.

Last bike-related plus of the day is that there's no toll charge for motorbikes on the Forth Road Bridge. You have to slow down to a trundle until the toll operator registers your passing, but that's all. Look, it's only 80 pence for a car — and even that's northbound only, so effectively 40 pence each way — but you're still getting something for free that car drivers have to pay for, so it just feels good, okay?

The M5. North to look for Speyside distillery again on the way to Dufftown and then Glen Garioch at Old Meldrum. In quest terms, this is a culminant trip, a raid into the distant hills and forests to a place of richness, a descending upon, to lift the treasure. I'm fairly brimming with anticipation, though I'm just a tiny bit nervous too, in case the cupboard is bare (of course, I could just have rung up and checked, but somehow that seemed like cheating).

Near Kingussie I finally find the way to the Speyside distillery, but it's up a steep, rough track with

424

formidable-looking stones and rocks where decent law-abiding tarmac ought to be. If I'd brought the Defender I'd be up there without a second thought, but in the M5, with its foot-wide low profiles, it's just asking for trouble. I continue towards Dufftown instead.

Another hot day on Speyside, but this time it's not unseasonable; it's early August and the whole of the British Isles is having a proper summer heatwave. Records are being broken, tarmac is melting, rail tracks are buckling. I haul into the car park at Glenfiddich and buy so much whisky I'm invited to come to the rear door of the shop to load up from a pallet. This is the Havana Reserve I've decided is pretty much the bee's knees. How good to make its acquaintance again.

Then I head east, for Old Meldrum, road-bagging as I go. This means spending at least some time on the A96, the much-used and much-abused main road between Aberdeen and Inverness.

There is an alternative way; the rail way, and that Aberdeen-Inverness line is also quite a good route for distillery-bagging, swinging through so much of Speyside. A book called *The Iron Road To Whisky Country* makes it sound like the only way to travel, though if you want to get round lots of distilleries, a car still seems the obvious choice. Especially if somebody else can do the driving.

Old Meldrum (innocent of the gratuitous "Old" charge — it's just the name of the town) is a pleasant little place on a low hilltop, deep in the fine farming land of Formartine. Formartine. Now there's a word, a

425

place I'd never heard of. It's symptomatic of my relative ignorance of this whole corner of the country that the name of this regionette is completely new to me. It's not an old country name, at least not one that I'd ever heard of, and yet there it is, on a couple of Ordnance Survey maps, and easily Googled — there's a Formartine football team — so obviously the right name for the district but just one I'd never heard of. Whatever; Old Meldrum is home to what is now the most easterly distillery in Scotland, given that the old distillery at Glenugie near Peterhead has closed.

Glen Garioch, it turns out, is a real contender for undiscovered gem; a little-known belter. It has had its share of ups and downs, closures and changes over the years, and the expressions reflect some of that variability; not so much in outright quality but in the differing spectra of tastes they present. The peatiness has come and gone over the years for a start, but it may be making a comeback, depending where Morrison Bowmore/Suntory want to go with this particular distillery's expressions. In the relatively recent past, certainly the bottles-still-available past, Glen Garioch has presented, at fifteen and 21 years old, as one of the last of the old-school Highland whiskies, full of peat and smokiness. This is balanced by lots of fruit and herbs and a degree of sweetness with a long, rich finish. More recent expressions may not be so olde-worlde characterful — much less peat for one thing — but the spirit being laid down over the last few years appears to be returning to its roots, which in Glen Garioch's case you would swear you can smell. Entirely worth seeking out.

To Oban by train. Ann and I take the Fife Loop from North Queensferry to Waverley, the Embra-Glasgow shuttle service to Queen Street, then the combined Fort William/Oban West Highland train, which splits at Crianlarich.

I've always liked trains. When I was a child I loved going down to the station at North Queensferry and climbing the steps of the footbridge to wait for a train to pass underneath. This was the early sixties, so most of the trains were hauled by steam engines. The steam and smoke exploded out around you as the engine's funnel slid beneath the metal plates protecting the bridge's wooden structure. For a few moments you were completely enveloped in a oil-scented white fog of warm steam and coal smoke, just lost to the world, ears ringing. I think I fell in love with that feeling of wild abandonment, that noise, that smell, that sense of power and raw, released energy — those of you who've read my book *The Bridge* might recognise this description. When they started using diesel multiple units for the Fife Loop, our school playground would stop as we all stood and stared, fascinated, at this strange engine-less group of carriages coming trundling across the Bridge.

The first part of the journey to Oban is unremarkable, leaving Queen Street and looping round from north to west, through the undelightful schemes before coming back down towards the Clyde after

Dalmuir and Kilpatrick (I get a good look at that Art Deco-ish sports pavilion I spotted while I was trying to find a way to Auchentoshan distillery). The line heads under the Erskine Bridge — as elegant and minimalist as the Forth Road Bridge is dramatic and muscular — and then along the shore towards Dumbarton, where those red summits of the Inverleven distillery rise like bricky echoes of Dumbarton Rock, then heads along the coast again, with Port Glasgow, Greenock and Gourock present across the river and the hills and mountains of Argyll visible in the haze down river. The line starts to rise after the outskirts of Helensburgh, then clatters along the hillside. Out of the town we head towards the sheer bloody disfiguring awfulness that is Faslane, the greatest physical manifestation on British soil of our Not Even Remotely Independent Deterrent; our US-owned, Brit-managed McNuke franchise.

Last rant before the end.

I have been in Faslane. Ann and I stopped off at the base once to see my cousin Katrine when she was Press Relations Officer there — she's a Lieutenant Commander in the Navy, and, as I write this she is, thankfully, just back unharmed from the Gulf (another whisky connection; Katrine's father, my uncle Peter, ex Fleet Air Arm, used to fly the private plane for the Distillers Company). Faslane is home port to the giant submarines which carry the US/UK Poseidon missiles with their Multiple Independent Re-entry Vehicle warheads (how nice to find something that claims to be Independent that actually is).

It's a big place full of impressive buildings. There's one colossal shed that can house an entire mega-sub, and then raise the whole 30,000-tonne bulk of the thing right out of the water. So, massive, Thunderbirds-worthy machinery, entirely worth the ten billion of hard-earned taxeroos that went into the whole system. The base is full of helpful people, too; we'd limped in with a flat tyre on the Drambuie 911 after some arguably over-optimistic road-bagging on some very small and badly maintained roads in the hills not far away, and the guys from the base Engineering section helped me change the wheel (for one of those horrible space saver tyres — we had to crawl back to Fife at 50. I almost fell asleep).

Meanwhile the guys in the Officers' Mess were, Ann reported, to a man unfailingly courteous, pleasant and witty. She loved the way they called Katrine "Ma'am", too.

Tyre changed, we had lunch with the base commander, another deeply professional and quietly impressive guy, with a good line in deprecating, humanisingly funny stories about the base, like how the government gave him more money per head to feed the guard dogs than the men, and how some bored MoD police, sent out to a distant part of the site to make sure traffic was sticking to the base speed limit, had turned their radar gun on a guy out running, and put him on a charge for exceeding said speed limit (if I recall correctly, he was let off and they were reprimanded for wasting a superior's time).

We had a good lunch in stimulating company and as we left to make our slow way home, past the peace people's caravans outside the gates, I remember thinking that, given the fact that we had these weapons of mass destruction, and the whole Poseidon missile and sub system to house, deploy and launch them, the men and women we'd met on the base were exactly the sort of responsible, sensible, well-trained, eminently sane and thoroughly capable people I'd want to be in charge of them.

The point — for crying out bleedin' loud — is that we shouldn't have the damn things in the first place. They're a moral obscenity, and it's only one of their less poisonous consequences that all these smart, capable people devote their undoubted talent, sometimes their entire careers, to maintaining such horrors in preparation for a day they too hope will never come. I have enormous respect for these people, but, frankly, when I hear some bunch of bag-arsed feminist nutters have thrown a load of equipment off a Navy barge, or taken hammers to the nose cones of fighter bombers on an airbase, they're the ones I truly admire.

I suppose my dad would say they were pissing into the wind, too. But that's not the point.

The ugliness that is the whole McNuke Statelet takes a long time to go; there are further jetties up Loch Long, fuel tanks for conventional ships dotting the hillsides below the rising track and then the entrances to the

430

deep ammo stores disfiguring Gleann Culanach. The views of Loch Long do a lot to ameliorate the grisly presence of this awfulness.

I travelled this way once just before New Year, maybe twenty years ago, with Jim and various other members of the Greenock card school, on our way for Hogmanay at Les's. There had been a lot of snow over the previous few days, but on the evening we travelled it became a still, clear night with a full moon. Through opened windows we looked from the gently rocking train down to the ink-black loch under the pitch star-pitted sky, with the mountains on the far side of the loch shining pale blue-white under the moon and the trees all dark but dusted with the snow. The old train's engine became almost silent for a while, sound soaked up by the trees round a bend ahead as we coasted down towards the head of the loch, just the clicking of the carriage wheels left. A few tiny navigation lights winked, lost in the emptiness and the silence.

Another time, again in winter but on this occasion in the bright milk light of day, the train was crossing the waste that is Rannoch Moor, where the whole line floats on sunken, bundled branches, when it startled a whole hundred-or-more herd of deer. They went leaping away across the page-white snow, dark bodies like liquid shadows, as though made from some quickened negative of mercury.

Then there was the time Jim and I sat across the table from each other on the same journey, completely stoned, and had an Extreme Close-Range Water Pistol Fight.

Ah well. Boys and toys.

It's a hottish journey in the train, even with all the windows open (no AC for the West Highland Line, though on the few occasions when you'd welcome it, you'd really welcome it). The views are worth it though.

Oban. We stay at the Caledonian Hotel, as it's close to the station. Once dowdy, the place has become positively funky. Our room has a view over the harbour even better than the one at Kirkwall, and a big free-standing bath in the generously sized bathroom, with a separate shower big enough to bend over in for soap retrieval purposes without the risk of impaling oneself on the plumbing. Lots of stripes and bright colours. And themed, too, in a nautical and sailorish sort of way. There are some nice little flourishes; our room on the third floor has a wee turret with a single curved window, and the curtains hang from the rail via boating shackles rather than ordinary curtain rings.

The view is magnificent, across the arms of the busy town spread out enfolding the harbour, with sheltering Kerrera just off shore, Lismore, Morvern and Mull in the distance. A few long banks of mist spill over the far sea, brilliant white in the August light.

Oban's proper urban distillery, even more so than, say, Tobermory, however it's still very close to the sea, or at least the harbour. Good Visitor Centre, interesting tour (unique double worm-tub condensers, so there) and a well-stocked shop very definitely in Modern Vernacular style, with walls of thin-slabbed greenish glass, pale wood abounding, well up-tarted iron columns and lots of steel stanchions. All a bit cramped

432

and crammed in, with a bustling town around it and a cliff behind, but interesting. Busy, at you might expect, given that it's in the centre of one of the West's prime tourist spots and the whisky itself is well promoted as part of the UDV/Diageo Classic Malts range.

As a dram, Oban is an interesting amalgam, with hints of Island — even Islay — and Highland characteristics. The standard expression is a 14-year-old with only a thimble of peat and wee breeze of sea about it. It has lots of caramelly, smoky sweetness, a sort of luscious thickness in the mouth and a reprise of seaweed towards the end. A little pot of gold at the end of a fabulous railway line.

The wait for the journey back isn't too much fun, though the reason for the final delay is not one you could blame on Scotrail. The 1320 train had almost every seat reserved and so we stay in Oban — strolling, shopping and sitting in the bar — until the 1810 is due to leave. There is, however, a problem. There's been a bad road accident just out of town which has created a huge tailback (and caused the wee roads I've referred to as the Oban bypass to jam up for hours). Our train driver is on the wrong side of the jam. For a while there's talk of the train being cancelled. Oh well, I tell Ann, we'll just stay another night, what the hell. We already know the Caledonian is fully booked for tonight, but I just walk round to the Tourist Information Centre, attractively housed in an old church . . . only to discover that Oban is having one of its Full nights, with no hotel rooms or B&Bs left. There might be some people left who didn't normally do B&B

433

who would put stranded tourists up, but even they
might all be full . . .

Redman's Blues.

Les and Aileen did this once years ago, when somebody
from the Fort William tourist office got their number
and — in some desperation — rang up about ten
o'clock in the evening to say, look, they had all these
people and nowhere to put them up for the night (Fort
Bill Full); could they help out?

So the McFarlanes played host to a very nice young
Japanese couple for a night. Les and Aileen are
educated as well as educating types, but their Japanese
is limited. To Hai, Sayonara and various brand names,
basically. Their guests' English was, if anything, even
more sparse. Still, a bed was made up, breakfast was
provided the next morning and the nice Japanese
couple insisted on paying even though the McFarlanes
were embarrassed and reluctant.

However.

I should mention that our pal Ray had been staying
that night too, there for the weekend. Ray, being
himself, could not resist singing what he claimed was
an old authentic Gaelic folk song for the nice young
Japanese couple, in a spirited performance, with
actions, which they duly recorded on their camcorder.
So, somewhere in Tokyo, or wherever, there was once a
video of Ray singing. We like to think the nice Japanese
couple had various friends round to see the videos they
took while in Scotland, and so watched this. Ray sang

the following, or something very like it, to the tune of *Oh Flower of Scotland*: "Ocha-lomine loashin, soagoo-phuid eadeskin, sheakital oot' an arhubitallin . . ."

Calamine Lotion. I'm saying no more. Work it out.

Anyway, so; maybe no way out by rail today, no way out by road for hours (we couldn't hire a car — I'd not thought to bring my driving licence), and nowhere to stay. Yikes! Maybe we could get on the next ferry out and hire a cabin on a long round trip to Barra or somewhere. Maybe I should investigate the taxi fare to Fife. Maybe Ann could call her Islay Air pal Lorna and ask for the name of a good helicopter pilot . . .

The train driver gets through. He arrives at the station to considerable — and non-ironic — applause, which you can't imagine happens all that often. It's another hot journey, even as the sun sets. We arrive home just before midnight, still a bit frazzled and sweaty.

From our house, a reasonable time to Oban by car is not much over two hours. By train it's nearly six. Unless you miss or haven't booked on one train and have to get the next in which case it becomes eleven.

If it could have, I'm sure that the M5, tucked up in its garage all this time, would have shaken its suspension and rolled its headlights.

CHAPTER
SIXTEEN

A Secret Still

The search for the perfect dram leads to the quest for the secret still, just because whisky and the making of it is largely about tradition, about history, and so much of whisky's past is written in the vanishing ink of clear, illegal, governmentally unsanctioned raw spirit. There is a feeling that by finding and tasting spirit produced recently from a small, domestic-scale still hidden in the hills, half buried with heather turfs by the side of a stream, the way they all used to be, somehow it will be possible to connect with a romantic past that modern-day whisky is still informed by and may well benefit from comparison with.

The search for the perfect dram leads to beautiful or honestly workmanlike distilleries scattered throughout the length and breadth of Scotland, their presence signalled by tall chimneys, acres of warehouses and white-on-brown tourist signposts, it leads you to Visitor Centres full of smiling, helpful people in tartan, it leads you to audio-visual displays, carefully lit blonde wood and gleaming stainless steel, it leads to precisely laid-out car parks, dainty flower beds, neatly stacked displays of whisky marmalade and whisky mustard and

436

whisky fudge and bottles and decanters made in the shape of stills, it leads you to cash registers and credit card terminals and plastic bags with the distillery's web address printed on them.

The quest for a secret still — inspired by a single lead, a years-old report from somebody who knows somebody — leads to a long journey in the slack water between summer and autumn and a breeze-stroked hillside with the smell of the sea curling from the distant shore. It leads to a short track and a locked gate, a clamber and a hike and a feeling of exposure, walking up the grassed strip between deep ruts, the soil and the slow-swaying grasses damp from earlier showers. It leads to a straggled collection of disused buildings, an old farm, all tumbled, broken down. It leads to tall grasses, banks of nettles and ancient bales of square-mesh wire, flattened by time and infested with weeds; to crumbling stone walls, half rough-casted, and to rotting wooden window frames, the glass so long shattered and resmashed the ragged, finger-high margin left feels nearly edgeless, merely cold.

The interiors are mostly open to the clouds, some mounded with chaotic, waist-high rubble, one sloped with rusting corrugated iron, one still mostly shielded from the elements; a half-intact floor and a view up the slope towards a small stream, angling beneath a low hill crowned with a dry-stane dike on the skyline, its silhouetted stones filigreed against a still bright sky of slowly sliding clouds.

The room looks like an old kitchen. There's a wide chimney and a gaping dusty hole where an old cast-iron range might have been. A chipped Belfast sink under the window stands on rough-looking naked bricks, badly cemented. The single tap turns but nothing comes out. There's no pipe beneath the plughole anyway, just a hole in the floorboards. No suspicious-looking pipe work or lumps of peat, no old copper water tanks lying around, not really anything that looks out of place or could be dual use.

Outside again, by the back doorstep, as another shower comes in over the fields, there are a few slim ears of barley, growing in a tiny brittle posy. Pale straw gold but flimsy-feeling, they are dry and light in the hand, barely more than husks.

Probably blown here from a far-away field.

A few grains, as a souvenir.

So a secret, still. I suppose I effectively tasted what I was looking for — raw spirit — at Macallan and Old Pulteney and a few other places — whisky straight out of the still. I seriously doubt that the stuff these guys make would taste any worse than what might come out of an illicit still, and to the extent that genuine peatreek might have tasted different, it would probably have tasted worse.

Of course, it isn't really the same, but I can live with this.

Time for some closing thoughts.

I like malt whiskies. And the malts I've come to truly love while researching this book are those which in a sense have least to do with Scotland. What I mean is that the whiskies I've really fallen for are those that have taken on the majority of their character from drinks made in other countries; from American bourbon, or Spanish sherry, or Portugese port, or French wine or Cuban rum. They are still very much single malts, they are still very much Scotch, but it's the interplay between the raw spirit as made in Scotland and those other tastes brought in from abroad that have made the greatest and most enduring impression on me.

I love this assimilative aspect of whisky. I love the fact that single malts, those apparent paradigms of purity, actually show far more variety in taste than any blend, that they are much more influenced by outside factors than any other type of alcoholic drink made without the same seemingly limiting strictures of law and tradition. I love the fact that no other drink I've ever heard of has the same sort of ability to *absorb* (I mean, flavoured vodkas? Really). Maybe they could, of course; I'd guess that brandy or vodka or bourbon or any other spirit finished in wildly different barrels sourced from around the world could and would display the same amazing spectra of tastes and subtleties as single-malt whisky, but the point is that whisky already does, and we should treasure this, indeed we need to celebrate the fact.

Whisky really is an international drink in that sense too, and this ability to accept and combine with distinctive flavours from elsewhere, to enhance them and be enhanced by them, is, potentially at least, an important symbol.

The Scots as a people are the result of a great blending and marrying over the millennia, of Picts, Vikings, Angles, Saxons and countless others, and Scots people have been leaving Scotland and venturing out into the rest of the world for centuries. Like the Irish, they often had to go without much choice in the matter, but go they did, and they blended in, as a rule, while tending to retain a distinctive flavour, an identifiable note, within those other conglomerations of people across the globe.

Those Scots — often poor and fleeing injustice, with their homes burned behind them, victims of a corrupt and persecutive legal system which was glad to see the back of them and would not have welcomed their return — were the economic refugees of their day; they were, effectively, asylum seekers. Where they were allowed to put down roots, they flourished. Where they were accepted, they added immeasurably to the intellectual, cultural and financial wealth of the countries which had taken them in. It is only to our shame that we even think twice about extending the same basic human decency, the same self-interested courtesy, to those in the same situation now as we were in then.

In any event, we need to relax now and again, and a lot of us need to get out of our heads, with a little chemical help. If we're sensible, we'll accept this and set things up so that when we, or others, indulge ourselves so, we'll be — or they'll be — protected from avoidable harm within a sensible set of agreed rules. So a legal framework is required which on the one hand stops the unscrupulous from adulterating whatever it is we're using for such recreational purposes, while on the other hand prevents us from inflicting the effects of our inebria on others, by, for example, driving, operating heavy machinery or taking flash photographs in wildly volatile environments.

We pretty much have this already with alcohol and tobacco, though arguably without the commitment to early education that might help prevent later abuse. The legal framework surrounding alcohol use needs to proscribe things like drunk driving because alcohol has such profound behavioural effects on us. The legal framework surrounding tobacco use is just there to try to stop the young getting hooked too early; tobacco is such a rubbish drug there's no real problem with it affecting your ability to drive a car beyond the trivial aspects of needing to glance down at the lighter or ash tray now and again.

I speak as an occasional user myself here, a social smoker, and let's face it, fellow tobacco junkies, it really must be the single most pitiful drug ever discovered. Its two most profound effects are that it gets you hooked and it's deadly. That's it.

Well, wow. Even ignoring the seriously weird shit you can experience through acid, ecstasy, bong-fulls of dope and all the other illegal stuff, just look at *drink* for goodness' sake! You get effects generally including but not limited to: dizziness, euphoria, double vision, a hilarious inability to stand, all-consuming, tearful love for the drunken bastard or bastards you're getting drunk with, the beer glasses effect whereby those of

441

your gender of choice all become incredibly if only temporarily attractive, and pink elephants!

And with tobacco?

The first fag of the day gives you a slight buzz.

Right.

After extensive research, I can definitely tell you that single-malt whiskies are good to drink. Some are very good to drink. A few are exceptional.

There is, of course, no perfect dram. Or there are lots, depending how you look at it. What apparently tastes like a perfect dram now might not taste so good later. What tastes like a brilliant dram to me might taste awful to you. Your mileage, as our American cousins say, may differ.

To sum up, then.

I still love the Islay whiskies, particularly the three south coasters: Ardbeg, Lagavulin and — most of all — Laphroaig.

I've come to suspect that floor maltings might indicate a really good whisky — Balvenie, Bowmore, Highland Park, Laphroaig and Springbank all still floor malt, and all are amongst the very best. Whether this is really something to do with the taste that only traditional floor malting can produce, or is just a sign, a signifier of something else, something to do with how traditions are applied in the contemporary world, the way that the whole technology of whisky-making, ancient and modern, is applied to the task, I confess I don't know, but I think the question is worth asking.

Being made on an island, or at least close to the sea, would seem a hopeful sign too. Even if you ignore all the Islays, Glenmorangie, Highland Park, Springbank and Talisker would support that argument by themselves.

Heritage, at least as a sign of vast accumulated experience, along with intense attention to detail, also make a difference, so Glenlivet (after a dip) and the ever-impressive Macallan would have to figure in any best of.

As a sort of meta-whisky — a virtual contender if you like — membership of the Scotch Malt Whisky Society and the close perusal of the Tasting Notes each season could easily produce at least one bottle per order which you'd swear was one of the very best you'd ever tasted, so it has to count as well.

Ultimately, the single malt that most impressed me without being outrageously expensive or simply unavailable was that 21-year-old Glenfiddich Havana Reserve. This is brilliantly different, complex, utterly assured whisky-making of the first order; a drink that tastes unimprovably stunning with no water added, yet maybe even better with a dash.

At 60 quid for a bottle (at time of writing, mid August 2003) it's not exactly cheap, but then look at it this way; there's over three times as much alcohol in a bottle of 40 abv whisky as there is in even a fairly powerful bottle of wine, and there's *way* more than three times the amount of taste per sip, even if you water it down. So if you'd splash out on a fifteen or twenty pound bottle of wine, there should be no problem handing over 60 smackers for a brilliant bottle of malt.

In fact, if I'm right and this stuff is the equivalent of Grange or Pétrus, it's a positive bargain; they work out at 60 quid or more for a single glass.

It is all subjective, of course, and what I like, you may not. Your own perfect dram may still be out there.

The search is half the fun.

444

Pronunciation Guide

Emphasis where underlined.

A'Bhuidheanach	Ab<u>u</u>denach
a'bunadh	ab<u>un</u>ad
Acharacle	Ach<u>a</u>rakill
Allt-A-Bhainne	Alt<u>abane</u>
Aonach Mor	A-noch <u>Mor</u>
Ardbeg	Ard<u>beg</u>
Auchentoshan	Ochent<u>o</u>shin
Auchroisk	Ochr<u>oysk</u>
Azshashoshz	Azsh<u>a</u>shoshz
Balvenie	Balv<u>e</u>nie
Bowmore	Bow<u>more</u>
Brechin	Br<u>ee</u>chin
Bruichladdich	Brooick<u>laddie</u>
Bunchrew	Bun<u>krew</u>
Bunnahabhain	Boonah<u>a</u>vin
Caol Ila	Kull-<u>ee</u>la
Cardhu	Kar<u>doo</u>
Champaney	<u>Champ</u>aney (champ as in champion)
champions	champey-oh-neys (Greenock fitba version)
Chivas	Tchivas (not Shivas)

445

Clynelish	Klineeleesh
Cluanie	Clooney
Corryvrecken	Kawrayvrekin
Craigellachie	Craigellachie
Creag Meagaidh	Craig Meggy
Crianlarich	Creeanlarich
Crinan	Crinin
Culloden	Kullawdin
Dallas Dhu	Dallas Doo
Drambuie	Drambyooay
Dulnain	Dulnain
Dunvegan	Dunvey-gan
Edinburgh	Embra
Edradour	Edradower
Eileen	Ayleen
Eilidh	Ayley
Finlaggan	Finlaggin
Fochabers	Fochabers
Football	Fitba
Gaelic	Gale-ik (though opinions differ. I prefer this because otherwise when you refer to some body as a Gael, you'd have to call them a gal. See?)
Gallanach	Gallanach
Glenaladale	Glenaladale
Glendronach	Glendronach
Glenfiddich	Glenfiddich
Glenfinnan	Glenfinnin

Glengarioch	Glengeery
Glenlivet	Glenlivit
Glenmorangie	Glenmorangey
Glentauchers	Glentawkirs
Gourock	Goorok
Grantown	Granton
Greenock	Greenock (not Grenock, Grinock or Grinik)
Gruinart	Greenart
Ileach	Eelich
Islay	Islela
Inverness	Inversneckie
Jura	Joora
Kingussie	Kingyoosay
Kylerhea	Kylereeah
Ladhar Bheinn	Ladder Ben
Lagavulin	Lagavoolin
Laphroaig	LaFroyg (also sometimes known as Leapfrog)
Ledaig	Ledaig
Lochaber	Lochahbir
Lochailort	Lochayelort
Lochnagar	Lochnagar
Lochearnhead	Lochearnhead
Machrie	Machray
Masham	Massam
Menzies	(as is, or, more correctly:) Ming-iss
Montrose	Montrose

447

Munro	Mun<u>ro</u>
Oban	<u>Oh</u>-bin (not Ob<u>aa</u>n; this is guaranteed to have Scottish people sniggering behind your back)
Portmahomack	Portma<u>ho</u>mack
Rothes	Rothies
Schiehallion	She<u>ha</u>leon
Shiel	Sheel
Shoogelnifty	the <u>Shoo</u>gles
Spean	<u>Spee</u>un
Tyndrum	<u>Tine</u>drum
Wyvis	<u>Wi</u>vis